GLOBAL COMPETITION BETWEEN AND WITHIN STANDARDS

Also by Jeffrey L. Funk
THE TEAMWORK ADVANTAGE

Global Competition Between and Within Standards

The Case of Mobile Phones

Jeffrey L. Funk

palgrave

First published 2002 by
PALGRAVE
Houndmills, Basingstoke, Hampshire RG21 6XS and
175 Fifth Avenue, New York, N. Y. 10010
Companies and representatives throughout the world

PALGRAVE is the new global academic imprint of St. Martin's Press LLC Scholarly and Reference Division and Palgrave Publishers Ltd (formerly Macmillan Press Ltd).

ISBN 0–333–97039–X

This book is printed on paper suitable for recycling and made from fully managed and sustained forest sources.

A catalogue record for this book is available from the British Library.

Library of Congress Cataloging-in-Publication Data
Funk, Jeffrey L.
    Global competition between and within standards: the case
of mobile phones / Jeffrey L. Funk.
        p. cm.
    Includes bibliographical references and index.
    ISBN 0–333–97039–X
    1. Cellular telephone services industry. 2. Cellular telephone
systems—Marketing. 3. Mobile communication systems—
Marketing. 4. Competition, International. I. Title.

HE9713 .F86 2001
380.1'4562138456—dc21

                                                                    2001036021

10   9   8   7   6   5   4   3   2   1

11   10   09   08   07   06   05   04   03   02

Printed in Great Britain by
Antony Rowe Ltd, Chippenham, Wiltshire

To my mother Laurel, my brother Steven, and my sister Suzanne

Contents

List of Figures   x

List of Tables   xi

Preface   xiii

List of Abbreviations   xv

1 Introduction   **1**

The Hybrid Model of Markets and Committees   2
The Mobile Communications Industry and
    the Success of Ericsson and Nokia   7
The Success of Standards and their Supporters   9
Committee- and Market-Based Competition in Mobile
    Infrastructure and the Success of Ericsson   14
Committee- and Market-Based Competition in Mobile
    Phones and the Success of Nokia   16
Research Methodology   18
The Organization of the Rest of the Book   18

**2 Key Theoretical Issues in Competition Within and
Between Standards**   **21**

Models of Technological Change   22
Standards: Market Competition   23
Standards: Committees   25
Investment Size as a Moderating Variable on
    Standards Setting   25
Interface Ambiguity as a Moderating Variable on
    Standard Setting   28
Committee-Based Competition Within Standards:
    Customer–Supplier Relationships and Switching Costs
    in Network-Related Products   29
The Role of Global Development in Committee-
    and Market-Based Competition   31
The Role of Product Line and Platform Management
    in Market-Based Competition   33

**3 Market and Committee Mechanisms in Setting
Global Standards**   **36**

An Overview of Mobile Communication Systems
  and Standards   38
The First Regional Standard: Scandinavia's NMT
  System   53
The First Generation Global Standard: America's
  AMPS   56
Failed Efforts to Create a Pan-European Analog
  Standard   58
The Creation of the Second Generation Global
  Standard: GSM   63
The Japanese Create Another Proprietary Standard   69
The Lack of a National Digital Standard in the US   72
Japan Tries a Little Harder, but Fails Again with PHS   76
Japanese and European Collaboration in
  Third Generation Systems   78
Summary   84

**4 Committee- and Market-Based Competition in the
Mobile Infrastructure Market**   **93**

Committee-Based Competition and the Early Years
  of the Mobile Infrastructure Analog Market   96
Consolidation by US Service Providers and Increased
  Market-Based Competition   99
Market-based Competition in the International
  AMPS and TACS Infrastructure Markets   104
The GSM Infrastructure Market   108
Infrastructure Competition in the US Digital Standards   124
Infrastructure Competition in Japan's Market   130
Summary and Discussion   134

**5 Committee and *Particularly* Market Competition
in the Mobile Phone Market**   **145**

The US Analog Market (AMPS): The Early
  Success of Japanese Firms and Motorola's Eventual
  Domination   148
The Success of Nokia, Motorola and
  Ericsson in GSM   157

The US Digital Phone Market and Nokia's
 Global Platforms 169
The Japanese Market 183
Summary and Discussion 194

**6 Third Generation and Mobile Internet Standards and
Competition in Third Generation Infrastructure and Phones 206**

Negotiations over the Third Generation Standard 208
Mobile Internet and Computing Standards 213
The Japanese Mobile Internet Market 220
Interface Competition as of Early 2001 223
Competition in Third Generation Infrastructure 225
Competition in Third Generation Handsets 234

7 A Proposed Model of Technological Change 246

Global Standards and the Competition
 Between Alternative Systems, Designs, or
 Interface Standards 247
Competition *Within* a Specific Standard,
 Design, or System 252
Interaction Between Competition "Between"and
 "Within" Alternative Standards 256

Appendix 1 Interviews 260

Appendix 2 Analysis of the First 20 GSM Orders 262

*Appendix 3 Example of Standard Setting in Other
 Industries That Require High Investments* 264

*Appendix 4 Large Investments and Interface Ambiguities:
 The Internet* 270

Bibliography 273

Index 277

List of Figures

2.1   A simple model of technological change   22
3.1   Outline of a typical mobile communication system   38
3.2   The number of countries starting services   42
3.3   Standard setting method by system   51
3.4   Evolution of standard setting method in major countries   52
3.5   Fraction of worldwide subscribers per year   55
4 1   Global customer base for major infrastructure suppliers   105
5 1   The evolution of successful product line strategies,
      volumes, and unit costs in the mobile phone industry   147
5.2   Shares of US analog mobile phone market   151
5.3   Positive feedback between price and volumes in the
      US analog market   152
5.4   Percentage shares of US analog portable phone market   153
5.5   Evolution of Nokia's GSM 900 MHz phone line   158
5.6   Evolution of Ericsson's GSM 900 MHz phone line   159
5.7   Evolution of Motorola's GSM 900 MHz phone line   159
5.8   GSM handset shares   162
5.9   Evolution of Nokia's TDMA-based digital phone lines   176
5.10 Weights (grams) of Japanese digital mobile phones   187
5.11 "Imputed" weight of Japanese digital mobile phones   188
5.12 Market shares for digital mobile phones in Japan   190
6.1   Key interfaces in mobile computing   215
6.2   The new tradeoff between richness and reach   221
6.3   Japanese vs. US and European approaches to the
      mobile Internet   222
6.4   New phones, higher speed data services and new
      PDAs will continue to change the reach and richness
      tradeoff   225
6.5   3G service schedules and thus the need for
      dual-mode phones   237
7.1   A new model of technological change for
      network industries   246

List of Tables

1.1 The role of committees and markets in the competition between and within standards in the mobile communications industry   2
1.2 Worldwide shares for all markets in 1997, 1998, and 1999   8
1.3 Mobile infrastructure market share rankings by firm and standard   10
1.4 Mobile phone market share rankings by firm and standard   11
1.5 The evolution of global standards   12
2.1 Types of actors involved with standards that require large investments   27
3.1 Evolution of mobile communication standards in major countries and year in which service began   39
3.2 The evolution of global standards   41
3.3 Service start dates for selected analog and digital standards and countries   43
3.4 Selected information for global and non-global standards   47
3.5 Openness: the number of sponsors per standard   49
3.6 The expected degree of competition between manufacturers (handsets and infrastructure) and service providers for each standard   52
4.1 Degree of continuity in vendor–customer relationships for various technological discontinuities in mobile infrastructure by region   95
4.2 Largest US service providers and their number of licenses as of January 1986 in the largest 90 US markets   97
4.3 Number of orders for each vendor by type of service provider in the largest 90 US markets   98
4.4 Market shares in early and subsequent orders   99
4.5 Evolution of major US carriers and their infrastructure suppliers   101
4.6 Number and percentage of orders by service provider and vendor as of May 1992 in the largest 90 and second largest 90 US markets   103
4.7 Early and subsequent market shares in the GSM base station market   108

4.8   Early and subsequent market shares in the GSM
switching market   108

4.9   Major *initial* suppliers for European GSM operators
who started both analog and digital services   111

4.10   Initial suppliers for each European country's first,
second and third European GSM operators that did not
start analog services   113

4.11   Base station and switching shares in the European
GSM 1800 market in 1997   118

4.12   Analog and GSM suppliers to Middle Eastern countries   120

4.13   Leading vendors for selected service providers when the
service providers have made *early* investments
in other service providers   122

4.14   US infrastructure shares in 1997   129

4.15   Japan's service providers, service start dates, and
infrastructure suppliers   130

5.1   A comparison of GSM 900 platform management
strategies for Nokia, Motorola, and Ericsson
between 1994 and 1997   163

5.2   Shares of the US digital phone market   170

5.3   Percent of common designs in Nokia's digital phones
by series   177

5.4   Amount of additional development resources needed
to modify Nokia's 900 platforms for the markets and
phones shown in Figure 5.9   178

6.1   Competing standards for some of the interfaces/
technologies shown in Figure 6.1   217

A.1   Number of interviews each year   260

Preface

The mobile phone industry is an exciting and fast-paced industry. While this makes for fun research, it also means that anything written becomes outdated long before it is published. I wrote most of the initial drafts of this book in the second half of 1999 and the first half of 2000. I planned to and have attempted to update the book many times since then as I have revised the arguments and historical sections of the book. However, as changes began to occur on an almost daily basis, I realized that this would be a very difficult task. Thus, many of the forecasts for the industry are quite simple and possibly outdated. In the first half of 2001, there were still large uncertainties with third-generation services (and their associated phones and infrastructure) and even second-generation mobile Internet services. In particular, the services implemented by Europe and the US (called WAP) appear to be a failure (and have a new name) while Japan's mobile Internet is booming. The success of the Japanese mobile Internet, in particular the success of i-mode, is probably the largest unknown in the market. It may provide Japanese firms with an opportunity to reassert themselves in the global phone and other markets within the mobile phone field. Further many of the problem that I have cited in the book have become much bigger problems in 2001. Emisson problems with product line and platform management in 1999 & 2000 led to its alliance with Sony inhandsetsin 2001. Lucents Subsidization of loans to service providers in the late 1990s in one reason for the downgrading of its debt in 2001.

Many people helped me with this book, too many actually to include their names. More than 200 individuals at more than 20 different firms provided me with a great deal of their valuable time and insights. This includes representatives from Alcatel, Bosch, Ericsson, Deutsche Telekom, Fujitsu, Hitachi, KDDI, Kyocera, Lucent, Matsushita, Mitsubishi, Motorola, NEC, Nokia, Northern Telecom, NTT Docomo, Philips, Sanyo, Siemens, Sony, and Toshiba.

There were also a number of other people who have provided me with immense help on the actual manuscript and ideas that led to the manuscript. Martin Kenney, Susan Sanderson, Jeffrey Liker, and Bruce Kogut provided me with comments on earlier versions of the text and many more people provided me with comments on earlier papers, such as Gerard Cronin, Patrick Donegan, Kentaro Nobeoka, and Joel West. Stephen Rutt, Keith Povey, Zelah Pengilley, and others at Palgrave helped me with the manuscript. Of course, any errors are my own.

July 2001   JEFFREY L. FUNK

List of Abbreviations

AMPS	Advanced Mobile Phone System
ARIB	Association for Radio Industry Business
cdmaOne	Code Division Multiple Access One
c-HTML	compact-Hyper Text Mark-up Language
C-Netz	C-Net
CoPS	Complex products and systems
CTIA	Cellular Telephone Industry Association
DAMPS	Digital Advanced Mobile Phone System
EDGE	Enhanced Data Rates for GSM Evolution
ETSI	European Telecommunications Standards Institute
FCC	Federal Communication Commission
FDMA	Frequency Division Multiple Access
GPRS	General Packet Radio System
GSM	Global System Mobile
ITU	International Telecommunications Union
MOU	Memorandum of Understanding
NMT	Nordic Mobil Telephone
NTT	National Telephone and Telegraph
RC2000	Radicom 2000
PCS	Personal Communications Services
PDC	Personal Digital Cellular
TDMA	Time Division Multiple Access
UMTS	Universal Mobile Telephone Service
WAP	Wireless Application Protocol
WML	Wireless Markup Language
WCDMA	Wide Band Code Division Multiple Access

1 Introduction

Standards play a critical role in network industries such as telecommunications, broadcasting, consumer electronics, the Internet, computers, and information systems. They define critical interfaces between complementary products and without the establishment of these standards new markets in the network industries rarely grow. Further, the emergence of a standard has a dramatic effect on competition in these industries. Firms that support the successful interface standard are typically rewarded with increasing market share and profits while the other firms are forced to either adopt the standard or compete in a shrinking market.

The standards literature divides standards into *de jure* standards that are created by committees and *de facto* standards that are chosen by markets. The commercialization of the product typically follows the creation of a *de jure* standard while with *de facto* standards, individual firms commercialize products and the market then determines the winning *de facto* standard (Asaba, 1995; Besen and Farrell, 1994; Farrell and Saloner, 1992; Khazam and Mowery, 1992).

However, it is relevant that the distinction between *de facto* and *de jure* standards is becoming less and less valuable. Due to the growing recognition by firms that standards are important, there are a growing number of committees, or at the minimum coalitions of firms, that are involved with creating *de jure* standards.[1] Firms participate in these committees to create what can be considered *de jure* standards but in the end it is still the market that determines the actual winning and thus *de facto* standard (Shapiro and Varian, 1999).

Further, most of the standards literature focuses on competition between two firms, the role that network externalities play in this competition, and a winner-take-all result.[2] In reality, there is not a single winner since many firms participate in multiple committees in order to cover all their bets. Not only does this mean that there is competition between committees, each of which may be promoting a different standard, there is also competition between the firms that are working in a single committee on the development of a single standard.

Table 1.1   The role of committees and markets in the competition
between and within standards (that is, between manufacturers)
in the mobile communications industry

	Committees	*Markets*
Between standards	1. Organizations create standards in committees	1. Markets choose winning standards where network externalities play big role
	2. Size and openness of committee are key variables	2. Competition between service providers and between manufacturers increases forecasted and actual installed base
Within Standards (that is, between manufacturers)	Firms compete to: 1. Understand the standard 2. Have their technology in standard and earn licensing fees from technology 3. Work with service providers on development, testing and implementation of new technology	Firms compete to: 1. Introduce superior products 2. Market their products to new customers 3. Develop new distribution channels 4. Create economies of scale

THE HYBRID MODEL OF MARKETS AND COMMITTEES

This book uses a hybrid model of markets and committees to explain
the competition both between and within standards at the global level.
Although several papers (for example, Farrell and Saloner, 1988) have
suggested that a hybrid system for setting standards can result in better
performance, this research is the first to do this empirically.[3] Moreover, this book uses the hybrid model to also explain competition
within a particular standard at the global level (see Table 1.1). It
examines how governments and firms use markets and committees at
national, regional, and global levels to create competitive advantage at
these different levels.

This book looks at these issues in the mobile communication industry, an industry with rapid technological change and high levels of
organizational complexity.[4] The third generation of technology is now

being implemented in spite of having a history of only twenty years. The organizations involved in this industry include governments, service providers, infrastructure manufacturers, phone manufacturers, and other technology suppliers. Of particular importance, service providers act as intermediaries between manufacturers and final users and in the competition between standards their decisions have a greater impact on the standards competition than the decisions of final users (that is, consumers). And the fact that many of these service providers must make very large investments in these systems (for example, many service providers expect to invest more than US$10 billion in third generation systems) makes them very risk averse and increases their desire for openness and large coalitions.

The hybrid model: global standards creation

This books shows how the hybrid model of setting standards, which uses both market and committee mechanisms, explains standard setting in the mobile communications industry better than a model that only employs one or the other mechanism. Committees are defined very broadly in that alliances and coalitions are defined as small committees. In the mobile communications industry, multi-firm, national, and regional committees selected mobile communication standards in some cases through the selection of national champions and in others through the evaluation and comparison of competing systems. However, due to the lack of a single overarching governance structure for setting global standards and the lack of authority in international standard setting bodies, it was market mechanisms, through increasing returns to scale, that have caused the emergence of global standards.

In particular, the creation of a single open standard by a large country (for example, the US) or region (for example, Europe) has been far more effective in creating global standards than promoting competition between multiple standards within a country or region as the US did in digital mobile technology. These single open standards were created in committees that contained a large number of service providers and manufacturers. The choice of a single open standard in an open standard setting process caused the *forecasted* installed base instantaneously to increase, making the standard more attractive to non-aligned firms. The choice of a single open standard by a large single country or region and the resulting high forecasted installed base are particularly important to service providers since they must make very large investments in these systems and thus they do not want to invest in a losing standard.

The expected and actual competition between service providers and manufacturers, which reflects the degree of openness in the committee, promoted market mechanisms since the expected and actual competition influenced the forecasted and actual installed base. The competition between service providers, in particular the awarding of new services licences, increased the forecasted and actual installed base since it convinced other countries and service providers in other countries that someone would actually start services that are based on the new standard. Competition between manufacturers convinced other countries that prices for infrastructure and phones would drop, thus enabling a growth in subscribers. Further, competition between manufacturers also increased the number of firms that were able to act as agents of diffusion in convincing non-aligned third party governments and service providers to adopt the standard as their own. As the "bandwagon" gained momentum with a large percentage of third party governments adopting the standard, even the countries that promoted alternative systems ended up adopting the global standard or a portion of the standard.

The hybrid model: competition between firms in a single standard

Firms also need to be concerned with both committees and markets, albeit from a different perspective than just competition between standards. As noted earlier, although most of the standards literature focuses on competition between two firms, the role that network externalities play in this competition, and a winner-take-all result, in reality, there is not a single winner and in fact many firms participate in multiple committees in order to cover all their bets. Not only does this mean that there is competition between committees, each of which may be promoting a different standard, there is also competition between the firms that are working in a single committee.

The competition between these firms who are working in a single committee occurs both at the committee and the market level. At the minimum, firms must participate in a committee in order to understand the standard and thus be able to develop products that are based on the standard. At a higher level, firms compete in committees to have their technology included in the standard and earn licensing fees while they simultaneously use their superior knowledge of this specific technology to develop superior products. On the other hand, it is generally argued that the greater the degree of openness in the standard, the greater the competition changes from standard-setting (that is, committees) to product competition (that is, markets) where product development, manufacturing efficiencies and other factors determine the winners (Shapiro and Varian, 1999, p. 231).

However, this book will find that the relative importance of committees and markets depends not just on the degree of openness in the standard but also on the degree of product complexity. A growing number of authors argue that competition in complex products and systems (CoPS) such as military systems, power plants, automated production systems, railway systems, and telecommunication systems differs significantly from that found in mass-produced commodity goods. Customer involvement in innovation tends to be high and suppliers, regulators and professional bodies often work together with customers to negotiate and develop new product designs, methods of production, and post-delivery systems. Switching costs are high, relationships between suppliers and customers may persist over many generations of products, markets are often bureaucratically administered, and direct competition is low in contrast to commodity goods, which are characterized by arm's-length market transactions.[5] Further, the concept of CoPS is not entirely new, as Woodward (1958, p. 279) describes in her seminal research into UK project-based companies in the 1950s: "those responsible for marketing had to sell, not a product, but the idea that their firm was able to produce what the customer required."[6] This book will find that this is an important part of committee-based competition, particularly in mobile infrastructure.

Mobile communications infrastructure is an example of a CoPS while mobile phones are an example of a traditional mass-produced consumer product. The greater complexity of, the fewer customers for, and the greater importance of first mover advantages with infrastructure cause committees to be more important for infrastructure than phones. Mobile infrastructure providers must simultaneously participate in the standard setting process and cooperatively develop the technology with the service providers. Since the cooperative development work with the service provider is done within the context of the standard setting work in the committee, this cooperative development work may be defined as part of the competition in committees and not markets. Further, in order to cooperatively develop the product with the service provider, the infrastructure providers must first obtain an order for an experimental product from a service provider in much the same way as Woodward's project-based companies. And this is complicated by the high switching costs of service-providers, where many service-providers have purchased multiple generations of infrastructure from the same supplier.

The lower complexity of and greater number of customers for phones cause markets to be more important for phones than for infrastructure. Firms must participate in the standard setting activities and thus committees are important to some extent, particularly for the initial phones. But the lower complexity of phones makes the relationships between phone manufacturers and the final consumers (that is, the market) more important than the relationships between phone manufacturers and service providers (that is, committees) particularly in comparison to the case of infrastructure. Thus, most of the competition between phone manufacturers revolves around the factors found to be important in traditional consumer products industries like automobiles, appliances, and consumer electronics. In particular, product line and platform management was found to be the key factor of success in the mobile phone industry.

The hybrid model: competition in a single standard at a global level

The way that competition occurs in both committees and markets becomes even more complex when it occurs at the global level as it does in the mobile communications industry. As mentioned earlier, although global committees exist, they do not have the power of enforcement and thus national and regional committees play a more important role than international committees in the telecommunications industry. This means that firms must participate in various national and regional committees. In fact, since the sources of standards have changed from the US in analog to Europe in digital and Japan in third generation technology, the most successful mobile communications infrastructure and phone firms have been participating in standard setting committees on three continents for many years and they have also created global development capabilities to support participation in these standard setting activities. Further, the market side of this is also very important; the most successful firms have also participated in these multiple markets for many years.

The relative importance of committees and markets at the global level is also influenced by both the degree of openness in the standard and the differences between CoPS and mass-produced products. The complexity of and low volumes for infrastructure causes there to be high switching costs even over multiple generations of technology. And coupled with the changing sources of new technology and standards in the mobile communications industry, the most successful firms were quicker to create close working relationships with service providers from a large number of different countries and regions, particularly the US, Europe and Japan. This enabled them to have the necessary relationships in place when the particular region became the source of the new standard. Participation in standard-setting committees and their relevant global development capabilities were a necessary complement to these global relationships with service providers.

For phones, relationships with service providers were less important than the way in which product line and platform management were carried out in the multiple markets. However, participation in committees was necessary and the level of openness in the committee did have an impact on the appropriate form of product line and platform management in at least one case. Further, the most successful firms were able to use their knowledge of multiple standards (through their participation in the relevant committees) to develop global platforms, which essentially allowed them to create global economies of scale in development, production, and purchasing. This is an important way in which firms can overcome the lack of influence that they often have on the technical specifications in an individual standard in a world where most standards are created in large committees. Firms with this global development capability can change the competition from competition within a single standard, including its relevant committees and markets, to competition at the global level.

THE MOBILE COMMUNICATIONS INDUSTRY AND THE SUCCESS OF ERICSSON AND NOKIA

Mobile communication is one of the fastest growing markets in the world. The number of subscribers had reached 450 million in the world by the end of 1999 and it was expected to exceed one billion by the end of 2003. Penetration rates have passed 45% in most developed countries and in Scandinavia, they have passed 60% with Finland's penetration rate now over 70%. Further, some believe that there will be more people connected to the Internet through mobile phones than through PCs by 2005. The growth in this industry and the story of how firms such as Nokia and Ericsson have succeeded is a fascinating one with lessons for many industries. Nokia is the leading producer of mobile phones and Ericsson is the leading producer of mobile infrastructure (base stations and switching equipment) in the world (see Table 1.2).

The fact that Scandinavia has the highest penetration rates and two of the most successful firms is not accidental. The early start of services (in 1981) and the rapid growth in the Scandinavian market gave Nokia and Ericsson an early edge over other firms. However, the story of their success is far more interesting than just an early start. For example, Japan was the first country to start services in 1979 yet its firms have achieved very little success in the industry. Motorola, Lucent and Nortel benefited from the relatively early start of services (1983), growth, and much larger markets in North America but they have not performed as well as Nokia and Ericsson.

The success of Ericsson and Nokia also has very little to do with the wireline industry where Ericsson has been fairly strong and Nokia has been a producer of small wireline switches. The two largest producers of wireline switches, Alcatel and Siemens, are far less successful in the mobile field than other firms such as Motorola, the second largest producer of mobile base stations and a firm that does not produce wireline equipment. Successful producers of cordless and other wireline phones such as Panasonic, Sony, and Sanyo are also not the leading producers of mobile phones; instead it is firms like Nokia, Motorola, and Ericsson.

Table 1.2   Worldwide shares for all markets in 1997, 1998, and 1999 (percent)

Firm	Infrastructure		Phones		
	1997	*1998*	*1997*	*1998*	*1999*
Ericsson	30	29	16	15.1	10.5
Lucent	13	14			
Motorola	15	12	25	19.5	16.9
Nokia	10	12	20	22.5	26.9
Nortel	13	11			
Siemens	5	5	3.6	2.9	4.6
NEC	5	5	5.0	4.2	3.2
Alcatel	4	4	2.5	4.3	4.2
Matsushita			7.3	8.2	5.4
Mitsubishi			3.0	2.8	3.4
Samsung				2.7	6.2

Source: DataQuest's Gartner Group ("Nokia Extends head in Cell-Phone Market, Dataquest Says," *Bloomberg News*, 2/8/2000) for phones. For infrastructure data is from firms.

The success of Ericsson and Nokia and even the relative success of other firms such as Motorola is a function of how these firms have competed in both committees and markets, including relationships with service providers in the case of infrastructure and effective platform management in the case of mobile phones.

THE SUCCESS OF STANDARDS AND THEIR SUPPORTERS

Firms benefit when their products or technologies become global standards. This has also been the case in the mobile phone industry where domestic firms have typically been the most successful firms in each standard and firms whose domestic standards have become global standards have the highest shares in that generation of technology. As shown in both Tables 1.3 and 1.4, the former is true in both infrastructure and in the phones themselves. In infrastructure, US firms have largely dominated markets for those standards that were created in the US such as AMPS, DAMPS, and cdmaOne. Similarly Scandinavian firms have dominated markets for their standard (NMT), European firms have dominated the markets for their standard (GSM) and Japanese firms have dominated the market for their standard (PDC).[7] A similar situation exists in handsets. Motorola has dominated the AMPS market (US standard), Scandinavian firms have dominated the NMT market (Scandinavian standard), European firms have dominated the GSM market (European standard), Japanese firms have dominated the PDC market (Japanese standard), and US and Korean firms have dominated the cdmaOne market.[8]

Further, the firms whose domestic standards have become global standards (see Table 1.5) have the highest share of the world market. US firms dominated the worldwide analog infrastructure and handset markets since AMPS (and its derivative TACS) was the global analog standard with Ericsson being the notable exception. European firms dominate the worldwide digital infrastructure and handset markets since GSM is the digital global standard with Motorola being the notable exception. The shares of US firms in the digital market will certainly increase if cdmaOne is adopted by a large number of countries while Japanese firms are expecting the success of W-CDMA to increase their shares of the worldwide market. Thus it is important for firms to have their domestic standard become a global standard.

The linkage between standards and firm performance is a major reason why academics and business people are interested in why

Table 1.3 Mobile infrastructure market share rankings by firm and standard

	Standard									
	Analog				GSM			Digital		
Firm	AMPS		NMT	TACS	900	1800	1900	DAMPS***	PDC	IS95 CDMA
	US	Non-US								
Lucent	1	4			7**			2		1
Motorola	2	2		1	4				4	2
Nortel	4	3			6*	3*	2*	3		3
Ericsson	3	1	1	2	1	2	1	1	2	
Nokia			2		2	1	3			
Alcatel					5					
Siemens					3					
NEC		5		3					1	
Fujitsu									3	
PKI					7**					
Matra					6*					

*After acquisition of Matra by Nortel.
**After acquisition of PKI by Lucent.
***DAMPS is typically called DAMPS in the US press. As discussed in Chapter 2, since GSM, PDC, and DAMPS are all based on TDMA technology, this book uses the term DAMPS.

Table 1.4 Mobile phone market share rankings by firm and standard

		Standard							
		Analog				Digital			
		US AMPS							
Firm	Overall (1997)	1989	1996	NMT (1991)	TACS (1994)	GSM (1998)	DAMPS (1998)*	PDC	cdma One
Nokia	1	10	2	2	2	1	1		2
Motorola	2	1 (16%)	1 (69%)	1	1	2			3
Ericsson	3	9	8	3	3	3	2		
Matsushita	4	2	6	5		7		1	
Sony/Qualcomm	5								1
NEC	6					9		3	
Siemens	7					5			
Alcatel	8					4			
Mitsubishi	9	3	5					2	
Philips	10			4		6			
Toshiba	11	4	9					6	

*DAMPS is typically called DAMPS in the US press. As discussed in Chapter 2, since GSM, PDC, and DAMPS are all based on TDMA technology, this book uses the term DAMPS.

Table 1.5 The evolution of global standards

Generation of technology	Communication standard	The standards country or region of origin	Number of adopting countries (end of 98)	Number and percent of each generation's subscribers as of December, 1998	
First generation analog cellular	AMPS*	North America (1983)	79	72.0	78%
	TACS*	Britain (1985)	25	15.0	16%
	NMT	Scandinavia (1981)	35	5.0	6%
Second generation digital cellular	GSM*	Europe (1992)	120	132.0	63%
	DAMPS	US (1993)	35	18.5	9%
	cdmaOne	US and Korea (1996)	15	23.0	11%
	PDC	Japan (1993)	1	36.0	17%
Low-mobility digital cellular	PHS	Japan (1995)	1	6.0	98%
Third generation digital cellular	Wide-Band CDMA*	Japan (2001)			

* Global standards.
Source: Current subscriber data is available from organizations that support various standards; historical data can be found in Garrand (1998), Telecommunications (1998), and Mobile Communications International (October 1999).

some products and technologies become standards. The book, and in particular Chapter 3, argues that a hybrid model of setting standards that uses both market and committee mechanisms can result in better performance than a system that only employs one or the other method. The role of a national or regional committee is to select a single standard through the evaluation and comparison of competing standards. The choice of a single open standard by a large nation or region is critical since it causes the forecasted installed base to increase dramatically, making the standard more attractive to non-aligned firms. Further, market competition is also important but it is not the competition between standards, rather it is the competition between service providers and manufacturers, that influences the forecasted and actual installed base. The competition between service providers, in particular the awarding of new service licences, increases the forecasted and actual installed base since it convinces the non-aligned firms that someone will actually start services that are based on the new standard. As is widely known, incumbents are often not the first firms to adopt a new technology.[9]

The relationship between the level of openness in the standard and the amount of competition between either service providers or manufacturers is the linkage between the committee and market mechanisms at least in the competition between standards. Open standards attract a larger number of service providers and manufacturers, thus increasing the amount of competition within the standard and the number of agents who can act as agents of diffusion.

This book argues that the choice of a single open standard by a large nation or region is particularly important in cases where large investments are required in a specific interface and thus intermediate firms like service providers are highly risk averse. It is argued that the degree of required openness and the size of the coalitions increase as the size of the investment increases. Where extremely large investments are required, for example in the mobile phone industry,[10] it is argued that openness and large coalitions become even more important. Large countries (for example, the US) or regions (for example, Europe) that adopt a single open standard are more likely to create a global standard than countries or regions that do otherwise.

This is why the choice of a single open standard, the introduction of competition between service providers and manufacturers (mobile infrastructure and phones), and the large US population caused more than 100 countries to adopt the US analog standard AMPS or a closely related standard called TACS. In digital however, the US government left the choice of a standard to firms while the European governments sponsored the creation of a single digital standard, GSM. Similar to the case of AMPS, the choice of this single open standard by Europe, the introduction of competition, and the large European population caused more than 130 countries to adopt GSM. In third generation technology, the Europeans have again chosen a single standard and awarded licences to new firms in order to spur competition. Here though, it was the key alliance between Ericsson, Nokia, and Japan's largest service provider NTT Docomo that caused Europe to choose W-CDMA.

However, the success of GSM or even AMPS is not the only reason for the success of Ericsson, Nokia, or even Motorola. In particular, as shown in Tables 1.3 and 1.4, these firms have managed to succeed not just in domestic standards but also in standards that originated in foreign countries. In mobile infrastructure, the success of Ericsson and to some extent Motorola has more to do with their effective competition in both committees and markets of which the former was found to be more important in the infrastructure market. This committee-based competition included the early creation of relationships with many service providers and their participation in foreign standard setting processes, both of which required the creation of global development capabilities.

COMMITTEE- AND MARKET-BASED COMPETITION IN MOBILE INFRASTRUCTURE AND THE SUCCESS OF ERICSSON

Chapter 4 describes how committee-based competition and the interaction between these committee- and market-based competitions play a stronger role in overall competition than just market-based competition by itself. As in many complex products and systems (CoPS), firms participate in standard-setting committees while they simultaneously develop technology in cooperation with a service provider due to the complexity of mobile communication standards. The documentation for many standards is more than ten feet thick and is created over many years. Unless company representatives are present when the details about the standard are decided and they are simultaneously doing product development with customers, they cannot understand the reasons for particular standardization decisions.

Cooperative development work with service providers is an essential part of the competition in committees since early orders for test and commercial systems are necessary to develop the experience in mobile infrastructure. Although in theory these early orders could be from new or existing service providers, Chapter 4 will find that *existing* service providers generally placed the earliest orders for mobile infrastructure. Therefore, committee-based competition has often determined the early orders largely through the continuity of vendor–customer relationships. Chapter 4 will show that there are high switching costs between the infrastructure and service-providers since most service providers have purchased multiple generations of infrastructure from the same infrastructure vendor.

Within a single generation of technology, the most successful firms used their early orders to create capabilities in market-based competition. Whether the early orders were obtained through committee- (through orders from existing service-providers) and/or market-based competition (through orders from new service-providers), it was necessary for firms to translate these early orders into superior products and other forms of capabilities for market-based competition. Firms that did this were able to create positive feedback where new orders led to superior products and the superior products led to new orders.

In a subsequent generation of technology, it is important to translate the capabilities of market-based competition in the current generation of technology into the capabilities of committee-based competition in the next generation of technology. Firms must participate in these next generation standard-setting committees while they simultaneously develop technology in cooperation with service providers, who for the most part are already existing service-providers with existing suppliers. This is of course problematic given the changing sources of each generation of technology. The US was the source of the analog standard AMPS, GSM was created in Europe, and W-CDMA services will be first started in Japan.

Therefore, in order to succeed in a subsequent generation of technology, firms need to develop relationships in a foreign country before the next generation of technology begins. Ericsson has done this through the early creation of global customer relationships (that is, relationships with service providers all over the world) and by using these global relationships to acquire early orders in both second (including GSM) and third generation standards. Global development capabilities and participation in foreign standard setting processes were necessary parts of these global relationships with service providers. Ericsson's faster creation of the customer relationships, development capabilities, and participation in standard setting at the global level are the major reason why Ericsson is a major supplier in more analog and digital standards than any other infrastructure supplier.

COMMITTEE- AND MARKET-BASED COMPETITION IN MOBILE PHONES AND THE SUCCESS OF NOKIA

Chapter 5 describes how market-based competition has played a more important role than committee-based competition in the competition between mobile phone providers. Other than the relatively closed standards like Japan's PDC, committee-based competition has only played a strong role during the early years of the standards. Some firms were unable to compete due to their lack of participation in a standard setting process while others initially obtained high shares through their relative strength in committee-based competition.

Market-based competition has played a much more important role than committee-based competition in the global mobile phone competition due to the high levels of openness in the key standards and the relative simplicity of the product, at least as compared to mobile infrastructure. Market-based competition determined the winners in the global standards AMPS and GSM and even in other standards such as NMT, DAMPS, and cdmaOne.

In this market competition, product line and platform management has been the critical method of competition, even more so than product development where Japanese firms can still develop phones in about the half the time that Western firms take. And the appropriate product line and platform management has changed as the industry has evolved from a small-scale regional-based industry to a global industry and there are still important regional differences. It is the evolution of the industry and the regional differences that are interesting since they largely determine the appropriate form of product line and platform management.

Changes in volumes and costs have caused the appropriate product line/platform management strategy to change and also market leadership to change from the Japanese firms in the mid-1980s to Motorola (from the late 1980s to the mid-1990s) and to Nokia in the mid-to late 1990s. The Japanese firms initially dominated the US analog phone market, which was by far the largest phone market in the world. They acquired a 70% share of the US AMPS market by the late 1980s through a continuous improvement strategy that they have used in many industries. However, Motorola managed to reverse this trend and acquire almost a 70% share of the market by 1996 by introducing a strategy of volume discounts and rapid price decreases in the late 1980s as the US market was changing from a business to a personal market.

The GSM market changed even more quickly from a business to a personal market and Motorola, Nokia and Ericsson were the first to recognize this and rapidly reduce prices. Further, they began to subsidize low-end models to obtain economies of scale while making their profits at the high end of the market. This strategy makes it difficult for firms to gradually move from the low end of the market to the high end of the market as the Japanese did in a variety of industries such as automobiles and consumer electronics during the 1970s. Chapter 5 will also show how differences in platform strategy and implementation explain the superior performance by Nokia in GSM as compared to Motorola and Ericsson.

In the worldwide digital phone market, Nokia's use of global platforms provides it with a distinct competitive advantage. While Ericsson has been able to also use global platforms to some extent, Motorola, the other European firms, and the Japanese firms are still struggling to understand and subsequently introduce global platforms. For the same amount of engineering resources, Nokia is capable of developing 50% more phones than Ericsson and more than twice the number of phones as Motorola, the other European firms, and the Japanese firms. Thus, while Motorola was struggling to change its emphasis from analog to digital phones in the US in the late 1990s, Nokia was introducing a steady stream of phones for multiple frequencies for the different standards in the European, US, and Japanese markets (see Table 1.4).

Nokia's global platforms provide an interesting twist to the relative importance of markets and committees. Since Nokia is able to develop phones for multiple standards from a single platform, they are less dependent on having their technology adopted in a specific standard. Not only does the current standards literature largely focus on two-firm competition, the research on competition in committees largely focuses on how firms can have their technology be made part of a standard. Nokia's creation of a global development capability, which is certainly a part of the market-as opposed to the committee-based strategy, further reduces the importance of committee-based competition in the mobile phone market.

RESEARCH METHODOLOGY

Between 1993 and 1999, data have been gathered and theories have been tested and revised numerous times using the case study approach (Eisenhardt, 1989; Yin, 1989). The initial research focused on management of the phone development process and how firms could reduce development times and costs and improve product quality. Seventeen interviews were carried out with five Japanese cellular phone producers in 1993 and 1994 (Funk, 1997). During this time period, the importance of industrial standards to competition in the cellular phone industry was recognized and thus the research goals were broadened. More than 100 interviews with more than twenty different firms were carried out between 1996 and 1999 in Japan, Europe, and the US (see Appendix 1 for details).

The analysis of standards depended on published material[11]and interviews with firms. The analysis of infrastructure included an analysis of orders, which were found in published sources[12] and confirmed in interviews and press releases. The analysis of phones depended on interviews and data on phones, of which the latter were found in magazines and other home pages.[13]

THE ORGANIZATION OF THE REST OF THE BOOK

The second chapter discusses several key theories that play a role in the hybrid model of markets and committees. It provides background on the literature on standards, customer–supplier relationships (particularly with respect to switching costs), global development, and product line/platform management. The third chapter describes why certain mobile communication standards such as AMPS and GSM have become global standards while other standards have not fared as well. It also describes how Europe ended up choosing NTT Docomo's third generation standard. Chapters 4 and 5 describe why certain firms have succeeded more than others for mobile communication systems and phones in each of these standards.

Chapter 6 returns to the issue of third generation systems and discusses the final battles between various third generation standards and the factors that will most likely determine the winners and losers in third generation infrastructure and handsets. It finds that in spite of US advantages in Internet-based technology, the US has many disadvantages. The European domination of the standard-setting processes for digital systems and the mobile Internet, the European and Japanese domination of the third generation standard-setting process, and early moves to the mobile Internet by Japanese consumers will make it difficult for US firms to succeed in third generation systems and phones. More than 30% of Japanese mobile phone subscribers were using phones to access the Internet (albeit on a limited basis) as of late 2000 with this number expected to reach 80% by the end of 2001.

Chapter 6 also discusses the competition to create mobile computing and mobile Internet standards and how this battle is following a very different path from the mobile communication standards battles. As opposed to large government-led or at least government-sponsored coalitions, the competition to create mobile computing and mobile Internet standards is characterized by a large number of loose alliances. This is because there are many key interfaces and the competition between different interfaces will probably prove to be more important than the competition between different standards within a specific interface.

Chapter 7 uses the hybrid model of committees and markets to propose a new model of technological change. This new model of technological change includes not only the hybrid model of committees and markets but also simultaneous competition "between" and "within" standards.

Notes

1. For example, 55 firms created the digital video camera standard, more than 100 firms created the 8-millimeter video standard, and two competing DVD standards were created by more than 50 firms each (Yamada, 1997).
2. For instance, see Katz and Shapiro (1985; p. 427), Besen and Farrell (1994; p. 121).
3. The hybrid model of markets and committees was first applied to standards creation in the paper (Funk and Methe, 2001).
4. Many people have argued the telecommunication industry presents paradigmatic cases of standard-setting in large technological systems (David and Steinmueller, 1994). This industry is therefore an important setting for understanding the idiosyncrasies of standard-setting processes (Antonelli, 1994) as well as setting a base line for generalizations on standard-setting in other industries (David, 1995).
5. Although Hobday (1998) was the first person to make this argument, the special issue (August 2000) of *Research Policy* that was devoted to "Innovation in Complex Products and Systems," is one example of the

growing interest in the distinction between CoPS and mass-produced products.

6. Woodward, 1958, p. 23, and quoted in Hobday, Rico and Tidd, 2000, p. 795.

7. There are several exceptions including Ericsson's strength in DAMPS, Motorola's and Nortel's strength in GSM, and Ericsson's and Motorola's strength in PDC.

8. There are several exceptions including Motorola's strength in NMT and GSM and Nokia's strength in DAMPS and cdmaOne.

9. For example, see Tushman and Anderson, (1986); Utterback (1994).

10. For example, Japanese service providers are each expected to spend more than US$10 billion to implement third generation services that are based on W-CDMA. Keitai Denwa, Jisedai kyousou makiake, NTT Docomo ga jigyou shinsei – IT toushi keninyaku. Docomo's new business in next generation phones is pulling IT investment, *Nikkei*, p. 11, 4/4/2000.

11. For example, see Garrard (1998) and Paetsch (1993). In addition, the analysis of the analog era depended on keyword searches of the *Financial Times*, *Handelsblatt*, and *Le Monde*.

12. For example, data on analog orders were obtained from *Cellular Business* and the US Office of Telecommunications and data on digital orders were obtained from *Mobile Communications*.

13. For example, see *Mobile Choice, What Mobile*, and *Telecommunications* (Japanese).

2 Key Theoretical Issues in Competition Within and Between Standards

This chapter looks at a number of theoretical issues that play a key role in this competition between and within standards. It begins by placing the competition between and within standards within the context of the technology change literature. The technology change literature argues that standards are created in response to the emergence of new technologies, often called technological discontinuities. The chapter examines the theoretical issues surrounding this competition between standards, including the literature on the roles of markets and committees in the competition between standards and the hypotheses that investment size and interface ambiguity moderate the role of these committees and markets.

Chapter 2 then goes on to point out that little work has been done in the area of competition within standards. In fact, the technology change and standards literature largely implicitly assumes that market competition *within* a standard begins as soon as the competition *between* standards is completed. This book will show that this is an oversimplified view of technological change and argues that these competitions occur simultaneously. Moreover, the competition within standards occurs both within committees and markets.

For mobile infrastructure, committee-based competition plays a more important role than market-based competition and the relationships between customers and suppliers play a large role in this committee-based competition. And due to the changing sources of standards, competition has occurred in committees on three continents and development centers were needed to support participation in these various committees. Thus, this chapter discusses the literature of customer–supplier relationships, the role of switching costs in these relationships, and global development.

For mobile phones, market-based competition has played a more important role than committee-based competition and product line and platform management at the global level have played a large role in this market-based competition. Thus, this chapter concludes with a discussion of the literature on product line and platform management including the development of global platforms. At the end of this book, Chapter 7 proposes a new model of technological change that pulls together some of this literature and shows how competition occurs within and between standards at the committee and market level.

MODELS OF TECHNOLOGICAL CHANGE

Figure 2.1 shows a simple model of technological change. Following a technological discontinuity, alternative product forms compete for dominance due to the large amount of market and technological uncertainty that exist. Thus product innovation is relatively rapid and production processes are highly flexible and labor intensive. The emergence of a standard or dominant design often causes this competition to change dramatically. The industry enters an era of incremental change where products and processes are incrementally improved (Abernathy and Utterback, 1978; Abernathy and Clark, 1985; Anderson and Tushman, 1990, Christensen and Rosenbloom, 1995; Tushman and Anderson, 1986; Utterback, 1994). Thus, competition often changes from product or service performance to the effective use of complementary assets such as marketing, distribution, competitive manufacturing, and after-sales support (Teece, 1986). Japanese firms are the leaders in many of these industries such as automobiles, consumer electronics, machinery and steel.

However, in the network-related industries, which will most likely play the dominant role in the world economy in the twenty-first

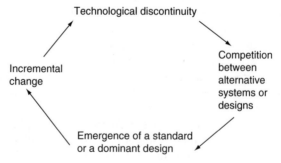

Figure 2.1   A simple model of technological change

century, firms must deal with a continuous stream of technological discontinuities.[1] These industries include the Internet, computers and information systems, broadcasting, telecommunications, and others. Often, just as one of these industries has entered an era of incremental change, a new technological discontinuity emerges which starts the process over again. Thus, the issue of how to recognize and adapt to these technological discontinuities is a more important managerial challenge than managing incremental improvement in these industries.

Standards play a critical role in the technological discontinuities that occur in the network industries; they define critical interfaces between complementary products and without the establishment of these standards new markets in the network industries rarely grow. Further, the emergence of a standard or dominant design has a dramatic effect on competition in these industries. Firms that supported the successful interface standard are typically rewarded with increasing market share and profits while the other firms are forced to either adopt the standard or compete in a shrinking market.

As discussed at the beginning of Chapter 1, the industrial standards literature divides standards into *de jure* standards that are created by committees and *de facto* standards that are chosen by markets. Committees create *de jure* standards and typically the commercialization of the product follows the creation of such a *de jure* standard. With *de facto* standards, individual firms commercialize products and the market then determines the winning *de facto* standard (Asaba, 1995; Besen and Farrell, 1994; Farrell and Saloner, 1992; Khazam and Mowery, 1992).

STANDARDS: MARKET COMPETITION

Much of the research on standards competition focuses on the pure market competition in the selection of *de facto* standards (David and Greenstein, 1990; Grindley, 1995). Four important findings have emerged from this research. First, independent firms negotiate the exchange of technology in an attempt to create "bandwagons" to develop products based on this technology (Farrell and Saloner, 1985) where both incumbents and new entrants (Kogut *et al.*, 1995) often play a key role in these negotiations. Price performance mechanisms and increasing returns to scale drive the installed base and thus the choice of industrial standards (Arthur, 1989).

Installed base is important since the value of a product to one user often depends on how many other users there are. In these cases, it is said that the product exhibits network externalities or network effects. The network can be either physical such as in telecommunication, transportation, or power systems, or virtual such as in the network of Wintel, VHS, and DVD users. Users often enjoy positive externalities or benefits when a new user joins the network since there is another person to communicate with or exchange compatible information (for example, files or tapes). Further, when economies of scale exist as they often do in the network industries, new users indirectly cause the availability to rise and the price to drop of hardware and even more so of software (whether it is software for computers or content for VCRs) (Farrell and Saloner, 1985). These positive externalities magnify small advantages in installed base and cause products to become the forecasted and thus *de facto* standard even when the installed base as a percent of total potential users is rather small. In many cases, this can lead to the product quickly acquiring close to a 100% share as in the case of the Wintel standard in PC operating systems and applications software (Shapiro and Varian, 1999).

Second, it is recognized that the choice of an open or closed policy plays a major role in the competition between standards because this policy can affect the installed base (Asaba, 1995; Grindley, 1995). Firms that adopt an open policy rather than a closed policy are more likely to obtain an early installed base for their products. An open policy is more likely to attract producers of complementary products and customers who may not want to become dependent on a single firm (Farrell and Saloner, 1986; Hayashi, 1992). Because of network externality effects, products that obtain an early installed base are more likely to become industry standards than other products (Katz and Shapiro, 1985).

Third, there is also a tradeoff between compatibility and performance. Making a product compatible with previous generations typically reduces performance and vice versa. The optimal tradeoff between performance and compatibility depends on the degree to which one must be sacrificed for the other and the number of new users (Shapiro and Varian, 1999).

Fourth, market mechanisms do not always succeed in setting a standard.[2] It has been determined conceptually (Farrell and Saloner, 1988) and shown empirically that it is often difficult for a single firm to create a standard (Farrell and Saloner, 1986). For example, in studies of the radio (see Berg, 1989) and TV broadcasting industries (Crane, 1979; Pelkman and Bueters, 1986), no single standard emerged.

STANDARDS: COMMITTEES

There also exists research on committee-generated standards. This research is mostly done from the standpoint of whether the committee work results in the establishment of a standard. Much of this work has been case study-based and has focused on how "anticipatory standards" are set (David and Greenstein, 1990). From these studies a number of institutional factors have been cited as playing a role in whether a standard is successfully chosen or not.

Since committees generally operate on a consensus basis in deciding on standards, institutional factors that improved the possibility of consensus resulted in standards being chosen (Sirbu and Zwimpfer, 1985; Besen and Johnson, 1986; Weiss and Sirbu, 1990; Funk and Methe, 2001). As summarized by Funk and Methe (2001), previous research has found that technology and market uncertainty, coalitions, ease of licensing, and other strategic considerations increased the livelihood of a standard being chosen.

Studies have found weaknesses in the committee-based standard-setting process as well (David and Greenstein, 1990). In particular, David (1986) found that government-based committees had very narrow windows of opportunity to influence the standard-setting process. These windows often occurred at times when the committee had the least amount of information available, rending them "blind giants" (David, 1986). Funk and Methe (2001) argue that movement away from consensus rule and the inclusion of users may be ways around the "blind giant" problem. Of relevance to this book have been the moves by the European Technology Standards Institute (ETSI) to avoid these problems by streamlining its decision-making process. ETSI has moved away from consensus rule to a strong majority rule (71%) and has opened up its membership to include a wider group of telecommunication stakeholders, in order to speed up its decision-making process and assure inter-operability (David and Steinmuller, 1994).

INVESTMENT SIZE AS A MODERATING VARIABLE ON STANDARDS SETTING

This book argues that although the hybrid model for setting standards is useful in a wide variety of situations, setting standards in cases where large investments are required in a specific interface is significantly different from cases where smaller investments are required or the critical interfaces are ambiguous. It is argued that the degree of required openness and the size of the coalitions (that is, the amount of competition between manufacturers and service-providers) increase as the size of the investment increases. As discussed in Chapter 1, the relationship between the level of openness in the standard and the amount of competition between either service providers or manufacturers is the linkage between the committee and market mechanisms at least in the competition between standards. Open standards attract a larger number of service providers and manufacturers, thus increasing the amount of competition within the standard and the number of agents who can act as agents of diffusion for the standard.

Very large investments have been and still are required in industries such as broadcasting (For example, digital television and radio, and high-definition television), transportation systems (For example, intelligent highway vehicle system, railroads, electric or hydrogen vehicles), power systems, and fixed wireline and mobile communication systems.[3] To a lesser extent, large investments are also required in consumer electronics (such as video tape recorders, CDs, digital video disks), computers, and other telecommunication (such as, wireless private branch exchanges, local area networks) products. Large investments are needed to create the infrastructure, content, production systems, and/or software.

What is unique about these industries is that large investments are often necessary *just* to offer basic services. And these large investments must be made by a variety of firms although the service and content providers typically must make the largest investments. For example, as shown in Table 2.1, these industries often require the development of industrial equipment, consumer equipment, and contents or services.

In these cases of extremely large investments, it is argued that large countries (for example, the US) or regions (for example, Europe) that adopt a single open standard and create competition between manufacturers and service providers are more likely to create a global standard than countries or regions that do otherwise. One reason for this is that incumbents will often not make the necessary investments in new technology unless there is a single open standard and a threat of new entrants.

Table 2.1   Types of actors involved with standards that
require large investments

Industry	Industrial equipment	Consumer equipment	Service or contents
Television or radio broadcasting	Television or radio transmission equipment producers	Television or radio receiving equipment producers	Television or radio program providers
Intelligent highway vehicle system	Information transmission or automobile control equipment producers	Information receiving equipment producers	Information and/ or highway control service providers
Fixed or mobile communication	Switching, base station, and transmission equipment producers	Phone producers	Fixed or mobile phone service providers
Video tape recording, digital video discs	Recording equipment producers	Playback equipment producers	Movie producers

Although in some cases, firms by themselves may be able to create such a single open standard and ensure competition between firms in these industries that require very large investments, in many cases, it is only the government that will be able to ensure all of these conditions. Thus its involvement may increase a country's chances of creating a global standard. Clearly there are potential problems with government involvement in these commercial activities. However, both the large number of regulated monopolies and the use of public resources such as land and frequency spectrum have caused many governments to be historically involved with these industries. This makes it easier for firms and consumers to accept government involvement. Further, what if one large country such as the US or one large region such as Europe or Asia (with Japan as the most likely leader) appears as if it can create a large installed base through government sponsorship of a single open standard and the awarding of new licences to ensure competition? Should governments of other countries or regions remain uninvolved or should they became involved and risk the chance of sponsoring an inferior system that is chosen for political reasons? Further, in these cases, should firms encourage governments to sponsor single open standards and if so how?

The mobile communications industry is an ideal industry to look at these issues due to the very large investments required and the large amount of technological change in this industry. For example, Japanese service-providers are expected to spend more than US$10 billion to implement third generation services that are based on W-CDMA.[4] On the other hand, the purchase of home video games, facsimile machines, personal computer software, or modems only involves a several hundred-dollar investment. Clearly, the former involves a much larger risk than the latter and these high risks cause firms to be careful in their choice of technology. A firm does not want to invest US$10 billion in a technology that will not be adopted by a large number of other users due to the existence of network externalities. The larger the number of service-providers that adopt W-CDMA, the larger the number of countries in which the Japanese handsets can be potentially used and the lower the future cost of handsets and infrastructure to the Japanese service-provider.

INTERFACE AMBIGUITY AS A MODERATING VARIABLE ON STANDARD SETTING

Many standard setting battles involve ill-defined interfaces and it is argued that this causes standard setting to occur quite differently than where the interfaces are well-defined. In most of the examples mentioned so far for mobile phones (interface between phones and base stations), broadcasting (interface between transmitters and receivers), and many types of consumer electronic products (CDs, tapes, and so on), the interface is fairly well-defined so the competition focuses just on this interface.

However, it is hypothesized that as uncertainty increases in what constitutes the key interface, the variety of relevant committees and markets will increase, as will the variety of alliances. As is discussed in Chapter 6, there are a number of interfaces involved with mobile computing and the mobile Internet and thus in addition to competition between various standards in each interface there is also competition *between* the various interfaces. In the mobile computing and mobile Internet markets, these interfaces include the interface between the users and various types of handsets (man–machine interface), the interface between the handsets and application programs (operating systems), or the interface between the handsets and the Internet (browsers and language for representing contents). The various types of handsets (that is, various types of markets) include mobile phones, PDAs, and handheld games, and if the wireline Internet is included, the list also includes desktop PCs, desktop games, digital televisions, and appliances. Due to the large number of interfaces and the competition between these interfaces, these handset manufacturers, software producers, and content providers are participating in a large variety of committees, markets, and alliances to determine the relevant interface standards.

Up till now, Chapter 2 has discussed competition *between* standards both in markets and committees and it has hypothesized two moderating variables: investment size and interface ambiguity. Chapter 2 now addresses theoretical issues that impact on the competition *within* standards both at the committee and market level in the mobile communications market. Although there clearly is a large literature aimed at market-based competition, there is little literature that ties the committee-and market-based competition together in the competition within a standard. The following three sections discuss three theoretical issues that impact on the competition within standards and at the end of this book, Chapter 7 will tie these aspects of committee- and market-based competition that occur within standards together with the competition between standards.

COMMITTEE-BASED COMPETITION WITHIN STANDARDS: CUSTOMER–SUPPLIER RELATIONSHIPS AND SWITCHING COSTS IN NETWORK-RELATED PRODUCTS

The focus on competition between two firms in the standards literature assumes that competition within a standard is relatively unimportant. This book argues that competition within standards occurs both in committees and markets and these competitions occur simultaneously with the competition between standards. It will find that committee-based competition in the form of high switching costs and long-term relationships between customers and suppliers plays a stronger role in mobile infrastructure than market-based competition. Mobile infrastructure providers must simultaneously participate in the standard setting process and cooperatively develop the technology with the service providers. Since the cooperative development work with the service provider is done within the context of the standard setting work in the committee, this cooperative development work may be defined as part of the competition in committees and not markets.

The cooperative development work between infrastructure and service providers may be considered a part of customer–supplier relationships, a popular topic in the field of Total Quality Management and supplier relationships in management books in the late 1980s. These studies of the automobile and other assembly industries found that it is easier to maintain than develop new relationships with customers and it is important to work with suppliers on improvements in quality, lead-time, and costs (Juran, 1992).

However, customer–supplier relationships are different and perhaps even more important in network-related industries such as computing, information, telecommunications, power, and transportation systems. Not only are these products complex, compatibility with other products is critical and thus switching costs are high (Williamson, 1975; Klemperer, 1995, Shapiro and Varian, 1999). Consumers and in particular firms must incur large durable equipment, software, training, maintenance, and information costs when they change suppliers of a product that has high switching costs. Thus, long-term relationships between customers and suppliers are common where firms often buy multiple generations of network-related products such as computers, telecommunications equipment, defence systems, automated production systems, and power systems equipment from the same vendor due to these high switching costs (Hobday, 1998).

Firms and consumers can be "locked in" at the technology (that is, standard) and/or the vendor level. One reason for creating standards is to eliminate or reduce vendor lock-in. For example, the creation of standards for many consumer electronics products such as video tape recorders, compact discs, and digital video disks has virtually eliminated vendor lock-in while to some extent creating technology lock-in. Of course, if a firm controls a particular standard (such as Microsoft controls Windows), the technology lock-in may eliminate vendor lock-in at one level (in the case of Windows, the computer level) while leading to vendor lock-in at another level (Microsoft) (Shapiro and Varian, 1999). In some cases such as the case of mobile communication systems that is described in this book, the complexity of the standard can lead to lock-in at both the technology and vendor level.

Technological discontinuities can reduce the degree of vendor lock-in and thus change customer–supplier relationships. This is partly since incumbents are often slow to invest in new technologies particularly when the new technology renders existing competencies useless or cannibalizes existing sales.[5] Large performance advantages in the new technology may also make switching costs meaningless, particularly when there is little compatibility between the old and new technologies. Thus, a long-standing managerial question has been how incumbents can survive when technological discontinuities may render existing competencies useless.

Incumbents have several advantages, however. They often control the committees that set standards and, due to switching costs, their customers may not necessarily want to change vendors, particularly if their vendor is not extracting monopoly profits from them. Incumbents can use their influence in these standard-setting committees to increase the amount of compatibility between the old and new technologies, thus raising switching costs. And even if there is no compatibility, the incumbents' influence in these standard setting committees can enable them to maintain a technological advantage over new entrants or at the minimum have technological parity (Besen and Farrell, 1994; Farrell and Saloner, 1998; Shapiro and Varian, 1999).

Influencing standard-setting committees is even more difficult at the global level, however. As discussed in Chapter 1, the sources of standards have changed from the US in analog to Europe in digital and Japan in third generation technology. Therefore, the most successful mobile communications infrastructure and phone firms have been participating in standard-setting committees on three continents for many years and they have also created global development capabilities to support participation in these standard-setting activities.

THE ROLE OF GLOBAL DEVELOPMENT IN COMMITTEE-AND MARKET-BASED COMPETITION

Most firms continue to globalize their operations in order to respond better to local needs and make better use of local capabilities. Historically, most firms have first globalized their marketing functions in order to obtain a better understanding of local needs. Manufacturing is often the second function to be globalized for either access to low-cost labor or for political reasons. For example, telecommunication firms have often agreed to locally produce equipment (and sometimes purchase local parts) in order to obtain both wireline and mobile equipment orders while in Japan, overseas production became a national strategy during the late 1980s to avoid trade friction with the US.

Development is typically the last function to be globalized since there are clearly large advantages to centralized development. However, specific needs that arise overseas typically require and have led to the establishment of overseas development centers. Further, many multinational firms have acquired overseas development capabilities through mergers and acquisitions. Thus, the main issue that the current literature on global development focuses on is how firms can effectively and efficiently utilize this technology on a global scale.[6]

While this book does not dispute the importance of this topic, it argues that in the network industries, the issues of standards, switching costs, and relationships with customers are an important part of this debate on global management and global development. And the mobile communications industry is an ideal industry with regard to these issues partly since it is dramatically different from the wireline telecommunications industry where most of the firms came from. Historically, these firms have developed technology in their home countries and adapted the technology for foreign markets when necessary. Since these adaptations have been relatively minor, most of the development work has been done in each firm's home country and most vendors have been able to sell the same, albeit relatively proprietary wireline equipment to most countries.[7]

In the mobile part of the telecommunications industry, however, different countries have chosen different mobile communications standards due to the use of different frequency bands, other needs, and the desire by domestic firms to promote their proprietary technology. Thus, it has been very difficult to sell the same or similar equipment to all carriers in the world except in the cases where the standards adopted by an equipment vendor's country have become global standards. This has caused global development to be more important to the mobile than to the wireline switching industry. But by itself global development does not appear to have played an important role in competition between mobile communication system providers. Rather, global development capability has primarily been important when it has been used in combination with participating in foreign standard setting processes and creating global relationships with carriers.

In mobile phones, global development capability is needed for a slightly different reason than with mobile communication systems. Although participation in the standard-setting process is also necessary, the product is simpler, continuity in customer–supplier relations is not a major issue (except perhaps in Japan), and competition is largely market-based. Within this market-based competition, a major issue is how to understand the similarities and differences between phones in order to develop global platforms.

THE ROLE OF PRODUCT LINE AND PLATFORM MANAGEMENT IN MARKET-BASED COMPETITION

It is widely recognized that effective product line and product platform management can lead to lower manufacturing, material, and development costs and shorter development times. Effectively designed platform products include "a set of common subsystems and interfaces from which a stream of derivative products can be efficiently developed and produced."[8] Firms can use these platform products to expand their product line either horizontally into other market segments or vertically (either up or down) into different price levels for a given segment in the market. Moving to higher price levels requires the addition of functionality while moving to lower price levels requires the removal of functionality. In both cases, common subsystems are achieved through the classifying and analyzing of subsystems, the identification of common customer needs and technologies,[9] the use of modular design, and the mapping of functional requirements to physical architecture[10].

However, the existing literature on product line/platform management has largely focused on industries such as the automobile or appliance industry that are not part of the network economy. And it is expected that the appropriate form of product line/platform management will be different in the network than non-network industries since the cost structures of these industries are different. The network economy is characterized by high fixed and low marginal costs and by rapidly declining costs both due to economies of scale and technological progress. Extreme cases are found in industries such as the information (For example, publishing, broadcasting, and the Internet), telecommunication, and airline industries where the marginal costs are almost zero when compared to the fixed costs. And when there is competition, prices often fall toward marginal costs. This is why the price of encyclopedias has dropped dramatically, why many Internet content providers give away information for free[11] and why mobile phone service providers heavily subsidize phones. Further, as the ratio of operating to fixed costs drops to very low levels, firms must price according to value, not cost, in order to recoup their large investments in fixed costs. The challenge is to segment users according to their willingness to pay.[12]

Similar situations, albeit less extreme, also exist in manufacturing industries that are experiencing rapidly declining costs due to both economies of scale and technological progress. Industries such as the consumer electronics, computer, electronic game, and mobile phone industries are experiencing rapidly declining costs due to both economies of scale and technological progress in such areas as semiconductor devices, discrete electronic parts, batteries, displays, magnetic and optical disk drives, and optical fibre. In these industries, performance–price improvements of 30 % per year are not uncommon and it is in these industries that this book's discussion of product line/platform management has the most relevance.

These high fixed and rapidly declining marginal costs that are spreading from the service side to the manufacturing side of the network economy will change the manner in which these manufacturing firms carry out product line/platform management. It is already common for firms to price initially below cost on the expectation that costs will drop. Effective platform management expands the applicability of this strategy. Firms can develop a wide variety of custom or derivative products from a common platform product; the common platform of course provides the high volumes and thus rapidly declining costs.

Also of interest, the use of common platforms also provides manufacturers with a large amount of flexibility in pricing since there is a large amount of cost interdependencies between models. Manufacturers can set prices according to customer value rather than cost. They can subsidize low-end models to obtain economies of scale while making profits at the high end of the market through creating a brand image and pricing by value or, in other words, customer willingness to pay.

The effective implementation of such product line/platform management strategies in the network economy, particularly the manufacturing side of the network economy, requires a number of issues to be addressed. When should firms introduce volume-based discounts? How and when should they begin expanding their product lines? How many derivative projects should be carried out using a single platform, how should the products be priced, and can a particular strategy act as an entry barrier to other firms? And what are the variables that determine the answers to these questions?

Moreover, can firms develop global platforms and should they try to? Automobile firms have struggled for years to develop global platforms without success. What are the factors necessary to develop these global platforms? Chapter 5 will find that firms with this global development capability can change the competition from competition within a single standard, including its relevant committees and markets, to competition at the global level.

Notes

1. Anderson and Tushman, 1990; Christensen, 1998; Shapiro and Varian, 1999.
2. See Funk and Methe (2001) for a more detailed discussion of these issues.
3. The specific interfaces include the transmission protocol for television, radio, and communication signals and the protocol for controlling vehicles in an intelligent vehicle system.
4. See page 20 n. 10.
5. Anderson and Tushman, 1990; Tushman and Anderson, 1986; Utterback, 1994.
6. For example, see *Innovation Management: Strategies, Implementation, and Profits* by Allan Afuah, Oxford University Press, 1997; *Managing Across Borders: The Transnational Solution*, 2nd edn by Christopher A. Bartlett and Sumantra Ghoshal, Harvard Business School Press, 1998.
7. One exception has been NTT Docomo which has made a number of unique technical decisions that has forced NEC and Fujitsu to develop different types of equipment for the Japanese and foreign markets (Fransman, 1995).
8. Meyer and Lehnerd, *The Power of Product Platforms*, The Free Press, 1997, p. xii.
9. Ibid.
10. Ulrich, 1995.
11. Shapiro and Varian, *Information Rules: A Strategic Guide to the Network Economy*, Harvard Business School Press, 1999.
12. For example, airlines use the volumes in economy class to fill the planes while they make their profits in business and first class: Shapiro and Varian, *Information Rules: A Strategic Guide to the Network Economy*, Harvard Business School Press, 1999.

3 Market and Committee Mechanisms in Setting Global Standards

This chapter shows how the hybrid model of setting standards explains standard setting in the mobile communications industry better than a model that only employs one or the other mechanism. For the most part, national and regional committees selected mobile communication standards, where market mechanisms, through increasing returns to scale, caused the emergence of global standards.

This chapter also argues that the choice of a single open standard by a large country (for example, the US) or region (for example, Europe) has been far more effective in creating global standards than promoting competition between multiple standards within a country or region. The choice of a single open standard by a large country such as the US or a region such as Europe has caused the forecasted installed base for the specific standard to rise dramatically, thus providing the stimulus for starting the so-called bandwagon effect. The degree of openness in a standard is reflected by the number of service-providers and manufacturers that participate in the creation of the standard.

This degree of openness also provides the linkage between the committee and market mechanisms in the creation of standards. The expected and actual competition between service-providers and manufacturers is of course related to the number of firms that participate in the creation of the standard. And this expected and actual competition promoted market mechanisms since it influenced the forecasted and actual installed base for the standard. The competition between service-providers, in particular the awarding of new services licences, increased the forecasted and actual installed base since it convinced other countries and service-providers in other countries that someone would actually start services that are based on the new standard. Competition between manufacturers convinced other countries that prices for infrastructure and phones would drop, thus enabling a growth in subscribers. Further, competition between manufacturers also increased the number of firms that were able to act as agents of diffusion in convincing non-aligned third party governments and service-providers to adopt the standard as their own.

The creation of a large forecasted installed base was particularly important in this industry due to the large investments associated with implementing mobile communication systems, which make service-providers very risk averse. Most service-providers have been unwilling to adopt a standard until many other service-providers have announced their intention to adopt the specific standard. This is why the choice of a single standard by a specific country or region along with expected competition between manufacturers has been necessary to start the bandwagon for a specific mobile communication standard.

Both governments and firms can and did influence the start of this bandwagon through their effect on the mix and role of committee or market mechanisms at the national level. However, although it goes without saying that firms play the most important role in creating, choosing, and diffusing standards, in many cases it is only the government that will be able to start this bandwagon when a single standard and competition between manufacturers are necessary. In this case, government involvement may increase a country's chances of creating a global standard. While most people would agree that governments should attempt to increase competition, the degree to which they are involved with doing this and choosing a single standard is problematic. Government involvement may be able to facilitate the creation of a single open standard and the existence of competition but it may also encourage the selection of an inferior system for political reasons. In what situations should governments be involved with setting these standards and how should they be involved?

Government involvement will probably be more effective and accepted in industries where they have played an historical role. In telecommunications, governments have traditionally played a strong role through the existence of regulated monopolies. They have typically determined the wireline standards and prices or at the minimum have had a large influence on the standards and prices through their control of the committees that make these decisions. However, the deregulation of telecommunications and other industries that started in the 1980s has caused many governments to redefine their roles in these industries. Thus, while governments have also played a strong role in the mobile communications industry, these roles have changed dramatically since the early 1980s, allowing one to compare the various methods used by governments and firms. In some cases governments have determined the standards, in others the degree of openness in creating a standard, or even when they have left the choice of standards to the marketplace, they have influenced the choice of a standard by their allocation of a specific frequency band. Further, at the minimum, governments have determined the number of licences to award per market and thus determined the degree of competition. In turn, this has enabled them to indirectly influence the prices, demand, and installed base for the mobile communication services.

AN OVERVIEW OF MOBILE COMMUNICATION SYSTEMS AND STANDARDS

All mobile communication systems have a number of similar charac-teristics as shown in Figure 3.1. Voices are transmitted between the handsets and the base stations via analog or digital signals using a variety of frequency bands (450MHz to 2GHz).[1] The switching sta-tions transfer calls between different base stations (calls between mobile phones) and between a mobile and wireline system (calls be-tween mobile and fixed line phones). Further, they also transfer the control for a call between base stations as users move between areas that are controlled by different base stations. Service providers manage these mobile communication systems along with a variety of other technical systems that are needed to provide mobile communication services (such as billing systems). Infrastructure suppliers provide the base stations, switching equipment, and network management systems. Handset suppliers provide the handsets. Although many firms supply

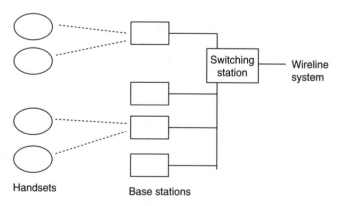

Figure 3.1   Outline of a typical mobile communication system

Table 3.1   Evolution of mobile communication standards in major
countries and year in which service-began

Country	1st generation analog cellular	2nd generation digital cellular	3rd generation digital cellular	Low mobility cellular
US	AMPS (83)	DAMPS (92), GSM (95), cdmaOne (96)	Various standards	None
Japan	NTT (79) TACS (89)	PDC (93) cdmaOne (98)	Wide-band CDMA (2001)	PHS (95)
Scandinavia	NMT (81)	GSM (92)	Wide-band CDMA	None
Great Britain	TACS (84)	GSM (92)	Wide-band CDMA	Telepoint (89)
Italy	RTMS (85) TACS (89)	GSM (92)	Wide-band CDMA	None
France	RC2000 (85) NMT (89)	GSM (92)	Wide-band CDMA	None
Germany	C-Netz (85)	GSM (92)	Wide-band CDMA	None

Source: Garrard, 1998.

both infrastructure and handsets, it is uncommon for infrastructure or handset suppliers to be involved in the management of carriers.[2] Mobile communication standards define some or all of the interfaces that are shown in Figure 3.1.

Technological change in the mobile communication industry

Table 3.1 shows the evolution of three generations of mobile communication standards in the countries that contain the world's leading producers of telecommunication equipment. First generation analog services were first started in Japan in 1979, in Scandinavia in 1981, and in the US in 1983. France, Germany, Great Britain and Italy started services in 1985. Second generation digital services were first started in 1992 in Europe and by 1995 digital services were being offered in more than 100 countries. The major advantage of digital systems (second generation) over analog systems (first generation) is in voice quality and in the level of efficiency that they use the frequency spectrum. Since frequency spectrum is a limited resource, frequency spectrum efficiency is important. Digital systems also generally have better voice quality and data transmission capabilities. Low mobility digital systems such as Japan's Personal Handyphone System (PHS) are a low-cost version of second generation digital systems. They are cheaper to install than conventional digital systems in densely populated areas[3] but the phones cannot be used in fast-moving vehicles. Thus, they have been mostly considered applicable to densely populated areas in Asia. Third generation systems are expected to include higher than existing frequency spectrum efficiencies, better voice quality, and much higher than existing data transmission rates (greater than 1Mbps) than second generation cellular systems, along with multi-media capability and global roaming.

The actual standards that these countries adopted are quite confusing even to those who know the industry well. Acronyms are widely used and often the names of the standards change over time and/or are different depending on whether the publication is a US-or European-based publication. Therefore, this book will introduce the names of these standards gradually with a focus first on global standards.

The evolution of "global" standards

Table 3.2 shows the evolution of mobile communication global standards. This book defines global standards in terms of both their number of subscribers and the number of countries adopting that standard. The system with the largest market share is usually said to be the standard. However, if a country, such as the US, with a large market sets a standard, then it may appear that its system is the *de facto* global standard in spite of the standard's small global presence. Consequently, this book argues that for a standard to be a global standard, the number of countries adopting that standard as well as its number of subscribers is important.

AMPS and GSM, W-CDMA, and to a much lesser extent NMT and cdmaOne can be defined as global standards since a large number of countries have adopted them and they have acquired a significant fraction of the subscribers. AMPS (originally developed in the US) and GSM (originally developed in Europe) are clearly global standards in terms of both the number of adopting countries and the number of subscribers. Service-providers in most European and Asian countries have announced that they will start services that are based on W-CDMA, albeit actual services will not be started in many countries until 2002.

In the case of NMT (developed in Scandinavia), although there were only five million subscribers to systems based on the NMT standard at

Table 3.2 The evolution of global standards

Generation of technology	Communication standard	The standards country or region of origin	Number of adopting countries (end of 98)	Number and percent of each generation's subscribers as of December 1998	
First generation analog cellular	AMPS* TACS* NMT	North America (83) Britain (85) Scandinavia (81)	79 25 35	72.0 15.0 5.0	78% 16% 6%
Second generation digital cellular	GSM* DAMPS cdmaOne PDC	Europe (92) US (93) US and Korea (96) Japan (93)	120 35 15 1	132.0 18.5 23.0 36.0	63% 9% 11% 17%
Low-mobility digital cellular	PHS	Japan (95)	1	6.0	98%
Third generation digital cellular	Wide-Band CDMA*	Japan (2001)			

* Global standards.
Source: Interview and author's analysis.

the end of 1998, it was the first system to be adopted by multiple countries. Six countries, beginning with Scandinavia, had introduced NMT systems before services based on AMPS were started. By the end of 1993, 36 countries had introduced NMT systems. cdmaOne (originally developed in the US and implemented in Korea) may become a global standard although the numbers of subscribers and adopting countries are still very low compared to AMPS and GSM.

Data for DAMPS, PHS, and PDC are included in Table 3.2 for comparative purposes. DAMPS (digitalized version of AMPS) was originally developed in the US while PHS and PDC were developed and still primarily used in Japan. It should be pointed out that DAMPS is often called TDMA (time division multiple access) in the US where it, cdmaOne and GSM are the three digital standards that

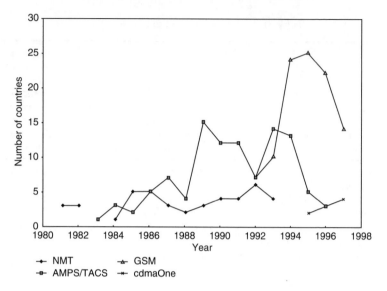

Figure 3.2   The number of countries starting services based on the major standards by year

are used in the US. This book uses the term DAMPS since TDMA is actually a technology and not a standard. In fact, GSM, PDC, and DAMPS are all based on TDMA technology. The term TDMA began to be used for DAMPS in the US in order to distinguish it from CDMA (code division multiple access) technology after CDMA became a candidate for adoption by service-providers. The first system to be based on CDMA technology was originally called IS95 CDMA and is now primarily called cdmaOne, the term used in this book. W-CDMA is of course also based on CDMA technology.

Figure 3.2 shows the number of countries that started services based on these global standards for each year between 1981 and 1997 and Table 3.3 shows the names of these countries. As shown in Figure 3.2, in 1987, the number of countries beginning services based on AMPS and TACS surpassed NMT; a situation that has continued until the beginning of the twenty-first century. In 1994, the number of countries adopting GSM for the first time passed AMPS and TACS and this situation is expected to continue for several years.

The general trend from NMT in the mid-1980s to AMPS/TACS in the late 1980s and early 1990s to GSM in the mid-1990s can also be found in an analysis of most major regions in the world. In the

Table 3.3 Service start dates for selected analog and digital standards and countries

Standard	1981	1982	1983	1984	1985	1986	1987	1988	1989
NMT	Sweden, Norway, Saudi Arabia	Denmark, Finland, Spain		Austria	Luxembourg, Netherlands, Oman, Tunisia, Malaysia	Iceland, Turkey, Thailand, Indonesia	Belgium, Morocco, Switzerland	Cyprus	France, Algeria, Cambodia, Faroe Is.
AMPS			US	Canada, Korea		Australia, Virgin Is., Israel	Cayman Is., Bermuda, Dominican Republic, Singapore, New Zealand, Thailand	Venezuela, Zaire	Chile, Curacao, Argentina, Antigua, St. Kitts, Mexico, Dutch Antilles, Brunei, Taiwan
TACS				Hong Kong	Ireland, UK		Bahrain	Macao, China	Sri Lanka, Japan, Malaysia, Taiwan, Mauritania, UAE
Others	Japan (NTT–1979)				Germany, France, Italy	S. Africa (CNETZ)			Portugal (CNETZ)

(Contd.)

44

Table 3.3 Contd.

Standard	1990	1991	1992	1993	1994	1995	1996
NMT	Andorra, Croatia, Hungary, Slovenia	Czechoslovakia, Estonia, Russia	Greenland, Latvia, Lithuania, Poland, Uzbekistan, Estonia	Belarus, Bulgaria, Romania, Ukraine			Cook Is., Honduras, Panama
AMPS	Barbados, Grenada, Guatemala, Peru, St. Lucia, St. Vincent, Pakistan	Bolivia, Guadeloupe, Jamaica, Martinique, St. Martin, Uruguay, Trinidad & Tobago, Indonesia, Lebanon, Philippines	Montserrat, Paraguay, Burma, Cambodia, Guam, Russia, Vietnam, Gabon, Brazil	Aruba, Belize, Cuba, El Salvador, Guinea, Nicaragua, Surinam, Bangladesh, Kazakhstan, Laos, Sri Lanka, Burundi	Colombia, Costa Rica, Ecuador, Ghana, Madagascar, Georgia, Uzbekistan, Turkmenistan, Nauru	Angola, Benin, Central Africa, Zambia, Papua New Guinea	
TACS	Italy, Malta, Spain, Austria	Kuwait, Singapore	Ghana, Nigeria	Kenya, Yemen	Philippines, Zaire, Gambia		

GSM	Denmark, Finland, France, Germany, Italy, Portugal, Sweden, UK	Greece, Ireland, Luxembourg, Switzerland, Norway, Austria, Australia, New Zealand, UAE, Hong Kong	Belgium, Iceland, Holland, Hungary, Russia, Turkey, Morocco, Tunisia, S. Africa, Azerbaijan, Iran, Qatar, Kuwait, Pakistan, Brunei, Indonesia, Philippines, Cambodia, China, Thailand, Laos, Vietnam, Fiji, Cameroon	Bulgaria, Croatia, Cyprus, Gibraltar, Lithuania, Spain, Andorra, Georgia, Bahrain, Lebanon, Egypt, Jordan, Lesotho, Namibia, Uganda, Nigeria, Tanzania, Malaysia, Macao, India, Seychelles, Sri Lanka, Taiwan, US, Canada	Albania, Bosnia, Czech Republic, Slovakia, Latvia, Macedonia, Montenegro, Poland, Libya, Saudi Arabia, West Bank/Gaza, Cote d'Ivoire, Ghana, Zimbabwe, Malawi, Mauritius, Bolivia, Mongolia, Serbia, Tunisia, Venezuela, Kenya	Bangladesh, Djibouti, Israel, Mozambique, Nepal, Romania, Taiwan, Syria, West Bank, Armenia, Estonia, Senegal, Madagascar, Georgia	Venezuela, Peru, Cape Verde, Burkina Faso, Zimbabwe
cdma One				Hong Kong, US	Peru, Canada, Korea	Singapore, China, Zambia, Yemen	Israel, Philippines, Mexico, Indonesia, Brazil, Japan

mid-1980s, four Asian countries adopted NMT versus two for AMPS or TACS while between 1988 and 1993 twelve countries adopted either AMPS or TACS. From 1994 onwards, seventeen Asian countries adopted GSM versus only two countries for AMPS and TACS. In Africa, four (all in North Africa) countries adopted NMT in the 1980s versus three countries for TACS. Between 1990 and 1993, five countries adopted AMPS or TACS, and after 1994, seventeen countries adopted GSM against two for TACS or AMPS. In the Middle East (which overlaps with Africa), four countries adopted NMT versus four for AMPS and TACS until 1993. From 1994, however, eleven countries have adopted GSM versus none for NMT and AMPS/TACS.

South and Central America and Europe have slightly different diffusion patterns than Asia and Africa. Almost all of the South and Central American (including the Caribbean) countries initially adopted the US AMPS for historical rather than political reasons. Similar to wireline standards where South and Central American countries have for the most part adopted US standards, virtually all of the South and Central America countries also decided to allocate the same frequency band (800 MHz) as the United States to mobile communication services.[4] This includes Cuba and Nicaragua who clearly would prefer not to support an important US policy.

European countries have primarily emphasized NMT and GSM for technical as opposed to political reasons. Only Great Britain, Ireland, Spain, Austria, and Malta adopted the AMPS/TACS (in this case TACS) standard. In Western Europe, this is probably due to the early success of NMT (eleven countries adopted it during the 1980s) and the adoption of unique standards by France, Germany, and Italy. The emphasis on NMT and GSM is even more pronounced in Eastern Europe and the old Soviet republics (at least the northern ones) where systems based on NMT 450 were installed even in the early 1990s (see discussion below).

Characteristics of global standards

As shown in Table 3.4, the systems that became mobile communication global standards had relatively high levels of early installed base[5] and openness. This is similar to most other products or standards that have been the subject of books and articles on industrial standards. One measure of openness is the number of sponsors, that is, the number of participants in the standard-setting process. Table 3.5 summarizes the number of sponsors for a number of mobile communication standards.

Table 3.4 Selected information for global and non-global standards

Generation of technology	System	Introduction date	The standard's country or region of origin	In country or region of origin soon after introduction		Degree of openness
				# of subscribers (1000s)	Penetration rate (%)	
First generation analog systems	AMPS	1983	US	680 (86)	0.27 (86)	High
	NMT	1981	Scandinavia	330	1.5	High
	TACS	1984	UK	122	0.18	High
	C-Netz	1986	W. Germany	17	0.03	Low
	RC2000	1985	France	10	0.02	Low
	NTT	1979	Japan	75	0.06	Low
	RTMS	1985	Italy	4	<0.01	Low
Second generation digital systems	DAMPS	1992	US	3.5 (92)	<0.01 (92)	High
				80 (93)	0.032 (93)	
				480 (94)	0.192 (94)	

(Contd.)

Table 3.4 Contd.

Generation of technology	System	Introduction date	The standard's country or region of origin	In country or region of origin soon after introduction		Degree of openness
				# of subscribers (1000s)	Penetration rate (%)	
	GSM	1992	Western Europe	500 (92) 1400 (93) 4700 (94)	0.20 (92) 0.56 (93) 1.9 (94)	High
	PDC	1993	Japan	<10 (93) 200 (94)	<0.01 (93) 0.50 (94)	Low
	cdmaOne	1995	US and Korea	1100 (96) 7400 (97)	0.37 (96) 2.5 (97)	Low
Low-mobility digital cellular	PHS	1995	Japan	4900 (96) 6900 (97)	3.8 (96) 5.5 (97)	Medium
	CT-2	1994	Hong Kong	175 (96)	<0.1 (96)	High

Source: Garrard, 1998; Telecommunications, Various years: Paet Sch 1993.

Table 3.5 Openness: the number of sponsors [1] per standard

| Generation of technology | Standard | Initial sponsors | |
		Service providers	Manufacturers
Analog	NTT	NTT	NEC, Fujitsu
	NMT*	Four Scandinavian PTTs	>10 firms from Europe, the US, and Japan
	AMPS* [2]	> 50 service-providers	>10 firms from Europe, the US, and Japan
	C-Netz	Deutsche Telekom	Siemens, PKI
	RC2000	France Télécom	Matra
	RTMS	Italy's PTT (SPI)	Italtel, Telettra
	MATSE	None	AlcaTel & Philips
Digital	GSM*	13 European PTTs	>10 firms from Europe and the US
	DAMPS	All members of CTIA	>10 firms from Europe, the US and Japan

(Contd.)

Table 3.5 Contd.

Generation of technology	Standard	Initial sponsors	
		Service providers	Manufacturers
	PDC	NTT DoCoMo	NEC, Fujitsu, Motorola, Lucent, Ericsson
	PHS	NTT Personal, DDI Pocket, Astel	>10 Japanese firms
	cdmaOne[3]	Initially (early 1990s), None	Initially (early 1990s) Qualcomm, Hughes
	PACS	None	
Third generation	DoCoMo W-CDMA	>10 service-providers from Japan, the US, Asia, and Europe	>10 firms from Japan, the US, Asia, and Europe
	TD-CDMA	None	>10 firms from Japan, Europe, and the US
	CdmaOne 2000	Initially (May 1997) None	Initially (May 1997), Qualcomm, Motorola, Lucent, Nortel

* Global standards.
1. Sponsors are defined as the participants in the standard setting process.
2. Although the FCC defined the specifications, many firms submitted proposals and were the initial providers of service, phones, and infrastructure.
3. Qualcomm had licenced its technology to 14 service-providers and 16 manufacturers by mid-1996 (Garrard, 1998).
Source: Interview and author's analysis.

This book differs from other research in this area in that this chapter will show how a hybrid system of committees and markets leads to greater levels of early installed base and openness. Figure 3.3 uses Table 3.4 to classify the standards as relatively closed (single or few sponsors), relatively open (many sponsors) or committee-based (where the actual standard-setting process is also open and a single standard is chosen). This is a bit confusing in that the committee-based method of standard setting is one type of committee mechanism, in this case the most successful type. All of the global mobile communication standards (AMPS, GSM, and W-CDMA) are committee-based standards (with international participation) that are for the most part sponsored by governmental agencies. Further, several of the global and non-global standards have evolved towards a more open or committee-based standard setting process throughout their life in order to gain support.

Figure 3.4 uses Figure 3.3, Table 3.4, and other information to also summarize the evolution of the standard-setting processes in several major countries. Most of Europe and Japan moved from a relatively closed approach in analog standard setting to a committee-based approach that is open to both domestic and foreign participants in second and third generation digital standard-setting. On the other hand, the US has moved from a committee-based approach in analog to complete free market competition in second and third generation digital standard-setting. This is one reason why Europe's GSM system became the second generation standard and cooperation between Europe (Nokia and Ericsson) and Japan (NTT DoCoMo) have probably made W-CDMA the third generation standard as opposed to a US-developed second or third generation system.

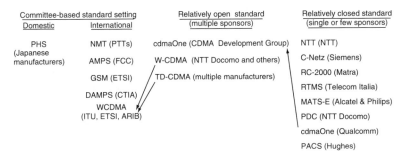

Figure 3.3 Standard-setting method by system (sponsors in parentheses, arrows show the evolution of the standard)

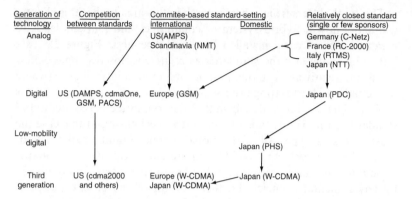

Figure 3.4   Evolution of standard-setting method in major countries (standards are in parentheses and arrows show evolution both within and between generations)

The critical market-based mechanisms are expected and actual competition between manufacturers and service-providers in the market. These factors also have a strong impact on forecasted and actual installed base in much the same way that the adoption of a single standard by a country or region does. Although the degree of competition is of course related to the degree of openness, this is not the only effect that governments have on competition. Since governments have largely determined whether phones will be rented or purchased and the number of licences to award, they have also had a strong effect on the degree of competition in phones and services through these policies.

Table 3.6 summarizes the degree of competition in phones and services for each of the standards. As shown in Table 3.6, the systems that became mobile communication global standards had relatively high levels of competition between both manufacturers and service-providers. For example, the expected and actual awarding of new licences by European countries during the competition between second and third generation systems has increased the forecasted and actual installed bases for their systems. Similarly, the expected and actual awarding of new licences in Japan and announcements by NTT DoC-oMo that it would aggressively implement W-CDMA have also lead to large forecasted and probably large actual installed bases for W-CDMA in Japan. On the other hand, the expected and actual lack of licences in the US when DAMPS was being created and third generation systems were being considered is a second reason why Europe

Table 3.6 The expected degree of competition between manufacturers (handsets and infrastructure) and service-providers for each standard

Generation of technology	Country and standard (*global standard)	Expected degree of competition	
		Service providers (i.e., new licences)	Manufacturers
Analog	Japan's NTT	Low	Low
	Scandinavia's NMT*	Medium	High
	US AMPS*	High	High
	Germany's CNETZ	Low	Low
	France's RC2000	Low	Low
	Italy's RTMS	Low	Low
Digital	Europe's GSM*	High	High
	US DAMPS	Low	High
	Japan's PDC	High	High
	Japan's PHS	High	High
	US and Korean cdmaOne	High	Medium
Third generation	Japan (W-CDMA)	High	High
	Europe (W-CDMA)	High	High
	US (cdma2000)	Low	High

Source: Interviews.

and Japan and not the US are the sources of the second and third generation standards.

The rest of this chapter shows how a hybrid model of committees and markets is more effective than an emphasis on one or the other. It begins with competition between various analog systems including the first analog system to be adopted by multiple countries, called NMT.

THE FIRST REGIONAL STANDARD: SCANDINAVIA'S NMT SYSTEM

The Nordic Mobile Telephone (NMT) standard was the first standard to be used by multiple countries and to be adopted by countries other than those who created the standard. The reason for its relatively strong success is that the Scandinavian companies and Ministries of Telecommunications (MPTs) adopted a single open standard and it created a relatively large amount of competition between manufacturers and to some extent service-providers. The single open standard was created in an open standard-setting committee process in which both domestic and foreign companies could participate.

The Scandinavian companies and MPTs had been cooperating on mobile communications since the 1950s. In 1969, they established the Nordic Mobile Telephone Group and by 1975, a timetable for the implementation of the NMT system had been established that planned for service-to begin in 1981. An open specification that used the 450 MHz band was defined in 1977 in which operators were free to define their networks and manufacturers were free to design and manufacture equipment to these specifications. Although the Swedish Telecom Radio Laboratory did much of the early development work in Sweden, in 1977, firms were invited to submit proposals for the supply of base stations and switches for a commercial NMT system. Ten manufacturing companies made proposals including foreign firms such as Fujitsu, Hitachi, Motorola, and NEC.[6]

NMT service-began in late 1981 and early 1982 in Sweden, Norway, Denmark, and Finland. The choice of a single open standard by Scandinavia and the relative success of pre-cellular systems in Scandinavia led to relatively high subscriber forecasts (for that time) for NMT in Scandinavia. This caused several other countries to immediately adopt the standard. For example, Saudi Arabia decided to adopt NMT in 1981 (it actually started services before Sweden in September 1981), Spain decided to adopt NMT in early 1982 (services were started in June 1982) and the Netherlands, Belgium, and Italy were expected to quickly follow at that time.[7]

The strong early growth in subscribers in the NMT services also drove the further adoption of NMT by other countries. By the end of 1983, there were more than 75,000 NMT subscribers, which was more than any other standard in use at that time (see Figure 3.5). It was more than the number of subscribers in the US (70,000) and more than twice the number of subscribers in Japan (35,000) despite Japan's earlier start (1979) and much higher population. By the end of 1984 there were about 150,000 subscribers, which was almost four times as many as in Japan and only slightly less than in the US (170,000).[8]

The initial high growth rate was due to low handset (handsets were purchased, not rented) and service-charges and geographical and life-style characteristics in Scandinavia.[9] The operators set low service-charges due to their relatively optimistic forecasts for mobile services, competition from pre-cellular systems and through some pressure from the government.[10] The annual charges were dropped by 50% with the

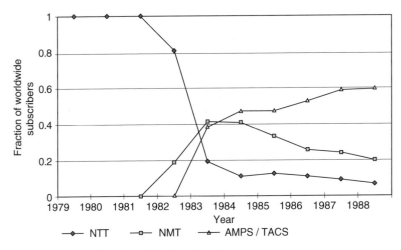

Figure 3.5   Fraction of worldwide subscribers per year

start of the NMT 900 service 1986;[11] this price reduction had been planned since early 1984[12] Even in 1989, Scandinavian service-providers, in particular Iceland and Denmark still had the lowest mobile phone charges in Europe.[13] Interestingly, unlike the US and Great Britain, the service-providers did not pay large activation commissions to retail outlets for acquiring subscribers.

As a result of this growth, a 900MHz NMT system was installed in the major Scandinavian cities and subsequently in numerous other countries in Europe, the Middle East and Asia. Specifications for the 900MHz system were created in 1984 and services based on the 900MHz system were started in the four Nordic countries in December 1986. A total of twenty countries had started services based on either the NMT-450 or NMT-900 systems by the end of 1987. Subsequently 23 other countries also started services based on these systems (see Figure 3.2). Many of these systems (NMT-450) were installed in the late 1980s and early 1990s when AMPS and TACS were primarily being installed in the world. This was due to the control of the 900MHz band by the military in Eastern Europe, trade restrictions to Eastern Europe, and the ease of providing inexpensive coverage with the NMT-450 system. Even in the early 1990s, it was not clear that mobile communication would succeed in Eastern Europe and the old Soviet Union.

Contrast the success of NMT with Japan's NTT system. In spite of a two-year disadvantage and a much lower population, NMT had more subscribers in Scandinavia and far more diffusion to other countries than Japan by the end of 1983 (see Figure 3.5). Although Singapore and Hong Kong bought small experimental systems from NEC that were based on the NTT system, no countries outside Japan began commercial services based on the Japanese standard. NTT used a proprietary system that had been developed by itself and a small number of Japanese suppliers that included NEC and Fujitsu. Not only did the lack of foreign participation and the small number of participants in the standard-setting committee process reduce the number of manufacturers that could act as diffusion for the NTT system, NTT controlled the patents and set fairly high fees. This made it even more difficult for NEC to sell systems overseas.

Further, there was almost no growth in subscribers in Japan until competition was introduced in the late 1980s for service-provider and in 1994 for phones. Japan's MPT (Ministry of Posts and Telecommunication)originally licenced NTT's mobile communication service order to create executive positions for MPT officials. It created nine regional companies not due to the expected growth in the system or the complexity of managing such a system; it created nine regional companies in order to create nine executive positions for MPT officials. Neither the MPT nor NTT believed there was a large market for mobile communication services in Japan and thus NTT did not install many base stations and both the MPT and NTT agreed to set user fees at high levels. The MPT wanted to set the fees high[14] in order to minimize the number of complaints and prevent people from subscribing who could not afford the service, and it rented the phones because it thought the purchase of phones would confuse users.[15] The MPT was apparently influenced by the Ministry of Transportation whose offices were adjacent to the MPT at the time. The MPT controlled the renting of phones and the awarding of spectrums like the Ministry of Transportation controlled vehicle licences.

THE FIRST GENERATION GLOBAL STANDARD: AMERICA'S AMPS

The Advanced Mobile Phone System (AMPS) became the first global mobile communication standard. Similar to the reasons for the success of NMT, the US adopted a single open standard and created a relatively large amount of competition between manufacturers and unlike Scandinavia also among service-providers. While there were also some differences in the way the standard was created, the more important difference was in populations. The large US population and its decision to adopt a single standard with competition among manufacturers and service-providers caused many other countries to adopt AMPS. The US did not, however, create the same type of manufacturer and carrier committee to develop the standard as did Scandinavia. Instead, firms like AT&T and Motorola and to some extent Millicom and EF Johnson independently did the original development work. Unfortunately, the licences to test and commercialize these systems were delayed due to the ten-year court battle between AT&T and the Justice Department and the arguments by non-AT&T companies that AT&T should not be allowed to offer services. Tests were finally carried out in the late 1970s beginning with AT&T, who tested a system in December 1978 in Chicago, IL. American Radio Telephone Service, a subsidiary of Motorola, conducted tests in Baltimore and Washington, DC, beginning in 1980, using a system that was very similar to the AT&T system. Millicom Services received the third developmental licence and conducted tests in Raleigh-Durham, NC using a completely different system from that used by AT&T and Motorola.[16]

The licences to commercialize these systems were further delayed until the Justice Department announced on January 8, 1982 that the regional operating companies, later known as the Baby Bells, would be spun off from AT&T on December 31, 1983. The FCC, through proposals from various firms, was the final judge on the technical specifications in the AMPS standard with most of the adopted ideas coming from AT&T and Motorola.[17] As is described later, the one disadvantage of this approach was that it did not enable the US to move towards a full committee approach for the update of AMPS or the creation of a single US digital standard.

Nevertheless, the decision in 1982 by the US to adopt a single open analog standard and award two licences in each region caused many other countries to choose AMPS over NMT. For example, it caused Canada immediately and Korea soon after to adopt AMPS and Great Britain immediately (in February 1993) and Hong Kong soon after to adopt a modified version of AMPS, called TACS. These countries predicted that the adoption of a single standard by the US, with its large population and high per capita income along with the introduction of competition would cause the number of AMPS subscribers to grow rapidly and quickly pass the total number of NMT subscribers. In particular, it was expected that there would be a synergistic effect between the growth in subscribers and a drop in service-and handset charges.

The relatively high growth rates in the US and Canadian subscribers also caused other countries to adopt the AMPS standard. Although their penetration rates did not rise as fast as in Scandinavia, the large populations of US and Canada caused the number of AMPS subscribers to pass the total number of NMT subscribers by the end of 1984 (see Figure 3.5). The growth in subscribers in the US and Canada was largely driven by falling service-charges through competition between carriers. The US and Canada both awarded two licences per market with Canada awarding nationwide licences and the US awarding licences in 305 Metropolitan (MSAs) and 428 Rural Statistical Areas (RSAs). The US approach probably slowed growth since it was not until 1989 that all of the licences were awarded.

FAILED EFFORTS TO CREATE A PAN-EUROPEAN ANALOG STANDARD

The rest of Europe was much slower than Scandinavia and the US to create and implement mobile communication systems. Thus, consumers and manufacturers in France, Germany, Great Britain, and Italy would have been better off if these countries had adopted the NMT or AMPS system. Unfortunately, of these countries, only Great Britain adopted this approach and France and Germany, who wanted to create a pan-European system, criticized it heavily. But even if these countries had been able to create a very large committee of service-providers and manufacturers that would select a single open standard and promote competition between service-providers and between manufacturers, it is doubtful that they could have created a global standard due to their late start. And France and Germany did not create a very large committee of service-providers and manufacturers that would select a single open standard and promote competition between service-providers and between manufacturers. Instead, they adopted the "industrial policy" position that was popular in the early 1980s; protect new industries until they are prepared to compete internationally. This resulted in the creation of proprietary systems and the setting of high charges by the service-providers and manufacturers; a situation that guaranteed that the systems created by France and Germany would not become global standards.

In late 1982, countries were considering the NMT system (Scandinavian firms), AMPS (US and other firms), NTT system (NTT), C-Netz system (Siemens), RC2000 system (Matra), and MATS-E (Philips and Alcatel), with their sponsors in parentheses. Spain had decided to adopt NMT while Italy, the Netherlands, and Belgium were expected to follow at that time. West Germany was investigating C-Netz[18] and France was funding Matra's work on integrating Corpac (car phone system) and Rarpac (private network system) into the RC2000 system. Although Thomson had done the early work on Corpac, Thomsons poor development work caused France Télécom (at that time it was called DGT or Direction Générale des Télécommunications) to transfer the contract to Matra.[19] Philips and Alcatel did not have and were never able to find a sponsor for their MATS-E system.

Great Britain adopts TACS

Debates about the appropriate analog standard intensified first in Great Britain due to the early liberalization of its telecommunications market including its decision in 1982 to licence two analog service-providers. British Telecom and Securior received one licence while Racal Electronics was the major owner in the firm that received the second licence, Vodafone.[20] Securicor and Racal favored AMPS while British Telecom was under pressure from other PTTs to adopt NMT-450 in spite of its capacity limitations. Ericsson countered these capacity limitation criticisms by proposing a higher capacity system that uses the 900MHz band. Ericsson argued that it could develop and install such a system by early 1985 while simultaneously it promoted the TACS system due to its early development of equipment for AMPS.[21] British manufacturers (in parentheses) pushed for the adoption of Japan's NTT system (GEC-Marconi) or AMPS (Plessey).[22]

Although there were many more technical debates concerning the various systems.[23] in February 1983 a modified form of AMPS called TACS was chosen[24] primarily for reasons of economies of scale. Vodafone wanted to use the AMPS standard since it expected the prices of AMPS phones to drop as the US market grew. However, it also wanted the European channel spacing of 25kHz instead of the US 30kHz. This required the creation of TACS. Although British Telecom initially disagreed and proposed the investigation of C-Netz and MATS-E that were still on the drawing boards, it eventually saw the logic in Vodafone's argument[25] and in the benefits of a fast installation.

Since France had sometimes indicated that it would follow Britain's lead in the choice of a standard, France briefly considered the adoption of TACS.[26] However, support for the TACS system did not last long. Some French officials reportedly believed that modifications to the

AMPS system would cause TACS service-to be delayed until January 1986, as opposed to the projected start date of January 1985 which is when the MATS-E system, under development by Alcatel and Philips since 1982, was expected to be ready. Further, there was more criticism than support for the British decision since many French and German leaders wanted Britain to join them in the creation of a joint system that would be developed by British, French, and German as opposed to just US (Motorola) and Scandinavian (Ericsson) firms. These criticisms coincided with increasing concerns that Europe was falling behind the US and Japan in the electronics sector.

French and German collaboration

By April 1983, France and West Germany had announced they would implement a hybrid of the MATS-E (Philips and Alcatel) and the C-Netz (Siemens) systems hopefully with support from Italy, Switzerland, and Belgium.[27] In November 1983, the French and German governments agreed to construct pilot systems using the 900MHz band around major urban areas in France and Germany as a plan to boost general electronic cooperation in Europe and liberalize European telecommunication markets. The equipment was to be supplied equally by French and German companies and it was expected that 100,000 subscribers would be using the system by the end of the decade.[28] CIT Alcatel and Thomson who had agreed to merge their telecommunication interests in September 1983 immediately began holding talks with Siemens about collaborating on the project. Since Siemens and Alcatel were already cooperating with a German subsidiary (PKI) of Philips on the C-Netz and MATS-E systems respectively, Philips was also expected to be involved in the project. The coexistence in West Germany of two different networks was recognized as a problem: a problem that later became a major reason for the eventual abandonment of the joint project. Other companies were also interested in the project[29] and the number of interested companies, who were to be picked from pairs of Franco-German firms, had expanded greatly by May 1984.[30]

However, in October 1984, the disagreements on standards and the potential advantages of digital technology caused the joint project to be delayed until Europe could create a pan-European digital system.[31] Firms and governments were unable to agree on a standard partly due to the different standards which firms such as Alcatel, Philips, Siemens, and Matra were promoting. In particular, the delicate compromise between Siemens and Alcatel disintegrated due to the sweeping reorganization of the French electronics sector. The Alcatel–Thomson partnership with Standard Elektrik Lorenz (SEL), which also involved the private French Société Anonyme de Télécommunications (SAT) and AEG Telefunken decreased Alcatel's interest in the MATS-E system since its new partners did not have a stake in this system.[32] The final nail in the coffin was when SEL (which believed it had advantages in digital technology),[33] AEG, and the Société Anonyme de Télécommunications of France proposed a digital development project. Subsequently, Alcatel decided to join this project, thus abandoning its earlier plan to collaborate with Siemens (which had no desire to abandon its C-Netz system).[34] Finally, the conclusion that such a digital system could be installed only a few years after an analog system convinced the French and German governments and companies to delay the implementation of a Franco-German system.[35]

The decision to delay the implementation of the joint French and German system (which included Alcatel's loss of interest in the MATS-E system) and the allocation of the 900MHz band to the digital system provided Matra an opportunity to implement its RC 2000 system with France Telecom.[36] This system along with Germany's (C-Netz) and Italy's (RTMS2000) systems was introduced in 1985. Italy's system was created by Telecom Italia, Italy's state-owned telephone company, and Italtel, which is also owned by the same government parent as Telecom Italia.[37]

The downside of government involvement in standard setting

In retrospect, the political maneuverings by the French and German governments and also companies were almost meaningless and demonstrate the problems with an overemphasis on the committee side of standard setting. Firms were so busy maneuvering to have their technology included in the standard that an open standard-setting process never materialized. And the governments were so concerned with creating a competitive advantage for their national champions that they were unable to create such an open standard-setting process where manufacturers and service-providers would eventually compete freely in the marketplace.

Further, it was already too late for France and Germany to create a global analog standard when they were trying to do so. By the end of 1984, there were more than 150,000 NMT subscribers in Scandinavia and 170,000 AMPS subscribers in the US. Neither France nor Germany had this many subscribers in their unique systems until the end of

1989. Further, each country's total number of subscribers at the end of 1989 was twice as many as they had originally forecast when they had first announced their intention to create a joint Franco-German system. Nevertheless, the 100,000 subscribers they forecast for the end of the decade was only slightly more than the actual number of NMT subscribers at the time of the forecast in November 1983.

Although France and Germany did not realize this at the time, the successful analog standards had already been chosen when they were trying to create global analog standards in 1984 that would provide their manufacturing firms with an advantage. Only South Africa and Portugal[38] adopted the C-Netz standards (neither system ever achieved more than 15,000 subscribers) and no country adopted Radiocom 2000 (Egypt and Qatar adopted MATS-E). Their firms would probably have been much more successful than they were in the analog era (and possibly also in the digital era) if France or Germany had been an early adopter of either the NMT or TACS systems. Their firms ended up wasting a great deal of resources on systems that never diffused to any extent.[39]

The British TACS market also grew much faster than the French, German and Italian markets due to the greater market competition between service-providers and handset manufacturers. While the latter markets only had one service-provider until the 1990s, in Great Britain there was competition between the two network providers Cellnet and Vodafone and competition between what were then called service-providers in Great Britain. The British service-providers purchased airtime from the network operators and signed up subscribers. They were free to offer a variety of services for different customer segments and they offered phones from different manufacturers. The phone prices dropped quickly since TACS is similar to AMPS and the US AMPS market was growing quickly. Thus, service-and handset charges dropped quickly and Great Britain had the highest penetration rate in Europe outside Scandinavia from almost the start of service-until 1997, when it was passed by Italy. Other European countries such as Ireland, Austria, Italy, and Spain also adopted TACS systems. By May 1991, there were more TACS subscribers in Europe than there were NMT subscribers. Further, both systems had far more subscribers than C-Netz (four times), RC2000 (five times) and RTMS (ten times).[40]

In retrospect, Great Britain's decision to adopt TACS was the right decision. Although the introduction of TACS made it more difficult for wireline British manufacturers like GEC and Plessey to become global players in the mobile communications industry, their lack of success in the wireline industry[41] probably meant that they also had little chance in the mobile communications industry. On the other hand, Britain's early start in mobile communication services has helped Vodafone become one of the leading suppliers of mobile communication services and ARM become one of the leading suppliers of chip sets for mobile phones in the world. Further, the early start of services and Britain's liberal policies towards foreign manufacturers caused many foreign manufacturers like Motorola, Nokia, Lucent, Ericsson, and many Japanese parts manufacturers to set up factories and development centers in Great Britain. Nokia's decision to locate much of its development in Great Britain is partly due to its acquisition of Technophone, a relatively successful British manufacturer of portable phones in the analog TACS market. These companies may provide jobs to more British citizens than either GEC or Plessey have ever provided.

THE CREATION OF THE SECOND GENERATION GLOBAL STANDARD: GSM

The Global System Mobile (GSM) is the global digital standard for mobile communications. Similar to the reasons for the relative success of NMT and AMPS in analog technology, Europe effectively used both the committee and market mechanisms to make GSM the global digital standard. In particular, it created an open standard-setting committee-based process where it adopted a single open standard and it created a relatively large amount of competition between manufacturers and service-providers. Nevertheless, it took a long time for Europe to create GSM and this long process reveals many of the challenges in trying to effectively use both committee and market mechanisms in an environment where there is little central authority. Responsibility for the committee-based aspects of GSM evolved from the Conference European Posts and Telecommunications (CEPT) to ETSI and this evolution was heavily influenced by the failure of France and Germany to create a pan-European analog standard and by the European Community, including its moves towards integration. The market-based mechanisms were promoted on a country-by-country basis and these differences reflected the different speeds at which deregulation in each individual telecommunication market proceeded.

The initial momentum for GSM came from CEPT, the German and French firms, and the European Commission. Two blocks of 25MHz in the 900 MHz band were set aside for mobile communications in 1978 by CEPT, the organization that represents telecommunication carriers in Europe. In 1982, at a CEPT conference, the *Groupe Spécial Mobile* was created. In December of the same year, representatives from eleven countries met for the first GSM meeting.[42]

Germany and France were initially the strongest promoters of a pan-European system. After they abandoned their attempt to create a joint analog system, they were determined to develop a unified digital system that would provide their equipment firms with a competitive advantage. Their plan was to convince other countries to support the project and award the development of trial systems to the German and French firms who had been involved with discussions concerning a joint analog system. In 1985, their PTTs funded the development of prototypes for different systems[43] and Italy agreed to join France and Germany (and thus Telettra and Italtel become involved with the projects). The UK joined the other three in May 1986 in return for access to the full test results.[44]

Eight prototype systems were evaluated in the fall of 1986 under supervision by the Permanent Nucleus of the *Groupe Spécial Mobile,* which later became Global Systems Mobile. These included four systems that had been developed by the Franco-German alliance and four more originating in Scandinavia. The results were presented at a GSM plenary session in Madeira, Portugal in February 1987 where fifteen countries (the members of CEPT) voted on a digital standard. Thirteen of the countries wanted a narrow-band system that had been developed by Ericsson while France and Germany preferred a wide-band system that had been developed by French and German firms.[45]

The impasse was broken through behind-the-scene discussions between Ericsson and French and German firms. Beginning in 1986, Ericsson had been speaking with Siemens (who had previously not joined any of the French and German industrial consortia due to its development of C-Netz) and LCT, a French telecommunications company (the French PTT was also involved) who had done some work with narrow-band TDMA.[46] Technology exchange agreements were completed with LCT in 1986 and with Siemens in January 1987 where it was expected that Ericsson's AXE and Siemen's EWSD switches would be combined in systems for the Scandinavian, German, and hopefully other markets.[47] These agreements helped convince the French and German governments to vote for the narrow-band technology;[48] on May 19, 1987 the CEPT chose Ericsson's narrow-band system.[49]

The choice of the Ericsson system probably provided Ericsson and to some extent Nokia with advantages over other European firms in the short term. Since Nokia had also been developing a narrow-band TDMA system that was similar to the Ericsson system, it also had advantages over the other European firms, in particular, the French and German firms who had to change their development from wide-band to narrow-band systems. However, with services not expected to start until 1991, the German and French firms had plenty of time to recover.

Simultaneously, the European Commission (EC) began to recognize that CEPT's goals were in line with its own goals. The EC was trying to create an economically-integrated Europe and they recognized that the implementation of pan-European telecommunication services is an essential part of an economically-integrated Europe. Five different analog systems were in use by the end of 1985 and the inability of France and Germany to complete an agreement loomed large in their minds. A report published by the EC in December 1985 supported GSM and it worked behind the scenes to ensure that many regulatory obstacles were removed and that activities were well-coordinated. The CEPT's and EC's activities resulted in the formal acceptance of the GSM system, its implementation by the European Council of Ministers in June 1987, and the creation of the Memorandum of Understanding (MOU) in September 1987.[50]

The evolution of GSM from a small committee in CEPT to its formal acceptance by the EC and the creation of the MOU may be interpreted as an expansion and strengthening of the formal committees used to create GSM. The signing of the MOU by thirteen European countries was a critical event in the creation of GSM since it demonstrated a commitment by the signatories to GSM and it provided a framework for introducing commercial services in July 1991.[51] The creation of the MOU was similar to the decisions by Scandinavia and the US to introduce single open analog standards that were created in open committees. The forecast of installed base for GSM immediately rose and GSM became the first digital system to acquire a forecasted installed base. Further, the decision to create ETSI, which is described next, represents a further expansion of the formal committees used to GSM in that the participants now included representatives from manufacturers.

The committee side: the creation of ETSI

The next critical event was the creation of the European Telecommunications Standards Institute (ETSI) in January 1988. Although the manufacturers had been involved with the creation of GSM through their testing of various systems, participation in the CEPT had been restricted to the monopoly European PTTs. The PTTs were not only responsible for operating national and international telecommunications services but also for supplying consumer equipment, writing regulations, and allocating frequency spectrum. Thus the creation of ETSI and the decision to allow any European firm that was involved with telecommunications to become part of ETSI dramatically changed the competitive landscape of the European mobile communications market. It enabled any firm that had research and development activities in Europe to participate in the creation of GSM.[52] Motorola was the first foreign participant and later many foreign firms participated and became agents of diffusion for GSM. As for ETSI, it gradually took over all the standards work previously done by CEPT and the work of the *Groupe Spécial Mobile* was formally transferred from CEPT to ETSI.[53] A phased approach was adopted in which the GSM specifications have been updated several times with new features and capabilities being added each time

The success of ETSI is partly due to the peculiar market structure behind ETSI and shows some of the complex interactions between committee- and market-based approaches. Most members of ETSI were either government-owned carriers who operated monopolies or manufacturers who had exclusive relationships with these service-providers. Further, the requirement to have research and development activities in Europe prevented many foreign manufacturers from participating in ETSI. Thus, most carriers and some manufacturers probably perceived that cooperation in ETSI did not pose large risks of entry or lost opportunities in other markets. In other words, Europe adopted a committee-based approach that was essentially open but in many ways the European manufacturers and service-providers perceived that it was closed and thus safe for them to participate. As we shall see later, the decision by many countries to award licences to new service-providers introduced competition on the service-side and Chapters 4 and 5 will show that the relationships between manufacturers and service-providers also changed in a variety of unexpected ways.

In terms of competition, a key issue for ETSI was intellectual property rights (IPRs). Initially, completing the development of the GSM specifications took precedence over IPR issues. However, it became clear that many existing patents were absolutely essential to the implementation of GSM. This brought the service-providers and the manufacturers into conflict. The service-providers wanted low patent fees in order to speed market development while manufacturers wanted to defend their development work. The issue came to a head when the service-providers asked the manufacturers to sign an agreement allowing the global free use of patents deemed essential to the implementation of GSM. Many manufacturers felt they had no choice but to comply with the service-providers since the manufacturers needed to sell their equipment to the service-providers in order to recoup their development costs.

The lone exception was Motorola, who had become a member of ETSI through its multiple development centers in Europe.[54] This was part of a more general trend in the US information/communication industries where many firms such as IBM and AT&T were for strengthening intellectual property rights due to the global success of Japanese manufacturers in many electronic industries.[55] These US firms, including Motorola, argued that patents should be exchanged on a "fair and reasonable basis" although no one actually provided a good definition of a fair and reasonable basis.[56] This conclusion required firms to conduct bilateral negotiations in which European firms were worried that Motorola, who had the most patents, would not let them use the patents outside Europe.[57] Eventually, a number of firms completed patent exchange agreements including Alcatel, Motorola, Nokia, and AEG.[58] The big losers were Japanese firms. Since they had not participated in the creation of GSM, nor had they been simultaneously developing GSM technology, they did not have any patents to exchange and were forced to pay licensing fees on handsets of between 6% and 10% as a percent of sales.

The market side: the awarding of new licences

Europe also effectively used market mechanisms in their creation of the second generation global standard. The creation of ETSI and its relative openness to participation by foreign manufacturers like Motorola and others created both competition in the GSM market and foreign agents of diffusion for GSM. The former was necessary for the prices of infrastructure and handsets to fall. The latter encouraged non-European service-providers to adopt GSM, particularly those who had close relationships with Motorola or another foreign manufacturer.

As for service-providers, the European countries had been pursuing deregulation of their telecommunications industries at different speeds throughout the 1980s with Great Britain the leader. The creation of

GSM accelerated this process of deregulation as countries realized that the new GSM services were a new and important market. By the end of 1990, four countries had awarded licences and more than ten countries had announced that they would do so.

The awarding of these new licences promoted market growth both inside and as is described in the next section outside of Europe. Fifteen carriers in nine countries started services in mid-1992. There were multiple carriers in Denmark, Finland, France, Germany, Portugal, and Sweden. The initial growth came from first Germany and second France where the analog services and handsets were the most expensive. In Great Britain and the Scandinavian countries, it took a few years for GSM handset prices to drop to the levels of analog handsets before the number of GSM subscribers began to grow. Nevertheless, it was the new licencees who grew the fastest in Denmark, Germany, Denmark, Portugal and Sweden.

Adoption overseas

However, the number of countries adopting GSM exploded long before the growth in Europe took off. Although there were only 1.4 million GSM subscribers at the end of 1993 (as compared to about 25 million AMPS/TACS subscribers), almost forty countries had decided to begin services based on the GSM standard by then. This was not due to political factors, however, as some people have suggested. For example, former European colonies actually adopted GSM to a lesser extent than non-former European colonies.[59]

Instead, the fast overseas adoption is the result of Europe's effective utilization of both committee-and market-based mechanisms, both of which drove the forecasted installed base for GSM. The forecasted installed base for GSM had been building since thirteen countries agreed to start services based on GSM in 1987. This forecasted installed base continued to build as ETSI was established in 1988, open specifications were created in the late 1980s and early 1990s, governments requested bids for first and second licences beginning in 1989, and governments introduced measures to ensure fair competition between the first and second carriers. There was a positive feedback loop between this forecasted installed base and the number of adopting countries that became difficult to stop especially when other standards did not quickly emerge. And when they did emerge, they were not able to generate large forecasted installed bases. This was due to failures on both the committee and market sides in both Japan and the US.

THE JAPANESE CREATE ANOTHER PROPRIETARY STANDARD

Although Japan made large changes in the market-based side of standard setting during the implementation of digital services, the committee-based side saw fewer changes and the lack of these changes has meant that not a single other country has adopted the Japanese digital standard, called PDC. Further, Japan's late start in creating and implementing a digital standard meant that Japan would have needed to make drastic changes in its committee-based approach to compete with GSM, which was firmly established by the time Japan started its own digital services. This slow start reflected failures in Japan's market-based side of standard-setting in the analog services. Thus, Japan would probably have been better off if it had adopted GSM, although here again failures in Japan's committee-based standards-creation prevented this from occurring.

The market side: Japan introduces competition

The growth in the Japanese analog market was slow, as discussed earlier in this chapter. At the end of 1989, Japan had about one-fifth the penetration rate of the US and Great Britain and one-fifteenth that in Scandinavia. This was one year after competition had been introduced: IDO had started services in the Tokyo and Nagoya regions and the DDI Cellular Group in the other regions of Japan. It was not until Japan allowed consumers to purchase rather than rent phones (through pressure from the US government) and two new operators started services in Tokyo, Kansai (Osaka), and Nagoya in mid-1994 that the number of subscribers began to grow at a reasonable pace. This competition between service-prices and handset manufacturers caused service-and handset charges to drop dramatically. And with additional competition from three PHS service-providers beginning in 1995, the number of total subscribers doubled each year between 1994 and 1996. By the end of 1998 Japan had one of the highest mobile phone penetration rates (if PHS is included) outside Scandinavia.

The committee side: another proprietary standard

PDC was largely developed and is still largely controlled by NTT DoCoMo. NTT began developing the specifications for the PDC standard in 1990 and these engineers moved to NTT DoCoMo when it was spun off from NTT in 1992. NTT DoCoMo then developed the detailed specifications for the PDC standard in cooperation with manufacturers in much the way that service-providers used to do in the rest of the world. For example, as discussed earlier, until ETSI was created in the late 1980s, European service-providers also determined most of the system and detailed specifications for telecommunication systems in Europe's CEPT and then gave orders to manufacturers to develop specific components for the system. It was only with the development of ETSI that manufacturers became the main developers of telecommunication standards in Europe.

Japan does have its version of ETSI, which is called the Japanese Association for Radio Industry Businesses (ARIB). And unlike Japan's analog standard, the Japanese MPT required this organization to ratify the PDC standard and DoCoMo to publish a set of specifications for the air interface. Other service-providers implemented their PDC services based on these published specifications. However, DoCoMo's superior financial resources and its power over the MPT have largely meant that the ARIB merely rubber-stamps DoCoMo proposals at the point when they are already being implemented by DoCoMo. Further, no specifications have been published for the network interface and even the air interface is far less defined than the GSM standard. The lack of detail in the PDC air interface has meant that handsets can only be used with one service-provider. As discussed at the end of Chapter 5, DoCoMo used the lack of definition and its superior knowledge of the PDC air interface to develop superior handsets in cooperation with its manufacturers. Naturally, foreign service-providers do not want to adopt a closed standard like PDC, which is dominated by a single service-provider.

However, even if DoCoMo had published a more complete set of specifications for the PDC standard and digital growth had started sooner, it would have been highly unlikely that other countries would have adopted PDC. When DoCoMo began developing the PDC specifications in 1990, GSM already had a large forecasted installed base and was probably already the *de facto* global standard. Making PDC a global standard would have required a strong effort to immediately enlist the support of foreign carriers and manufacturers and to create an open committee-based standard setting process. NTT DoCoMo and other Japanese firms made no efforts of this kind. In particular, manufacturers were the only firms with an interest in creating a global standard and they were largely excluded from the Japanese standard-setting process. Further, they probably did not have the necessary global perspective at this time to create a global standard.

What if Japan had adopted GSM?

It is interesting to speculate on what would have happened if Japan had allocated frequencies that are compatible with GSM and adopted the GSM standard instead of the PDC standard. Japanese consumers would probably have benefited from the adoption of GSM since Japan has a much more expensive cellular service-than European countries. Further, the adoption of GSM would have helped Japanese producers of mobile phones and infrastructure. The early adoption of the GSM standard may have solved the patent problems that were faced by Japan's mobile phone producers (see Chapter 5) and thus enabled them to be more successful than they are now in the GSM mobile phone market.[60] It would probably have also helped Japan's producers of infrastructure compete in the GSM market. The major weakness of GSM in the late 1990s was that its initial versions were not very efficient in terms of using the frequency spectrum. In terms of frequency spectrum efficiency, Japan (and particularly DoCoMo) now has the greatest needs and DoCoMo has introduced systems with the highest frequency efficiencies in the world. If Japan were using the GSM standard, Japanese firms would probably have been the infrastructure providers to develop such GSM infrastructure as opposed to European firms who are now steadily increasing the frequency spectrum efficiency of GSM for the Asian markets where this is required.

The reason this did not occur is that Japan's decisions concerning its digital mobile phone standard were based on a compromise between a foreign ministry that wanted to appease the US government's demands for access and a national service-provider who wanted to maintain a closed standard in Japan. When IDO chose to adopt NTT's proprietary analog system in the late 1980s, the US government criticized IDO's decision and the decision by the Japanese government not to give DDI Cellular a nationwide service, partly due to Motorola's strong influence with the Reagan administration. Japan is sensitive to these criticisms and in this case it was very sensitive due to the ownership of IDO by Toyota, Japan's largest exporter to the US. Thus, IDO eventually installed TACS and, relevant to this discussion, the Japanese government decided to follow the US lead in the choice of a digital standard in order to avoid future conflicts. Thus, when the US Cellular Telecommunications Industry Association (CTIA) decided to base its digital standard on the TDMA work in the US (see discussion of the US standard-setting process below), Japan quickly followed.[61] In fact, Japanese engineers claim that the early versions of PDC were quite similar to the early versions of the digitalized version of AMPS, called DAMPS.

NTT DoCoMo also had little interest in adopting an open standard like GSM, which it did not develop. Although it did not like being told to adopt someone else's technology, this was better than being forced to adopt someone else's standard. This is partly for pride and partly to maintain a competitive advantage in the Japanese market. Technically speaking, GSM, DAMPS, and PDC are quite similar since they are all based on TDMA. But if DoCoMo had adopted an open standard like GSM or DAMPS, it would have been forced to develop a method of competing in the Japanese market that did not depend on control of the standard.

This analysis of the Japanese market demonstrates the importance of providing manufacturers and service-providers with equal power in the committees. If a service-provider is allowed to dominate the committee, a proprietary standard will emerge, which will raise the costs of the service-and make it difficult for manufacturers to act as agents of diffusion.

THE LACK OF A NATIONAL DIGITAL STANDARD IN THE US

In the late 1980s and early 1990s, the US moved in a completely different direction than Europe and Japan in terms of standard-setting and in terms of new mobile phone licences. While Europe moved to a committee-based standard setting process and Japan moved from a completely closed to a partially open standard, the US moved from a semi-committee-based standard setting process in analog to free competition in digital. In December 1988, the US Federal Communications Commission (FCC) announced that cellular service-providers would have the authority to introduce new cellular technologies at any time without prior regulatory approval. The only requirement was that the new system be compatible with the AMPS system. This decision reflected the free market emphasis of the Reagan administration and the growing belief that the success of the US firms in the information and telecommunications industries was due to "market" mechanisms. Further, in a retrospectively clear failure to understand how market mechanisms work in standard setting, while the European countries were aggressively introducing new licences in the early 1990s, the US government failed to do this until 1995 and thus also failed to promote adequate market mechanisms in the creation of a second generation digital technology.

DAMPS: a failure on the market side

Although the US service-providers were prepared for and wanted the right to choose their own digital standard decision, they recognized the value of a single open standard. After comparing a number of systems in 1988 including those that were based on TDMA (time division multiple access) and FDMA (frequency division multiple access), the CTIA (US Cellular Telecommunications Industry Association) selected a digitalized version of AMPS, called DAMPS. Like GSM, it was decided that this system would be based on TDMA.[62] The CTIA also released an outline of the specifications in mid-1990 that were formally accepted in November of the same year by its members.

At this point, the process of creating a digital system appeared similar to the European situation in 1987 when the general specifications for GSM were released. DAMPS was being created in an open standard-setting process like GSM. The major difference was the lack of new licences. Although the first applications for the PCS (Personal Communications Services) spectrum were submitted in 1989, the US did not begin awarding licences until 1995 and most services did not start until 1996 and 1997.[63] Contrast this with Great Britain where applications for 1800 GSM licences were first submitted in 1989 and 1800 services were started by 1993. The long US licensing process reflected the bureaucratic nature of the FCC, the fact that its procedures for awarding licences had to conform to principles of open government, decisions could be and frequently were challenged in court, and licences were awarded in 493 markets.[64] Like the analog era, the FCC believed that the large number of markets would encourage competition, thus increasing the chances that the best technology would emerge.

This left the implementation of DAMPS to the existing service-providers. And they had little incentive to install DAMPS except in the high-density areas of major cities where the first capacity shortages appeared.[65] Further, the analog compatibility requirement meant that phones were dual-mode phones and thus were heavier and more expensive to manufacture. As a result, DAMPS was only implemented as a temporary capacity solution in large cities where the service-providers heavily subsidized the sale of digital phones for heavy users. Only 0.1%, 1.5%, and 7.5% of the new subscribers in 1992, 1993 and 1994 respectively purchased digital phones.[66]

No process to select a single digital standard: a failure on the committee side

Shortly after the CTIA's decision to choose DAMPS, two new technologies began to draw attention in the US. First, Motorola proposed a narrow-band analog solution to the AMPS capacity problem that is typically called NAMPS. This enabled three times as many users for a given frequency band as with AMPS. Second and more importantly, it became clear that cdmaOne (then called IS95 CDMA or code division multiple access) had a number of advantages over DAMPS; these included several times higher frequency spectrum efficiencies, better voice quality, and better data transmission capabilities. Qualcomm had been lobbying the cellular industry since 1989 with proposals to use CDMA technology and in 1991, the CTIA carried out controlled tests of DAMPS, NAMPS, and cdmaOne and the results were presented at a CTIA forum in December.

This situation now sounds similar to the CEPT plenary session in February 1987 where fifteen countries voted on a digital standard for Europe. The key differences were that in 1987 the CEPT had authority to choose a system, licences for the new technology were going to be awarded, and the firms were able to agree on a compromise. In the US, however, the CTIA had no such authority to choose a system, no new licences were awarded until 1995, and the manufacturers were unable to find a compromise partly due to the fundamental differences between cdmaOne (based on code division multiple access) and DAMPS (based on time division multiple access). Further, it is also true that the large technical uncertainty in cdmaOne caused many carriers to stick with DAMPS. The result was that the CTIA did not choose a single system. It reiterated its support for the ongoing efforts to implement DAMPS while it recommended the development of cdmaOne technology.

The lack of a single digital standard created a large amount of uncertainty in the US and abroad in the early and mid-1990s. Other countries were afraid to adopt one of the US digital standards for fear that the other standard would eventually become the dominant US standard. And in general, the other countries were basically right in that neither standard has been able to generate a sufficient installed base in the US or abroad. In the US, the existing service-providers adopted DAMPS or cdmaOne while the new licencees adopted DAMPS, cdmaOne, or GSM. Globally, in mid-2000, more than 75% of cdmaOne subscribers were located in either the US, Korea, or Japan.

There are two reasons why the US was not able to choose a single standard before the new spectrum was auctioned and licences were awarded in 1995. First, in spite of cdmaOne's performance advantages, Qualcomm adopted a very closed policy and was unclear about the extent to which it would open cdmaOne. Although Qualcomm set fairly reasonable fees initially for the patents concerning infrastructure, these patent fees were raised after several firms purchased licences. Of greater importance, Qualcomm has set such high patent fees for the critical chips that are used in the handsets that it was able to control almost 100% of the US handset market (through its joint venture with Sony) well into 1998. This is one reason why Motorola's share of the US market dropped substantially in 1997 and 1998. Further, the price of the cdmaOne handsets as of mid-1998 was still three times the price of handsets (to consumers) that were available from US carriers who used different digital systems. This naturally discouraged many carriers in the US and other countries from adopting cdmaOne.

Second, there was also no process or desire on the part of the federal government to select a single standard; this was in spite of the benefits the US enjoyed with the selection of a single analog standard. In the early 1990s, it became widely accepted that the success of the US personal computer industry (and in particular Microsoft and Intel) was due to the unbridled competition between multiple standards. Thus, the US Federal Government's and the cellular industry belief in competition between multiple standards become even stronger during the 1990s. The US government, service-providers, and manufacturers underestimated the effect that the choice of a single standard by a large country like the US has on the forecasted installed base for the standard. Thus, the US did not develop an open committee-based standard setting process that is now clear was needed to adequately compete with GSM.

For example, if the US government had been able to create an agreement between US cellular operators and US manufacturers concerning the choice of cdmaOne as the US digital standard in return for low licensing fees for cdmaOne from Qualcomm, US consumers and manufacturers would have benefited. The choice of cdmaOne by the

US probably would have caused most providers of AMPS service-to adopt cdmaOne in South America, Asia, and Africa. It may have even caused some late entrants to the European market to adopt cdmaOne. Further, the lack of a single digital standard and the continuing lack of desire and process for creating a third generation standard have placed the US at a competitive disadvantage in the third generation market. I return to this subject after discussing another failed candidate for a global standard: Japan's PHS technology.

JAPAN TRIES A LITTLE HARDER, BUT FAILS AGAIN WITH PHS

Japan's Personal Handyphone System (PHS) is characterized as a low-mobility digital system because calls were originally very difficult and still are relatively difficult to handle in fast-moving vehicles. Thus, PHS represents a special form of second generation system where lower costs are achieved at the expense of mobility. The cost effectiveness of PHS is debatable considering the deficits being run by the PHS operators. The PHS operators are unfortunately dependent on NTT's wireline system, which is one of the most expensive, if not the most expensive, wireline systems in the industrialized world. As a result, the PHS operators paid half their revenues to NTT. Nevertheless, there is widespread agreement that the capital costs for PHS are lower than that for existing cellular systems in high-density areas. Not only are switching stations not needed but PHS base stations are much less expensive than existing cellular base stations. For example, a PHS base station that covers a 100-meter radius can handle three calls and costs about $2000 to implement. A cellular base station that can handle 100 calls, covering an area with a radius of 1 km, costs about $1M. Therefore, the base station cost per potential call is $600 for PHS and $10,000 for cellular. In low-density areas, where coverage, not capacity, is the issue, cellular systems have lower capital costs. The Japanese MPT would only approve a system that was one-fourth as expensive as cellular technology in order to open a new mobile communication market for the masses. This directive required Japanese firms to take full advantage of the low-cost potential of the small cell, small base station approach whereas Europe and North America decided to create personal communication systems that are almost identical to digital cellular. Because both North America and Europe have concluded that communication in a fast-moving vehicle is a necessary capability in a mobile communication system, their personal communication systems are theoretically more expensive than the PHS system.

These philosophical differences about mobile communication services provided PHS with an opportunity to become a global standard in low-mobility systems. In particular, PHS is well-suited for developing countries with high-population densities of which there are many in Asia. PHS was and still is considered similar or superior in performance to another low-mobility system, DECT (based on GSM), that has never been implemented on a commercial level. Nevertheless, PHS has only been adopted by one country outside Japan: Thailand began PHS-based services as of mid-1999 and this service-is not expected to be successful due to the Asian financial crisis.

PHS has failed at the international level primarily due to mistakes on the committee side while it has failed on both the international and national side due to mistakes on the market side. PHS is the only mobile communications standard that was developed using a committee-based approach but without any international participation. Although the standard-setting process was open to all Japanese manufacturing firms and service-providers from the beginning, the MPT delayed the opening of the standard to foreign firms in order to give Japanese manufacturers an advantage. Similar to the behavior often attributed to Japan's Ministry of International Trade and Industry,[67] foreign firms were not invited to participate in the standard setting process and the system specifications were not made public until one year after service-was started in July 1995. Quite naturally, most foreign manufacturers, including industry leaders such as Ericsson and Nokia, have criticized PHS. This has made it difficult for Japanese manufacturers to convince foreign carriers to adopt PHS, particularly when many of these foreign carriers are major customers of firms like Ericsson and Nokia.

Japan also made mistakes on the market side and this example shows the importance of having competition not only between service-providers and between manufacturers, but also between key suppliers. In PHS, while there has been sufficient competition between the three PHS service-providers, PHS is built on top of Japan's local telephone system where there is no competition. NTT, which is still partly owned by the Japanese government, has a monopoly in the local telephone market and is probably the most expensive provider of wireline service in the industrialized world. It has set very high connection charges for the PHS service-providers and there have been constant battles between the NTT and the PHS services providers over these charges.[68]

Further, the PHS carriers depend on NTT for fundamental changes in PHS and NTT has implemented these changes very slowly. For example, as the penetration rate for cellular phones (that is, non-PHS mobile phones) grew from about 3% in April 1994 when PHS was being designed to over 20% by late 1997, the number of people making calls to or receiving calls from cellular phones increased sharply. However, calls between PHS and cellular phones were not possible until mid-1996 and when they became possible they were nine times more expensive than PHS-to-PHS or PHS-to-wireline calls and three times more expensive than intra-cellular calls.[69]

The expensive PHS-to-cellular calls and high wireline connection charges are major reasons why two of Japan's three PHS carriers are not expected to become profitable in the near future. The latter makes it hard to reduce service-charges for calls between PHS and wireline phones, which is one reason why the number of subscribers has been declining from a peak of seven million in mid-1997. And both factors make it difficult to make money with the existing subscribers. The drop in subscribers and the continued losses discourage other countries from adopting PHS.

The reason for the delays in making cellular-to-PHS calls possible and the reason why these calls are still very expensive is that NTT has been very slow to implement appropriate switching equipment and it is generally believed that the MPT has not set appropriate connection charges. In particular, the fact that the Japanese government still owned more than 50% of NTT's stock (58.9%) in mid-1999 suggests that there is clearly a conflict of interest for the Japanese government in terms of setting appropriate connection charges and requiring NTT to install appropriate switching equipment. One wonders whether PHS was implemented to improve the financial situation of NTT or to provide mobile communication services to the mass public. The former interpretation would be consistent with Japan's slow moves to introduce competition into the local phone market even as NTT's high local phone charges slow Japan's growth in Internet usage and services.

JAPANESE AND EUROPEAN COLLABORATION IN THIRD GENERATION SYSTEMS

The changes in standard-setting approaches that were implemented in the 1980s and early 1990s in Japan, the US, and to some extent Europe intensified in the late 1990s. NTT DoCoMo initially moved towards an open model for standard setting, the US moved further towards a free competition model, and Europe further refined its committee-based approach through updates in the GSM standard. These changes in standard setting approaches led to a very unexpected outcome, the adoption of W-CDMA by the European Telecommunications Standards Institute (ETSI) in February 1998. This outcome was in spite of the fact that NTT DoCoMo's standard was not considered to be in the running by most industry observers until early 1997. This section describes how an alliance between NTT DoCoMo and Nokia and Ericsson led to the unexpected outcome. The alliance between these three firms can now be seen as an alliance between DoCoMo's relatively open model for standard setting and Europe's committee-based approach, which led to the actual standard being developed (as of late 2000) in a multiple committee-based approach that is coordinated by several international committees.

In 1992, the members of the International Telecommunications Union (ITU) voted to allocate frequencies for a third generation mobile communication system. This system was expected to provide global roaming and multi-media services. However, the US, Europe, and Japan have each used different forms of committee-and market-based mechanisms. In terms of committee-based mechanisms, Europe continued to strengthen its committee-based approach; it set aside the allocated frequencies and ETSI was expected to select a system in the late 1990s that Europe would propose to the ITU. As GSM began to diffuse throughout the world in the mid-1990s, most Europeans in the mobile communication field expected ETSI would propose an enhanced version of GSM and that it would be accepted by the ITU. Europe also promoted market mechanisms by planning to award licences for the new technology.

The US moved further towards a free competition model in which no process was established to select a third generation standard and no frequencies were allocated for third generation systems. Thus, it failed effectively to utilize either committee or market mechanisms. The US used the frequencies allocated by the ITU to third-generation systems in the early 1990s in the Personal Communications Services (PCSs) that were started first in 1995. Thus, it was not planning to award licences and implicitly was leaving the implementation of third generation services to the existing service-providers. It expected that the best third generation system would emerge from competition between existing service-providers. As systems based on cdmaOne began demonstrating their superior voice quality, data transmission, and use of the frequency spectrum in 1995 and 1996, most Americans in the mobile communication field expected that cdmaOne would become the *de facto* third generation global standard.

Superficially, Japan moved towards the European model by creating a committee in 1992 whose task was to define the Japanese proposal to the ITU and more importantly allocating frequencies for third generation services. At a more practical level, Japan's MPT pressured DoCoMo to either create or adopt a worldwide standard partly as a result of criticisms from abroad but also through its experience with PHS. This caused DoCoMo to adopt a much more open approach than it had done with PDC and eventually to create an alliance with Nokia and Ericsson and thus with Europe's open committee-based approach. This was important since DoCoMo's large share of the market meant that its decision to adopt a certain standard,[70] particularly if it was an open standard, would mean that Japan itself would be adopting a single open standard. On the market side, the Japanese government promoted market mechanisms by pushing for an early start date. Further, due to the large population densities and large penetration rates in Japan, NTT DoCoMo has repeatedly announced that it will install third generation systems very quickly in the major cities.

Still, by mid-1996, few participants in the global mobile communication field outside Japan believed that NTT DoCoMo had a chance of creating a global standard. Although NTT DoCoMo was attracting some support from Asian carriers (Korean and Chinese), most Europeans still believed that an enhanced version of GSM would win while many Americans believed that cdmaOne would win. However, even the possibility that cdmaOne would win was a large concern to Ericsson and Nokia who had previously decided not to participate in the cdmaOne infrastructure market. Their late entry would have made it difficult for them to become competitive particularly since they would be paying higher licence fees than the early entrants. Ericsson is the largest supplier of GSM and mobile communication infrastructure overall while Nokia is the second largest supplier of GSM infrastructure. The choice of cdmaOne as a third generation standard would have been a major loss to these firms.

The Emergence of the DoCoMo–Ericsson–Nokia Alliance

Ericsson and Nokia saw NTT DoCoMo's efforts as a way to increase their chances of success in the third generation market. Not only would collaboration with NTT DoCoMo enable them to participate on the creation of the standard, Ericsson and Nokia held an important trump card: Europe was planning to choose a single standard in late 1997 and award licences for this technology shortly thereafter. Ericsson and Nokia used this trump card to convince NTT DoCoMo to adopt the evolution path of the GSM network interface in place of DoCoMo's proposed ISDN interface; NTT DoCoMo announced this in March 1997. This was a major victory for Ericsson and Nokia in that it would enable them and other GSM infrastructure suppliers and service-providers to utilize a large amount of their existing technology in third generation systems. Naturally, this decision also increased the interest of GSM carriers in DoCoMo's standard.

Almost simultaneously, NTT DoCoMo announced the creation of a 12–member international development team and it was able to enlist the support of additional Asian carriers in April 1997.[71] With the announcement of an international development team and the decision to use the GSM network interface, private conversations revealed that Ericsson and Nokia would announce their support for NTT DoCoMo's system at a global mobile communication conference in Singapore in May 1997. This caused a four-firm US group consisting of Motorola, Qualcomm, Northern Telecom, and Lucent to belatedly announce their development of a wide-band version of cdmaOne called cdma2000. In fact, this decision was prepared so haphazardly that they failed to enlist the support of a single carrier before the announcement even though several carriers were angry that they were not consulted about the announcement.

Nevertheless, the US firms' proposal was too little and too late – the forecasted installed base for DoCoMo's system had already reached a critical mass. US firms argued that their proposed third generation system was compatible at the network interface with narrow-band cdmaOne and AMPS; thus it had the same advantages as a W-CDMA system that is compatible with the evolution of the GSM network interface. However, the US firms could not offer NTT DoCoMo or any other partner what European firms could offer (a decision by all concerned parties to adopt a single standard) since the US did not plan to choose a single standard or award licences for third generation systems. NTT DoCoMo had found it much easier to focus first on the European market and second on the US market since there would not be a US decision to adopt a single standard. The result is that US firms have had very little negotiating power throughout the entire third generation standard-setting process.

Following the announced support for DoCoMo's standard by Ericsson and Nokia, DoCoMo continued to receive support from additional carriers in Asian and European countries many of whom were then offering GSM services.[72] The support by these Asian GSM carriers (many of whom were partially owned by European carriers) for the DoCoMo proposal eventually caused many European carriers to vote for DoCoMo's proposal.

Late responses by other manufacturers

Other European manufacturers (such as, Siemens, Alcatel, Bosch, and Matra) were even slower than the US firms to recognize the growing support for W-CDMA and to create coalitions. Throughout much of 1997 they believed that an enhanced version of GSM would be the eventual choice for a third generation system in Europe and in the ITU. However, in addition to their lack of cdmaOne participation like Ericsson and Nokia, they also held the same trump card as Ericsson and Nokia: Europe's plan to choose a single standard in late 1997 and shortly thereafter award licences. Further, decisions in ETSI required 71% support and the wide-band CDMA proposal did not have this degree of support without these other manufacturers. This enabled European firms like Alcatel, Siemens, Italtel, Nortel-Matra, and Bosch along with Lucent, Motorola and Sony to propose a hybrid of TDMA and CDMA called TD-CDMA.

ETSI first voted in mid-December and W-CDMA only received 58% support. Although all ETSI members can vote, each member's voting power depends on their sales and thus large established service-providers and manufacturers have a distinct advantage. Most service-providers supported W-CDMA due to their desire for a quick implementation of services and the support for W-CDMA from the Asian carriers they had invested in. However, support from a larger number of manufacturers was needed to obtain a 71% vote. This required DoCoMo, Nokia, and Ericsson to negotiate with the European manufacturers and incorporate some aspects of their proposal. After again failing to achieve the necessary 71% vote on January 28, 1998, the following day a compromise was reached whereby the W-CDMA proposal would be used for outdoor applications and the TD-CDMA proposal would be used for indoor applications. The TD-CDMA proposal has subsequently become part of the W-CDMA standard.

In retrospect, both committee and market mechanisms were important along with the use of leveraging of these mechanisms by Ericsson and Nokia. In particular, decisions to choose or not choose a single open standard and promote or not promote early competition between manufacturers and service-providers played critical roles in the competition between candidates for the third generation standard. The Japanese government told DoCoMo, which had and still had in early 2001 almost 60% of the subscribers in Japan, to either create or adopt a global third generation standard. This was for all practical purposes an order to create a single open standard in a committee that was represented by more than 60% of the domestic firms. The Japanese government made early announcements about plans to award licences to three carriers. Europe also made plans to select a single standard that included the awarding of new licences. And most interestingly, Ericsson and Nokia used Europe's plans to select a single standard and the success of GSM as negotiating tools to convince DoCoMo to adopt the evolution of the GSM network interface. This is an interesting example of how firms can indirectly use committee mechanisms to promote their interests.

The US left the choice of a third generation standard and the start of services to the marketplace. Both of these factors reduced the negotiating power of US manufacturers in their support of cdmaOne. Further, no US service-provider had publicly announced its intention to start third generation services as of the end of 1999 and in fact most of them have publicly stated that they will not quickly introduce third generation services. Their late introduction of second generation services requires them to delay the introduction of third generation services. And a major reason for their delays in introducing second generation services was the long licensing process for the PCSs. This reveals not only mistakes in the use of committee mechanisms by the US government and its firms but also problems with fundamental government procedures and processes.

Interestingly, Korea has also suffered from the choice of W-CDMA by ETSI and this fact also reveals nuances with using the committee mechanisms. The Korean government agreed to implement cdmaOne in the mid-1990s in return for favorable patent fees from Qualcomm. The result has been a rapid growth in cdmaOne subscribers in Korea and there were more cdmaOne subscribers in Korea than in the US until mid-1999. Further, Korean firms are key suppliers of cdmaOne handsets and to some extent infrastructure in the world market. However, due to the expected success of W-CDMA and patent battles with Qualcomm,[73] the Korean government now publicly states that it made a mistake in the adoption of cdmaOne. Interestingly, if the US had adopted the Korean strategy, cdmaOne would probably have become a global standard on the level of GSM before the end of 1999. But Korea is too small a country to independently influence the global standard setting process. One Korean carrier who installed a cdmaOne system has subsequently elected to install a system based on the DoCoMo standard.

SUMMARY

The above examples demonstrate how a hybrid model of committee and market mechanisms has worked better at explaining the selection of mobile communication standards than the use of one or the other mechanism. Large countries (such as, the US) or regions (such as Europe) that created a single open standard in an international committee-based standard setting process and promoted competition between manufacturers and other key suppliers were able to create an early installed base and thus a global mobile communication standard. Scandinavia (NMT), the US (AMPS), and Europe (GSM) created their standards in committees that were relatively open to domestic and international firms. In particular, when they announced their plans to adopt a single open standard, the forecasted installed bases for these systems rose dramatically. These forecasts for installed base continued to rise as the countries or regions received participation from domestic and foreign firms in the standard-setting processes, awarded licences to multiple service-providers, started services that were based on the single standards, and experienced the synergistic effect from falling prices and an increasing number of subscribers.

The adoption of a single open standard also explains the evolution from NMT to AMPS and GSM. The decision by a very large and rich country, the US, to adopt a single open standard and competition caused many countries to adopt AMPS instead of NMT, which had already diffused to many small countries. The decision by Europe to create a single open digital standard, that was superior technologically to AMPS, and introduce competition caused the momentum to swing from AMPS to GSM.

Many of the failures illuminate the difficulties of effectively using the committee and market mechanisms. The PHS example shows the importance of international participation in the standard setting committees, particularly by those foreign manufacturers such as Ericsson,

Motorola, and Nokia who have the strongest ties to foreign service-providers. The PHS case also demonstrates the importance of key suppliers in generating market mechanisms; in this case, the wireline service-provider NTT was a key supplier of connections to wireline and cellular users. Further, both this case and the problems with delays in awarding licences in the US digital market show how many of these problems reflect fundamental procedural and process problems in their respective federal governments.

Many of the failures also demonstrate the problems with trying to catch up to and replace an already established standard. France and Germany tried to do this in the analog days with a system that was not really technologically superior to the existing system, which had already generated very large installed bases. Thus, in retrospect their consumers and firms would have been better off if they had adopted one of the established analog standards such as AMPS, NMT, or TACS. Japan should have also adopted GSM as opposed to creating a proprietary system. GSM was able to replace the analog standard, AMPS, through its superior technology (digital) and its effective use of committee and market mechanisms. However, the technological superiority of cdmaOne has not been sufficient for it to catch up and replace GSM. Its late start *vis-à-vis* GSM would have required very strong committee and market actions such as the wholesale adoption by a large country such as the US or by multiple small countries to get the bandwagon rolling. Korea is too small a country to get the bandwagon rolling for a new system. Interestingly, as we shall see in Chapter 6, in spite of continued emphasis by the US government that standards selection is best left to the market, it is primarily actions taken by the US government that have kept cdmaOne's international hopes alive.

This chapter also tells us something about the evolution of committee and market mechanisms in specific countries. Most of Europe and Japan moved from a relatively closed approach in analog standard setting to a committee-based approach that is open to both domestic and foreign participants in second and third generation digital standard setting. In the case of Europe, the success of Scandinavian's NMT system and more so the move towards European integration and more recently the success of GSM have provided motivation for this evolution. Japan's standard setting approach has evolved through a combination of overall deregulation in the economy, foreign pressure, the failure of PHS and learning by the MPT, the increasing role of foreign firms in Japan, and DoCoMo's open-mindedness. The US on the other hand has moved in the opposite direction due to both changes in overall US regulatory policy and the fact that the initial method used to create the AMPS standard was merely a semi-committee-based approach in which support for a full committee-based approach was not generated.

Finally, this chapter tells us something about the role that firms can play in standard-setting. The conventional view that standard-setting involves competition between two firms, each of whom tries to utilize network externalities by opening the standard and creating coalitions is clearing overly simplistic in the case of the mobile communications industry. Committee-based standards were far more successful than standards that were promoted by individual firms like Qualcomm's cdmaOne.

Interestingly, as we shall see in the next two chapters, most of the successful firms have not pushed a single standard. Instead they have primarily competed inside *multiple* regional committees to develop technology cooperatively with service-providers. Relationships with service-providers, participation in standard setting committees, and the creation of development centers that support these two factors in multiple regions are critical. Further, their participation in multiple committees recognizes that different service-providers desire different systems and thus the infrastructure-providers have supplied equipment that is compatible with a variety of standards. For example, the leading suppliers of GSM infrastructure and handsets did not push GSM at the expense of the analog standards. Ericsson, Motorola, and Nokia maintained their shares in the NMT, TACS, and AMPS markets as they competed in GSM infrastructure and phones. Further, to some extent these firms have also become major suppliers of products for other non-GSM digital standards such as the US DAMPS and cdmaOne and the Japanese (PDC) digital standard.

The notable exception to this debate is the role played by Ericsson and Nokia in the selection of W-CDMA by Europe's ETSI. This example further illuminates many of the problems with the two-firm model of standards selection in that Ericsson and Nokia utilized different sets of tools than merely opening the technology and building coalitions. These two firms were able to utilize Europe's international committee-based standard setting process including Europe's decision to adopt a single standard as a negotiating tool with DoCoMo. In return for their support of W-CDMA in ETSI they asked for DoCoMo to adopt the evolution of the GSM network interface. Although at some level this was merely building coalitions, Ericsson and Nokia would not have been able to do this without Europe's international committee-based standard-setting process and Europe's decision to adopt a single standard. The US firms did not have these negotiating tools at their disposal and thus were unable to convince DoCoMo to adopt the evolution of the US network interface.

Notes

1. The lower the frequency, the longer the distance the signal will travel.
2. Motorola is the main exception. It has invested in a number of service-providers. Further, it has been the main promoter of a satellite system called Iridium that provides mobile communication services from everywhere in the world. Other manufacturers have subsidized loans to many service-providers, which has led to financial problems.
3. The cost effectiveness of PHS is debatable considering the deficits being run by the PHS operators. The PHS operators are unfortunately dependent on NTT's wireline system, which is one of the most expensive, if not the most expensive, wireline systems in the industrialized world. As a result, the PHS operators pay half their revenues to NTT. Nevertheless, there is widespread agreement that the capital costs for PHS are lower than that for existing cellular systems in high-density areas. Not only are switching stations not needed but PHS base stations are much less expensive than existing cellular base stations. For example, a PHS base station that covers a 100-meter radius can handle three calls and costs about $2000 to implement. A cellular base station that can handle 100 calls, covering an area with a radius of 1 km, costs about $1M. Therefore, the base station cost per potential call is $600 for PHS and $10,000 for cellular. In low-density areas, where coverage, not capacity, is the issue, cellular systems have lower capital costs.
4. Personal communication with Ahti Vaisanen, Vice President of Third Generation Technology, Nokia Mobile Phones, 12/12/1997.
5. Also like other products, product and service troduction dates (that is, service-start dates), prices (that is, handset prices and service-charges), and per capita incomes have had a large effect on installed base (Paetsch, 1993).
6. Hulten and Molleryd, 1995. Subsequently, Ericsson developed a control unit for the base stations of another Swedish company that it eventually acquired, Magnetic, which was chosen as the primary supplier of base stations for the initial NMT system. Mitsubishi was the second supplier of base stations while Ericsson supplied the switches. Ericsson's AXE switch and its previous experience with the interim cellular systems were critical to this early order (Meurling and Jeans, 1984).
7. Jonquières, guy de and Paul Betts "The Mobile Phone Explosion," *Financial Times*, 1/10/1982, p. 18.
8. Garrard, 1998.

9. These geographical and lifestyle characteristics include high incomes, large rural populations (where there were no pay phones), easily achieved broad coverage with the 450 system, the large number of summer homes, and the quickly changing weather that can have fatal consequences. In particular, the owners of vacation homes that exist on the islands and mountains surrounding the major cities were the first major users. Readers who have entered the cities of Stockholm, Helsinki, and Oslo by boat will probably recall the large number of vacation homes on the islands surrounding these cities; most of these islands have never had wireline service. For example, Heinrich von Piere, Chairman of Siemens, claimed that the Scandinavian suppliers were lucky that the cellular boom started in the Nordic states "where all those isolated summer homes created an instant demand" (*Financial Times*, 17/10/1994, p. 4 of international telecommunications survey).

10. For example, service-charges were initially set at 1600 Swedish kronor (about $250) per year and 3.5 Swedish kronor (about $0.60) per minute in Sweden for an average annual charge of about 4000 to 5000 Swedish kronor (*Financial Times*, 15/5/1984, p. 18, world's fastest growing system).

11. Hulten and Molleryd, 1995; Paetsch, 1993. Sweden's service-charges were also affected by competition from Comvik which also started services in 1981 based on a different mobile communication system (the equipment was supplied by a US firm, EF Johnson).

12. *Financial Times*, 15/5/1984, p. 18, world's fastest growing system.

13. *Financial Times*, 5/4/1990, p. 6, Iceland tops OECD on Telecoms. One reason the Nordic service-providers were able to set low prices is that they financed the creation of NMT with profits from international calls. Although only 3% of their traffic were from international calls, these calls represented 30% of their profits (*Financial Times*, 10/7/1991, World telecommunications survey, p. 28, Mobile sector is Nordic flagship).

14. The MPT set a basic monthly charge of 40,000 yen (US$178 at 1982 exchange rates).

15. Wakabayashi, 1984.

16. This equipment was supplied by EF Johnson.

17. The AMPS standard defined the air interface and unlike Scandinavia, it did not define the interface between base stations and switching equipment.

18. See n. 7.

19. *Le Monde*, 14/2/1987, Les malheurs du radiotéléphone, p. S9c.

20. It was decided early on that British Telecom would have majority ownership in one firm (with Securcor) while several other firms would apply for the second licence. Initially, the front runner for the second licence was Cellular Radio, which was a joint venture between Air Call (private mobile radio services) and Cable & Wireless See also n. 7. However, Racal Electronics, Hambros Bank, Comvik, and Millicom ended up receiving the second licence after a last minute application due to their optimist views on mobile communications and by promising that much of the equipment would be made in the UK thus creating both service-and manufacturing jobs. Racal Telecom is a British firm with experience in the defense communications area and the new service-provider was called Vodafone (Meurling and Jeans, 1994).

21. *Financial Times*, 13/12/1982, p. 17, Ericsson defends the Nordic approach, by Geoffrey Charlish.
22. See page 88 n. 7.
23. For example, Philips claimed that its MATS-E system had three times as much capacity as AMPS. Motorola countered by arguing that it uses special switched 60 degree segment aerials that allow 25% channel reuse (of adjacent cells) as opposed to 16% with conventional AMPS. Further, Motorola's handsets also have seven automatically adjusting power levels whereas MATS-E only has one level which is very high causing its handsets to be too large. Low power levels are needed in order to avoid interference between cells when on top of high buildings and high power levels are needed in order to make calls from places far from a base station (*Financial Times*, 20/10/1982, p. 29, Motorola refutes Philips claims).
24. *Financial Times*, 22/2/1983, p. 6, DoI books an early call for cellular mobile radio export market, by Guy de Jonquières.
25. Meurling and Jeans, 1994.
26. Apparently the Industry minister, M. Jean-Pierre Chevènement, favored TACS with some support from Alcatel and Thomson while the Siemens system was supported by the Telecommunications Minister, Louis Mexandeau, who wanted German support for the French satellite, Telecom 1. Support for the Siemens system was in spite of the incompatibility between the 900 MHz frequencies that France had set aside for mobile communication and the 450 MHz band used in the Siemens system *Financial Times*, 22/2/1983, p. 6, DoI books an early call for cellular mobile radio export market, by Guy de Jonquières.
27. Interest in the MATS-E standard increased when it looked as though Alcatel and Philips would clinch a FFr 1.5 billion contract to supply Kuwait with a radio-telephone network based on the MATS-E standard; this was following an order from Qatar. Thomson-CSF also looked as though it was preparing to collaborate with Siemens on such a project *Financial Times*, 21/4/1983, p. 7d, Mobile phone team close to Kuwait deal, by David Marsh.
28. *Financial Times*, 30/11/1983, p. 32, France and West Germany in radio phone pact.
29. Matra and Bosch quickly agreed to submit a joint bid for a contract along with SEL, the West German subsidiary of ITT, which had already mounted an experimental 900 MHz radio telephone project *Financial Times*, 24/1/1984, p. 2, Radio-phone plan lures Franco-German bids, by David Marsh.
30. These companies included Matra and Bosch, Secre of the French Jeumon-Schneider group with Ericsson's West German affiliate, Société Anonyme de Télécommunications (SAT) of France with Standard Elektrik Lorenz (ITTs German subsidiary), and AEG Telefunken and Motorola subsidiaries (*Financial Times*, 15/5/1984, p. 19, Negotiations on Franco-German network).
31. *Financial Times*, 2/10/1984, p. 36, Franco-German discord delays radio-telephone network scheme.

32. *Financial Times*, 27/3/1985, p. 6, Cross border plan shelved, Meurling and Jeans, 1994.
33. *Handelsblatt*, 18/12/1984, SEL-Gruppe/System 12 für privat Nebenstellen Anlagen, p. 11.
34. *Financial Times*, 27/3/1985, Mobile communications survey 7, Tangled up in a cordless controversy.
35. Ibid.
36. This system, under development since 1981, uses the 400 MHz band *Financial Times*, 27/3/1985, mobile communications survey, p. 6, Cross-border plan shelved.
37. Both Italtel and Telettra made the handsets (Meurling and Jeans, 1994).
38. South Africa adopted C-Netz since few countries would do business with South Africa at the time. Portugal adopted C-Netz since it had better security than either AMPS, TACS or NMT.
39. For example, the RC-2000 project reportedly required 120 Matra engineers for four years of which two-thirds were devoted to software development (*Financial Times*, 6/5/1986, p. 19h. Mobile Communications Survey, European partners plan new network: efforts by France and Germany to create a pan-European system have been delayed)
40. Paetsch, 1993. A major problem with the C-Netz system was its poor quality and low capacity, which discouraged Deutsche Telekom from promoting the system aggressively *Financial Times*, 17/10/1994, p. 4 of international telecommunications survey. Close to 50 million users, Mark Newman.
41. Fransman, 1995.
42. Meurling and Jeans, 1994.
43. This includes ones proposed by AEG Telefunken, Standard Elektrik Lorenz, Bosch, ANT (a subsidiary of Bosch), SAT, Alcatel, and Philips *Handelsblatt*, 30/1/1985; *Handelsblatt*, 21/6/1985.
44. *Handelsblatt*, 12/10/85; 10/16/85; *Financial Times*, 16/5/1986.
45. Meurling and Jeans, 1994; Garrard, 1998.
46. Meurling and Jeans, 1994.
47. *Financial Times*, 21/1/1987, p. 4. Ericsson, Siemens plan mobile phone link-up.
48. Meurling and Jeans, 1994.
49. *Handelsblatt*, 21/5/1987.
50. Garrard, 1998.
51. The countries are Belgium, Denmark, Finland, France, Ireland, Italy, the Netherlands, Norway, Portugal, Spain, Sweden, the United Kingdom, and West Germany (Garrard, 1998).
52. Garrard, 1998.
53. The creation of the GSM standards was a long and arduous process. Digital systems are more complex than analog systems and it was decided very early to define not only the air interface but also the network interface. Further, billing and roaming, handset type approval, subscriber identification, privacy, security, short message services, and many other issues had to be handled by ETSI of which handset type approval ended up being the one key issue that caused a significant delay (almost one year) in the start of GSM services (Garrard, 1998).

54. *Financial Times*, 19/9/1989, Mobile Communication Survey, p. 4, A bill for rights, Peter Purton.
55. *Nikkei News*, 13/9/1994. Dejitaru Keitai Denwa, Nihonsei, Oushuu sannyuu ni deokure – Tokkyou ru-ru ni Bei Motoro-ra nado Hanpatsu, "Japanese digital phone manufacturers had a late start in the European market – US and others against the patent rules".
56. *Financial Times*, 19/9/1989, Mobile Communication Survey, p. 4, A bill for rights, Peter Purton).
57. (*Financial Times*, 19/9/1989, Mobile Communication Survey, p. 4, Wrangles hit flagship project, Della Bradshaw).
58. *Financial Times*, 13/7/1990, p. 3. Alcatel and Motorola in patents deal, William Dawkins).
59. Between 1993 and 1996, in total, 55 non-European countries started services based on GSM (61%) versus 35 for AMPS or TACS (40%). Of the former European colonies, 30 countries (57%) started services based on GSM as opposed to 23 countries (43%) starting services based on AMPS or TACS. Twenty-three of 32 former British colonies, 5 of 9 former French colonies, 1 of 9 former Spanish colonies, and 1 of 3 former Dutch colonies started services based on GSM (30 countries or 57%) as opposed to AMPS or TACS (23 countries or 43%).
60. Nikkei Industrial, 13/9/1994. Dejitaru Keitai Denwa, Nihonsei, Oushuu sannyuu ni deokure – Tokkyou ru-ru ni Bei Motoro-ra nado Hanpatsu, "Japanese digital phone manufacturers had a late start in the European market – US and others against the patent rules".
61. Further, following the release of the specifications for this standard (DAMPS) in early 1990, DoCoMo also adopted the Motorola coding and decoding technology *Nikkei News*, 5/6/1990 (p. 9. Motorola wins Japan phone race). NTT confirmed that equipment made by Motorola of the US will be the sole standard for the Japanese digital standard. Equipment made by NTT had come in a close second. Yamaguchi, NTT president, said the choice was based on technological considerations alone with no political influence on the Japan research and development centre for radio systems, which conducted the tests under the authority of the MPT. NTT claims it tried to sacrifice quality for price while Motorola achieved higher quality. Six other companies also submitted coding–decoding equipment for testing including Toshiba, NEC, Fujitsu, Matsushita, Mitsubishi, and Ericsson. Motorola is expected to licence technology freely to other firms.
62. This was somewhat of a victory for Ericsson and Nortel who had supported TDMA and a defeat for Motorola and Lucent who had supported FDMA 1/2/1989: Sizzling markets speed vendors in drive to digital cellular. *Electronics*.
63. In fact, all services had still not been started by late 1999 due to the bankruptcy of several firms who purchased frequency spectrum and the delays in re-auctioning the spectrum.
64. Garrard, 1998.
65. One of the major advantages of digital cellular is that it uses the frequency spectrum more effectively than analog cellular. But the low traffic and low population densities that existed and still exist in most

parts of North America meant existing service-providers expected few shortages of frequency spectrum in the near future. There is lower traffic in North America due to the fact that in North America owners of mobile phones must pay for receiving calls (in other countries charges are levied on outgoing mobile phone calls). Thus, many North American users do not pass around their phone numbers or turn their phones off and only use them to make calls.

66.   Garrard, 1998.

67.   Prestowitz, 1988; Johnson, 1982.

68.   For example, 40% of the revenues for the PHS carriers were being paid to NTT in the first two years of the PHS service-(only 9% for cellular firms) while these connection charges have represented a significant fraction of NTT's profits (Telecommunication, 1997).

69.   Even in mid-1998, they were still 4.5 times more expensive than PHS-to-PHS or PHS-to-wireline calls and 50% more expensive than cellular calls.

70.   NTT DoCoMo also has access to NTT's well-funded (by Japanese tax dollars) research programs and it was planning to operate services overseas (as a result of changes in NTT's charter). Koutaiiki CDMA, 2000 nen ni Tekiyou Sa-bisu, NTT Dokomo – Suishin Keikaku wo Happyou. NTT DoCoMo has announced its plans for Wide-Band CMDA services in 2000, 4/4/1997, p. 7. *Nikkei.*

71.   The team included Ericsson, Lucent, Fujitsu, NEC, and Matsushita, who were to develop infrastructure and Motorola, Nokia, NEC, Matsushita, Mitsubishi, Sharp, and Toshiba who were to develop handsets for the experimental systems. DoCoMo enlisted the support of Korea Mobile Phone, China Telecom, Australia Telstra, and Singapore Telecom and it announced that it had invited carriers from North America (including AT&T), Great Britain, Sweden, France, Germany, Italy, Thailand, Malaysia, Indonesia, and New Zealand to participate in the development of the W-CDMA system.

72.   This includes Japan Telecom in October 1997 and carriers in Indonesia in September 1997, the Philippines, Thailand, Italy in December 1997, and Hong Kong in January 1998.

73.   The Electronics and Telecommunications Research Institute (ETRI) of Korea claims that Qualcomm owes it royalties. In a 1991 agreement, Qualcomm agreed to pay 20% of the royalties that it receives from Korean firms that manufacture systems using the jointly developed technology to ETRI. However, ETRI claims that the agreement also applies to PCS frequencies (1900) and not just 800 MHz bands in Korea, foreign sales, and all Korean firms (not just Samsung, Lucky Goldstar, Hyundai, Maxon).

4 Committee- and Market-Based Competition in the Mobile Infrastructure Market

This chapter describes how committee-based competition and the interaction between these committee- and market-based competitions has played a stronger role in the overall competition between mobile infrastructure providers than just market-based competition by itself. Firms participate in standard-setting committees while they simultaneously develop technology in cooperation with service-providers.

Cooperative development work with service-providers is an essential part of the competition in committees since early orders for test and commercial systems are necessary to develop experience in mobile infrastructure. In fact, the shares of early orders for mobile infrastructure are very similar to the eventual breakdown of shares. In theory, early orders could come from either new or existing service-providers. This chapter will find that market-based competition has played a more important role than committee-based competition for obtaining orders from *new* service-providers. These service-providers have typically been the second and third firms to provide mobile services in a given country and thus they also have a tendency to differentiate themselves from the first service provider and purchase infrastructure from a firm that did not supply the first service-provider.[1]

However, the very fact that the *existing* service-providers have generally placed the earliest orders for mobile infrastructure has made committee-based competition very important, in many ways more important than market-based competition in mobile infrastructure. Committee-based competition has often determined the early orders, partly through the actual work on committees but also through the continuity of vendor–customer relationships. High switching costs and continuity in vendor–customer relationships are common in CoPS like mobile infrastructure. This chapter will show that there are high switching costs between the infrastructure and service-providers since most service-providers have purchased multiple generations of infrastructure from the same infrastructure vendor. And these switching costs and their associated required compatibilities have made it necessary for firms to offer both base stations and switching equipment.[2] Further, these high switching costs also exist to some extent when a service provider makes an *early*[3] investment in a second service provider in another country.

Within a single generation of technology, the most successful firms used their early orders to create capabilities in market-based competition. Whether the early orders were obtained through committee- (through orders from existing service-providers) and/or market-based competition (through orders from new service-providers), it was necessary for firms to translate these early orders into superior products and other forms of capabilities for market-based competition. Firms that did this were able to create positive feedback where new orders led to superior products and the superior products led to new orders.

In a subsequent generation of technology, it is important to translate the capabilities of market-based competition in the current generation of technology into the capabilities of committee-based competition in the next generation of technology. Firms must participate in these next generation standard-setting committees while they simultaneously develop technology in cooperation with service-providers, who most likely are existing service-providers with existing suppliers. This is of course problematic given the changing sources of each generation of technology. The US was the source of the analog standard AMPS, GSM was created in Europe, and W-CDMA services will be first started in Japan.

Therefore, in order to succeed in a subsequent generation of technology, firms need to acquire the relevant capabilities in committee-based competition in a foreign country before the next generation of technology begins. Ericsson has done this through the early creation of global customer relationships (that is, relationships with service-providers all over the world) and by using these global relationships to acquire early orders in both second (including GSM) and third generation standards. Global development capabilities and participation in foreign standard-setting processes were necessary parts of these global relationships with service-providers. Ericsson's faster creation of customer relationships, development capabilities, and participation in standard-setting at the global level are the major reason why Ericsson is a major supplier in more analog and digital standards than any other infrastructure supplier.

One remaining issue that is addressed throughout this chapter is the relative importance of committee-versus market-based competition in various regional markets and technologies. Although committee-based competition and the interaction between committee-and market-based competition has played a stronger role in the overall competition between mobile infrastructure providers than just market-based competition by itself, this relative importance was partly a function of the market and technology. An important part of committee-based competition is the high switching costs and thus continuity in vendor–customer relationships across multiple generations of technology. However, the degree of continuity in these vendor–customer relationships was not equal in all markets and technologies. This chapter will find that the greater the fragmentation of the market, the less the continuity in vendor–supplier relationships and thus the greater the importance of market-based competition.

This has been particularly true in the US market where the large number of initial licences eventually led to large amounts of merger and acquisition activity by the US service-providers. This activity caused US service-providers to acquire regions that were supplied by different vendors and thus they were forced to develop capabilities in managing multiple vendors. As summarized in Table 4.1, this has caused the US market to have far less continuity in these vendor–customer relationships than in other markets. This is in

Table 4.1   Degree of continuity in vendor–customer relationships for various technological discontinuities in mobile infrastructure by region

Technology or technological discontinuity	Degree of technological change/compatibility	Degree of continuity in vendor–customer relationships		
		US	Europe	Rest of world
Wireline to analog	High	High	High	NA
Within AMPS	None	Medium	High	High
Analog to GSM	High	NA	High	High
AMPS to DAMPS	Low	Medium	NA	High
AMPS to cdmaOne	Medium	Medium	NA	High
Within digital	None	Medium	High	High

NA: "Not applicable" due to either no adoption of the specific technology by the region or the incumbent suppliers did not offer the relevant technology/standard and thus it is difficult to assess the degree of continuity.

spite of the smaller technological discontinuity and greater compatibility between first and second generation systems in the US than elsewhere.

The remainder of this chapter discusses each major infrastructure market beginning with an analysis of competition in the analog market.

COMMITTEE-BASED COMPETITION AND THE EARLY YEARS OF THE MOBILE INFRASTRUCTURE ANALOG MARKET

The importance of committee-based competition in the early years of the analog market is shown by the large amount of continuity between wireline and analog infrastructure orders. Most of the early mobile communication service-providers in the industrialized countries gave their mobile analog infrastructure orders to the vendor that supplied their wireline system since most of the early service-providers were the national wireline service-providers (PTTs). These national wireline service-providers were the first firms to offer mobile communication services in Japan (NTT), Scandinavia (PTTs), the US (the Baby Bells), Canada (Bell Canada), Germany (Deutsche Telekom), France (France Télécom), and Italy (Italia Mobile Telecom). And the local wireline firms (names in parentheses) were the major suppliers of the mobile communications equipment to NTT (NEC), the Scandinavian PTTs (Ericsson and Nokia), Bell Canada (Nortel), Deutsche Telekom (Siemens switches and PKI base stations), France Télécom (Matra base stations and Alcatel switches), Telecom Italia Mobile in Italy (Italtel), and to some extent the US Baby Bells (Lucent[4]).

Committee-based competition in the infrastructure market was less important in the US than in other countries since the US introduced much more competition in the service market than other countries, particularly in the form of greater market fragmentation. The FCC (Federal Communications Commission) divided the US into 305 Metropolitan Statistical Areas (MSAs) and 428 Rural Statistical Areas (RSAs) and licenced two service-providers in each area. The wireline service-providers divided up the first licences while so-called radio-common carriers (RCCs), who had not been wireline service-providers, divided up the second licences in each area. Table 4.2 shows the names of the major service-providers and the number of licences they received in the largest ninety markets.

Table 4.2   Largest US service-providers and their number of licences as of January 1986 in the largest 90 US markets

Service provider	Number of licences
GTE*	14
Bell South*	13
Nynex*	11
Ameritech*	8
US West/New Vector*	8
RAM Broadcasting	7
Bell Atlantic*	6
United Telespectrum	6
Southwestern Bell*	6
Contel*	5
Pacific Telephone*	4
Southern New England Telephone*	3

*Wireline service-provider.

As expected, the competition for orders from the wireline service-providers emphasized committee-based competition while the competition for orders from the RCCs emphasized market-based competition. Lucent received most of the orders from the wireline service-providers, in particular the Baby Bells that were spun off from AT&T since it had supplied most of their wireline systems when it was Western Electric (see Table 4.3). Lucent obtained 30 of 55 or 55% of the original orders from the Baby Bells. It did not receive more of the orders since some of the Baby Bells had begun to see AT&T (at that time Western Electric) and thus Lucent as a potential competitor as the breakup of AT&T gathered momentum.[5] The two major exceptions to Lucent's dominance of the Baby Bell market were Bell South and US West. Bell South publicly announced in the early 1980s that it intended to distance itself from Lucent (then Western Electric) in wireline equipment since it saw AT&T as a future competitor.[6]

Lucent was much less successful with the other former wireline service-providers (that is, non-Baby Bells). Lucent only obtained eight of the 35 orders from these service-providers while Motorola obtained 23 orders.[7] This probably reflects committee-based more than market-based competition since these other wireline carriers had competed with AT&T for many years in the wireline field. Many of these non-Baby Bells had not bought from Lucent in the wireline field (Nortel and others were major suppliers) and thus probably did not want to buy from Lucent in the mobile field.

Table 4.3   Number of orders for each vendor by type
of service provider in the largest 90 US markets

Vendor	Former wireline carriers			Radio-common carriers
	Baby Bells	*GTE*	*Other*	
Lucent	31		8	17
Motorola	12	14	9	33
Nortel/GE	10			9
Ericsson				24
Other	2		4	7
Total	55	14	21	90

Market-based competition was even more important than committee-based competition in the RCCs since these firms were newcomers
to the telecommunications field. This market-based competition provided new firms with opportunities and Motorola and Ericsson were
the big winners. They supplied 63% of the radio-common carriers in
the 90 largest US markets.[8] Many of these RCCs were very small and
eventually merged with or were acquired by other carriers.

The market-based competition was also influenced by the tendency
in the US and elsewhere for the second service provider that is awarded
a licence to order their mobile infrastructure from a different vendor
than that used by the first licencee. In the US, different vendors serve
the first and second licencees in 80 of the 90 largest markets. In
Canada, Rogers Cantel ordered from Ericsson and Bell Canada
ordered from Nortel (GE supplied the base stations for Nortel).

The early competition in the analog market had a strong impact on
subsequent competition. Firms that obtained early orders were able to
develop the necessary experience and use this experience to obtain
subsequent orders. Both in the US market and the Scandinavian
standard NMT, there was also a strong correlation between the shares
of early and subsequent orders. As shown in Table 4.4, the vendor
shares for the first 31 US orders are very similar to the vendor shares
for all orders (shown as percent of population covered in mid-1991).
The largest change is that Lucent's share dropped and Ericsson's share
increased between 1983 and 1991.[9]

Similar results exist in NMT. Ericsson received orders from all of the
first six and 18 of the first 22 countries who offered NMT services
while Nokia received orders from five of the first 22 countries who
offered NMT services. Ericsson eventually became the major supplier

Table 4.4   Market shares in early and subsequent orders

Firm	Percent of first 31 orders	Percent of population covered as of mid-1991
Motorola	32	32
Lucent	45	34
Ericsson	6	19
Nortel	16	11
Other	0	4

to 29 of the 39 countries which have adopted NMT. Further, there was strong customer–supplier continuity; the same vendor supplied both the 450 and 900 systems for each service provider that adopted NMT.

There were slight differences, however, in the way the committee- and market-based mechanisms worked for firms in NMT and AMPS. Although in all cases, these successful firms created capabilities in market-based competition, some firms used their strength in committee-based competition to develop the capabilities in market-based competition while others were forced to obtain even their early orders through market-based competition. Ericsson (in NMT), Nokia (in NMT), and Lucent (in AMPS) used their early strength in committee-based competition, which came from their early involvement in the standard-setting processes and their relationships with wireline service-providers to develop capabilities in market-based competition. On the other hand, Ericsson and Motorola (both in AMPS) did not have relationships with wireline service-providers in the US so they were forced to rely on market-based competition to just obtain early orders from *new* service-providers.

CONSOLIDATION BY US SERVICE PROVIDERS AND INCREASED MARKET-BASED COMPETITION

The greater competition in the US market also caused market competition to be greater in the US than in other regions for other and fairly unexpected reasons. By dividing the US market into more than 700 areas, it created many more opportunities for vendors. Whereas in other countries, only one or in some cases two national suppliers of mobile base stations or of switching equipment emerged, in the US four companies emerged as major suppliers of mobile infrastructure.

Further, the existence of more than 700 markets appears to have caused the decentralization of vendor selection decisions. Although GTE and most independent wireline and RCCs bought from only one vendor, most of the Baby Bells purchased equipment from multiple vendors.[10]

More interestingly, the large number of markets has indirectly caused a continuous wave of mergers and acquisitions to occur in the US market which has strengthened the market-based competition among infrastructure providers. Initially these mergers and acquisitions were driven by the fact that a lottery was used to award licences and thus many firms applied for licences that only intended to sell those licences.[11] Subsequently, the mergers and acquisitions were driven by the desire to create a regional and in the long run nationwide coverage as service-providers recognized the high demand for roaming and the high roaming tariffs as profitable opportunities.

These mergers and acquisitions have in many cases changed the composition of vendors within a specific carrier (see Table 4.5). Most service-providers acquired markets that were served by different vendors and the equipment from these vendors was often incompatible at the network level partly due to the undefined network interface in the US AMPS standard. These incompatibilities caused many service-providers to have equipment replaced sometimes for performance reasons but often to improve compatibility in their networks.

For example, McCaw became the largest provider of cellular services in the US (before its acquisition by AT&T Wireless) primarily through the acquisition of Lin Broadcasting and small and sometimes independent carriers.[12] Ericsson and to some extent Lucent became the major suppliers to McCaw Cellular since McCaw acquired carriers who had been supplied by Ericsson and Lucent and since McCaw made an early strategic decision to use Ericsson equipment in order to solve compatibility problems. McCaw Cellular began replacing other vendors' equipment (including Lucent's equipment) with Ericsson equipment in 1986 first in Sacramento and Fresno and later in Florida (see Table 4.6).[13]

Other US service-providers followed a similar pattern. PacTel changed its suppliers from Lucent to both Motorola and Ericsson by replacing Lucent equipment and by acquiring RAM Broadcasting and General Communications Industries in the late 1980s.[14] In the 1990s, PacTel further diversified its infrastructure suppliers by forming a joint venture with Cellular Communications in 1990 in the Michigan and Ohio areas.[15] Bell South changed from only Motorola equipment to

Table 4.5 Evolution of major US carriers and their infrastructure suppliers

Carrier	Initial analog vendor	Changes in analog vendor	Digital system		Initial digital vendors	
Ameritech	Lucent	None	CDMA		Lucent	
Nynex	Lucent	None	BA/ NYNEX: CDMA	PrimeCo: CDMA	Lucent	PrimeCo: Motorola Lucent
Bell Atlantic	Lucent	Move towards Motorola with acquisition of Metro Mobile	CDMA		Lucent	
US West New Vector	Nortel and Lucent	Move towards Motorola with Nortel cancellations and Communications Industries	Airtouch: CDMA		Airtouch: NT, Lucent Motorola	
Pacific Telesis	Lucent	Move towards Motorola (General Communications Industries), Nortel (Cellular Communications) and Ericsson (Graphic Scanning in 1986 and RAM Broadcasting) through acquisitions and replacements	PacTel: GSM		Ericsson	
Bell South	Motorola	Move towards Ericsson (Graphic Scanning in 1990) and Lucent with acquisitions and replacements	DAMPS		Ericsson, Nortel	

(Contd.)

Table 4.5 Contd.

Carrier	Initial analog vendor	Changes in analog vendor	Digital system	Initial digital vendors
SW Bell	Lucent	It acquired Motorola-and Ericsson-supplied regions (Metromedia) but some were replaced with Lucent equipment	DAMPS	Ericsson
GTE	Motorola	Move towards Lucent (Contel Cellular) with acquisitions and replacements of Motorola equipment	CDMA	Motorola and Lucent
AT&T Wireless/ McCaw	Lucent and Ericsson	Move towards Ericsson with acquisitions and replacements with Ericsson equipment. Exception was acquisition of Lucent-supplied SNET.	DAMPS	Ericsson and Lucent
US Cellular 360 Communications	Nortel and NEC Motorola	None Originally called Centel, it acquired Motorola-supplied United Telespectrum and was acquired by and spun off from Sprint. Move towards Lucent with Alltel acquisition.	CDMA CDMA	Nortel Motorola

Note: Acquisitions are shown in parentheses next to their major vendor.

Table 4.6   Number and Percentage of Orders by Service
Provider and Vendor as of May 1992
in the largest 90 and second largest 90 US markets

Service provider	Lucent		Motorola		Northern Telecom		Ericsson	
	Top 90	2nd 90	Top 90	2nd 90	Top 90	2nd 90	Top 90	2nd 90
McCaw	11	12	5		2		14	14
PacTel			5	3			7	2
Bell South	3	1	9	3			4	4
SW Bell	4	3	3				2	
GTE			11	15	3	2		
Bell Atlantic	6	3						
Metro Mobile			12	2				
Ameritech	8	4						
Nynex	9	2	1		1			
SNET	4	1						
Centel			11	11				

other vendors such as Ericsson due to acquisitions (Graphic Scanning and American Cellular Communications) and problems with Motorola equipment. Southwestern Bell partly diversified from Lucent to multiple vendors between 1986 and 1992 as it acquired small independent carriers such as Metromedia who used other vendors such as Motorola and Ericsson.[16] GTE moved from one vendor (Motorola) to two vendors (plus Lucent) with the cancellation of some Motorola contracts and the acquisition of Contel in 1991.[17] Bell Atlantic also moved from a single vendor (Lucent) to two vendors (plus Motorola) when it acquired Metro Mobile in 1992.

Only a few service-providers stayed with one vendor for their analog equipment. Centel only bought from Motorola primarily since its acquisitions (for example, United Telespectrum in 1988) had also used Motorola equipment.[18] Two of the former Baby Bells, Ameritech and Nynex, increased the percentage of orders they gave to Lucent in the 1980s and 1990s through the replacement of other equipment with Lucent equipment in order to solve compatibility problems.

The overall result of these mergers and acquisitions has been a lower emphasis on continuity in customer–supplier relationships in the US mobile infrastructure market and thus a greater importance of market-based competition than in other countries. Interestingly, other countries that have divided their country into small mobile phone markets have also shown a lower emphasis on continuity in customer–supplier relationships. These include Mexico, Indonesia, Brazil, Russia, and China.[19] Thus, it appears that although committee-based mechanisms are in general more important for complex product systems (CoPS) than high-volume products, the fragmentation of markets may increase the importance of market-based competition in the CoPS.

MARKET-BASED COMPETITION IN THE INTERNATIONAL AMPS AND TACS INFRASTRUCTURE MARKETS

In the international market, the success of the US AMPS and its derivative TACS standards provided the suppliers of this equipment with large opportunities in the regions that adopted these standards. These regions include parts of Europe, South America, Asia, and Africa. And since many of the firms (such as Alcatel and Siemens) who had supplied these countries with wireline switches did not develop AMPS or TACS equipment (discussed below), orders were largely determined by market-based competition. But firms responded to these opportunities differently. Some firms like Motorola and Ericsson emphasized market-based competition to obtain these foreign orders while other firms remained focused on committee-based competition. And as we shall see later, the former two firms were able to turn this market-based strength into committee-based strength to obtain early critical GSM orders.

In AMPS and its derivative TACS, it was Motorola and Ericsson who became the leading suppliers of this infrastructure outside of the US. More than 90% of the world's AMPS and TACS subscribers outside the US are connected to their equipment. Motorola and Ericsson are the leading suppliers of TACS equipment primarily due to their success in the early TACS orders, the critical orders being from the British carriers, Cellnet and Vodafone. Although proposals were made by a number of other firms such as Siemens, Alcatel, Lucent, ITT (later acquired by Alcatel), Northern Telecom, and NEC,[20] Motorola and Ericsson obtained the first two orders since they worked harder to accommodate the needs of the British carriers and regulators. As was discussed in Chapter 3, both firms (Ericsson also proposed modified versions of NMT) worked hard to modify the AMPS

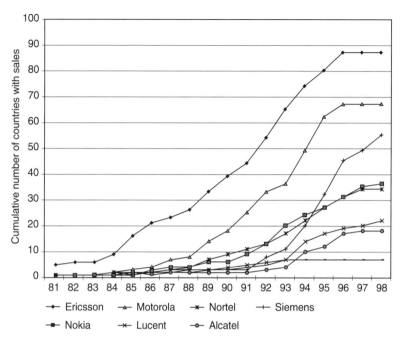

Figure 4.1   Global customer base for major infrastructure suppliers

standard for the British carriers while the other vendors largely tried to
sell their existing equipment.[21]

The success of Ericsson and Motorola in AMPS, TACS, and NMT
enabled them to begin creating a global customer base as shown in
Figure 4.1. Ericsson built its global customer base through the service-
providers who were early adopters of NMT and TACS. By the end of
1988, sixteen of the 21 and six of the 21 countries that had started
NMT and AMPS or TACS services respectively were using Ericsson
equipment. Between 1989 and 1992, 26 new countries (not counting
GSM) of which nine used TACS, six AMPS, and eleven NMT, started
services that used Ericsson equipment. As discussed below, many of
these analog orders led to critical GSM orders.

Motorola initially used market-based competition to obtain new
customers and subsequently committee-based expansions to expand
its relationships with the service-providers. Motorola built its global
customer base through sales of AMPS and TACS equipment, many of
which came through its own investments in carriers and work with

Millicom, which has invested in many other service-providers. Motorola received sixteen orders through its own investments in carriers, many of whom started AMPS services with the first being in Israel in 1985. These orders began to accelerate in 1989 just as AMPS and TACS services were started in many countries and orders from carriers with Millicom investments started. Although only ten countries had started analog services that used Motorola equipment as of the end of 1988, 24 new countries started services that used Motorola equipment between 1989 and 1992. Seven of these countries started TACS services, seven were-Millicom related services, and five were Motorola investments in service-providers that used AMPS.

Millicom is one of Motorola's best customers. Of the 24 service-providers who received early investments from Millicom, Motorola received fifteen of the 24 equipment orders.[22] Millicom and Motorola became involved in the late 1970s when cellular systems were first being tested in the US. In addition to this relationship leading to many AMPS and TACS orders, the relationship also helped Motorola obtain two key early GSM orders from Comvik in Sweden and Netcom in Norway. Motorola's sale of TACS infrastructure to other carriers also led as we shall see later to key digital orders from the Austrian PTT (GSM), Cellnet (GSM), and DDI in Japan (PDC).

Other firms were slow to change from committee-based to market-based competition, which was needed to create a global customer base. Nokia's global customer base did not begin expanding until it received a number of orders from new GSM carriers, particularly those who started 1800 services. Nortel's analog equipment was only installed in four and fifteen countries that had started analog services by the end of 1988 and 1992 respectively, with the majority of these being small Caribbean and Central and South American countries. Only three and five countries respectively had started analog services that used Lucent equipment by the end of 1988 and 1992. Siemens, Alcatel, Matra, PKI, and NEC were the slowest firms to develop a global customer base in spite of the extensive customer bases held by Siemens, Alcatel, and NEC in the wireline switch market.

These firms were slower to create a global customer base than Ericsson and Motorola for three reasons, all of which are related to their over-reliance on committee-based competition. First, they were too focused on their existing customers. For example, the early start of services in Japan should have helped Japanese vendors obtain an early entry into both the AMPS and TACS markets. As shown in Figure 3.5, there were more mobile phone subscribers for the Japanese standard (all in Japan) until it was passed in 1984 by NMT and subsequently by AMPS in 1985. However, like Lucent, Nortel, and the French and German suppliers, NEC[23] and Fujitsu were too focused on their national carrier. They were not interested in modifying their systems for the needs of the British and other foreign carriers since they believed that you worked with your national carrier, NTT, to develop a system and then try to sell that system to the rest of the world. While this worked to some extent for NEC, Fujitsu, Alcatel and Siemens in the wireline infrastructure industry where most countries use similar wireline equipment, the variety of different mobile communication standards requires vendors to develop equipment with a variety of carriers.

The second reason, which is related to the first, is that unlike Ericsson and Motorola, Alcatel, Matra, PKI, and Siemens were faced with late starts and slow growth in their domestic analog markets. However, the latter firms largely controlled the standards and thus they must be held partly responsible for the delays in service start, the lack of competition in the market and choice of proprietary and non-open standards.

Third, Motorola and Ericsson had already moved towards market-based competition in other products and both had a much larger *overall* global presence in the mid-1980s than the other two suppliers of AMPS infrastructure Lucent and Nortel, did in the US. The early growth in the US AMPS market and the adoption of AMPS by many countries should have encouraged Lucent and Nortel to move overseas. However, not only were they too focused on doing development work with their historical customers, the US and Canadian Baby Bells, they were also slow to move overseas in other businesses like the wireline switch business. While Motorola and Ericsson were obtaining more than a quarter of their sales from outside North America and Europe in 1985 respectively, the percentages for Lucent and Nortel were about 0% and 4% respectively. Further, Lucent and Nortel were not major suppliers of wireline equipment overseas even as late as 1990. For example, Lucent and Nortel did not have greater than 10% of the market share in wireline switching equipment in any region outside the US. Ericsson had greater than 10% of the market share in wireline equipment in five major regions in the world (Western and Eastern Europe, South America, Africa, and Asia). It was only in the US and Japan where Ericsson did not have greater than a 10% share of the wireline switching market.

108 Global Competition Between and Within Standards

Table 4.7   Early and subsequent market shares in the GSM base station market

Firm	Percent participation in base station orders for first 20 service starts	Percent participation adjusted for multiple vendors per service start	Percent of 900 base station European shipments in 1997	Percent of worldwide GSM base station shipments in 1997
Ericsson	50	31	36	34
Motorola	35	21	14	11
Nokia	30	19	25	27
Siemens	0	0	7	4
Alcatel	15	9	7	9
Nortel/				
Matra	10	6	9	10
Lucent			2	5
PKI	20	12		
Total	160	100	100	100

Table 4.8   Early and subsequent market shares in the GSM switching market

Firm	Percent participation in switching orders for first 20 service starts	Percent participation adjusted for multiple vendors per service start	Percent of European 900 switching shipments in 1997	Percent of worldwide GSM switching shipments in 1997
Ericsson	65	46	44	39
Nokia	20	14	18	19
Siemens	40	29	24	22
Alcatel	15	11	13	9
Nortel/Matra			1	9
Lucent				1
Total	140	100	100	100

THE GSM INFRASTRUCTURE MARKET

Committee-based competition also played a strong role in the GSM infrastructure market, particularly for the early orders where continuity in vendor–customer relations played an important role. Like the analog markets, there is a strong relationship between the shares in the early and later stages of the market and thus early success through continuity in vendor–customer relations was important. Tables 4.7 and 4.8 show percent participation in the first twenty orders and market shares in the 1997 GSM base station and switching markets respectively. Once the percent participation data is adjusted for the fact that many service-providers placed initial orders with multiple vendors, the market shares look very similar, particularly for the switch market. In the switch market, there is very little difference between the shares of the first twenty orders and the shares of shipments in 1997.

For the base station market, outside of Ericsson the shares for the first twenty orders and the 1997 market look somewhat different. Motorola's, Alcatel's and in particular PKI's shares have dropped while Siemens's, Nortel's and in particular Nokia's shares have in-creased. As described in more detail below, Motorola has received very few new orders for GSM base stations in Europe since Siemens ended its partnership with Motorola and began selling its own base stations in 1995. If Motorola's and Siemens' 1997 shares are combined, there is very little change in the percent participation in 1992 and market shares in 1997. The only real cases of change in market share are with PKI, Nokia, and Nortel. PKI was also Siemens' partner at the request of DeT Mobile, the newly formed mobile subsidiary of Deutsche Telekom. Due to problems with PKI's base stations, Siemens dropped PKI as a partner in 1992 and began working primarily with Motorola until it began selling its own base stations in 1995. Nokia's success with new carriers who were not highly represented among the first twenty service starts and Nortel's acquisition of Matra are the reasons for their increased market share.

Committee-based competition in the early orders

Committee-based competition determined most of the early orders. Critical early orders were obtained through early and active participa-tion in the standard-setting process and the simultaneous development of infrastructure with service-providers. These early orders were im-portant for gaining experience and mostly came from PTTs since they were the first firms to start services. They ordered trial systems from various suppliers in order to develop expertise in GSM and many of these orders for trial systems led to orders for commercial systems.

While Ericsson, Nokia, Siemens, Alcatel, PKI, Matra and Motorola were involved with the standard-setting activities from the beginning, Lucent, Nortel, and NEC had almost no involvement in the standard-setting process. This was due to their lack of a development center in Europe and their lack of interest in creating one. And firms such as

Lucent, who merely "developed the product for the specifications," failed in GSM since many of the key aspects of the standards were tacit as opposed to explicit knowledge.

However, provided that a firm did participate in the standard-setting process, it does not appear that the degree of participation has had much effect on competition.[24] Instead, the continuity in customer–supplier relations explains a significant fraction of the orders and in particular, success in the early orders. As shown in Table 4.9, in Europe, of the 27 European carriers who had offered both analog and digital services by 1998, 25 of the carriers ordered their *initial* digital equipment from at least one of their analog suppliers. For fourteen of these carriers, the analog and digital base station and switching equipment suppliers were exactly the same firms. For four other carriers, the major change in suppliers was the replacement of Motorola as a switch supplier with Alcatel or Ericsson.

These customer–supplier continuities were equally if not more important for the twenty earliest orders (see Table 4.10). Of the services that were started in 1992 and 1993, all sixteen of the service-providers who had offered analog services purchased equipment from at least one of their analog suppliers. Further, in seven cases the analog and digital base station and switch suppliers were exactly the same and there were only two cases where firms were actually replaced as a base station or switch supplier.[25] This large amount of continuity in customer–supplier relations made both previous analog orders and alliances with vendors who had received analog orders very important.

Ericsson and to some extent Motorola were initially more successful than the other firms in GSM since they had more analog orders and created more alliances (with vendors) than the other vendors did (see Appendix 2 for more details). Ericsson benefited from both its analog orders and its alliances with Matra, Italtel, and British firms. Motorola benefited from its previous work with Millicom and its alliance with Siemens. And as described later, these early orders were very important for creating the necessary capabilities in GSM infrastructure.

Market-based competition for orders from second and third service-providers

Market-based competition played a much stronger role in orders from the second and third service-providers to start services in a specific European country. Many of these service-providers had not offered analog services and none of them had offered wireline services. Thus,

Table 4.9 Major *initial* suppliers for European GSM operators who started both analog and digital services (continuities are shown in italics)

Country	Operator	System	Analog Suppliers		GSM Suppliers	
			Base station	Switch	Base station	Switch
Austria *	Mobilkom	TACS	*Motorola*	Motorola	*Motorola*	Alcatel
Belgium	Belgacom	NMT	*Nokia*	Nokia	*Motorola* *Nokia*	Siemens
Croatia	PTT	NMT	Ericsson	Ericsson	Siemens	Siemens
Cyprus	Cyp. Tele.	NMT	*Ericsson*	*Ericsson*	*Ericsson*	*Ericsson*
Czech Republic	Eurotel	NMT	*Nokia*	*Nokia*	*Nokia*	*Nokia*
Denmark *	Tele Danmark	NMT	*Ericsson*	*Ericsson*	*Ericsson*	*Ericsson*
Estonia *	EMT	NMT	Nokia	*Ericsson*	*Ericsson*	*Ericsson*
Finland *	Telecom Finland	NMT	*Ericsson* *Nokia*	*Ericsson* *Nokia*	*Ericsson* *Nokia*	*Ericsson* *Nokia*
France *	France Telecom	Radiocom	Matra	Matra *Alcatel*	*Alcatel* Matra	*Alcatel* Ericsson
France *	SFR	NMT	*Nokia*	*Nokia* Alcatel	*Alcatel* Nokia	*Alcatel*
Germany *	DeT Mobile	C-Netz	PKI	Siemens	*PKI Alcatel* Motorola	Siemens
Hungary	Westel	NMT	*Ericsson*	*Ericsson*	*Ericsson*	*Ericsson*
Iceland	PTT	NMT	*Ericsson*	*Ericsson*	*Ericsson*	*Ericsson*
Ireland *	Eircell	TACS	*Ericsson*	*Ericsson*	*Ericsson*	*Ericsson*

(Contd.)

Table 4.9 Contd.

Country	Operator	System	Analog Suppliers		GSM Suppliers	
			Base station	Switch	Base station	Switch
Italy *	Telecom Italia Mobile	TACS	Italtel / Ericsson	Ericsson	Italtel / Ericsson	Ericsson
Latvia	LMT	NMT	Nokia	Nokia	Nokia	Nokia
Netherlands *	PTT	NMT	Ericsson	Ericsson	Nokia / Alcatel	Ericsson
Norway *	Telenor Mobile	NMT	Ericsson	Ericsson	Ericsson / Nokia	Ericsson
Portugal *	TMN	C-Netz	PKI	Siemens	Motorola / PKI	Siemens
Serbia	Mobtel	NMT	Ericsson	Ericsson	Ericsson	Ericsson
Slovakia	Eurotel	NMT	Nokia	Nokia	Ericsson	Ericsson
Slovenia	Mobitel	NMT	Ericsson	Ericsson	Ericsson	Ericsson
Spain *	Telefónica	TACS	Motorola	Motorola	Motorola / Ericsson	Ericsson
Sweden *	Telia	NMT	Ericsson	Ericsson	Ericsson / Nokia	Ericsson
Switzerland *	Swiss PTT	NMT	Ericsson	Ericsson	Ericsson	Ericsson
UK	Cellnet	TACS	Motorola	Motorola	Motorola	Ericsson
UK *	Vodafone	TACS	Ericsson	Ericsson	Ericsson	Ericsson

* Services which were started in 1992 and 1993.

113

Table 4.10   Initial suppliers for each European country's first, second and third European GSM operators that did not start analog services (new suppliers for that country are in italics)

Country	Operator	Base station suppliers	Switch suppliers
Austria	Mobilkom*	Motorola	Alcatel
	Mobistar	*Siemens*	*Siemens*
Belgium	Belgacom	Motorola, Nokia	Siemens
	Mobistar	*Nortel*, Motorola	*Nortel, Alcatel*
Czech Republic	Eurotel	Nokia	Nokia
	Radiomobil	*Motorola*	*Siemens*
Denmark	Tele Danmark*	Ericsson	Ericsson
	Sonofon*	*Nokia*	*Nokia*
Estonia	EMT	Ericsson	Ericsson
	Radiolinja	*Nokia*	*Nokia*
Finland	PTT*	Ericsson, Nokia	Ericsson, Nokia
	Radiolinja*	Nokia	Nokia, *Siemens*
France	France Tel.*	Alcatel, Matra	Alcatel, Ericsson
	SFR (Cegetel)*	Alcatel, *Nokia*	Alcatel
	Bouygues	Nortel-Matra	Ericsson
Germany	T Mobil*	PKI	Siemens
	Mannesmann*	*Ericsson*, PKI	*Ericsson*, Siemens
	E-Plus	*Nokia*	*Nokia*, Siemens
Greece	Panafon	Ericsson	Ericsson
	Telestet	Ericsson	Ericsson
Ireland	Eircell*	Ericsson	Ericsson
	Digifone	*Nortel*	*Nortel*
Italy	Tele. Italia Mobile*	Italtel, Ericsson	Ericsson
	Omnitel	*Nokia*	*Nokia*
Latvia	LMT	Nokia	Nokia
	Baltcom	*Nortel*	*Nortel*
Netherlands	PTT	Nokia, Alcatel	Ericsson
	Libertel	*Ericsson*	Ericsson
Norway	Telenor*	Ericsson, Nokia	Ericsson
	Netcom*	*Motorola*, Nokia	*Siemens*
Portugal	TMN*	Motorola, PKI	Siemens
	Telecel*	*Ericsson*	*Ericsson*
Slovakia	Eurotel	Ericsson	Ericsson
	GlobTel	*Nortel*	*Nortel*
Spain	Telefónica*	Motorola Ericsson	Ericsson
	Airtel	Ericsson, *Siemens*	Ericsson, *Siemens*
Sweden	Telia*	Ericsson Nokia	Ericsson
	Comvik*	*Motorola*	*Siemens*

(Contd.)

Table 4.10   Contd.

Country	Operator	Base station suppliers	Switch suppliers
Sweden (cont.)	Europolitan*	Nokia	*Nokia*
UK	Cellnet	Motorola	Ericsson
	Vodafone*	Ericsson	Ericsson
	One-2-One	Ericsson	Ericsson
	Orange	*Nokia*	*Nokia*

* First 20 service starts.

many of them had not developed strong relationships with a specific infrastructure vendor.

Further, the fact that many of these second and third service-providers purchased their equipment from a different vendor than did the first service provider also suggests that market-based competition played a stronger role than committee-based competition in these orders. Many of these second and third service-providers did this in order to differentiate themselves from the service-providers who had already started services. As shown in Table 4.10, the base station suppliers for the second, third, or service provider were different from the base station supplier for the previous carriers in sixteen out of 23 cases. The same is true for switches (sixteen out of 23). Most of the exceptions were in France and Germany where the preference for committee-based competition (that is, domestic suppliers) caused most carriers to place orders with all of the major domestic suppliers.[26]

Nokia became the leading supplier of equipment to the new carriers through its early focus on market-based competition. It did this both in terms of its marketing and product approaches. On the marketing side, while other carriers focused on their previous customers or carriers in whom one of their previous customers was a major investor, Nokia began sending "tiger teams" to the countries that were discussing the awarding of a new licence. These tiger teams identified the most likely winners and worked with them to determine the best way to win a licence and compete in the marketplace. Of the first twenty service starts for GSM, seven of them were new carriers. Of the five new carriers that did not have investors who effected the vendor selection, Nokia received three of these orders versus two for Ericsson and one for Siemens (in Germany with Ericsson). Many of the subsequent new service-providers received licences in the 1800 band. Nokia received orders from three of the first four licencees in the 1800 band. Their success in these and subsequent contracts made Nokia the leading supplier of 1800 equipment until 1998 when it dropped to number two (see below for more details).

On the product side of market-based competition, Nokia has also been able to develop a relatively strong switch for mobile communication systems in spite of its brief history in the wireline field. Nokia started in the transmission area and in the 1970s began developing a digital switch for small wireline service-providers of which there were more than 60 privately owned local telephone companies in Finland at that time. By using Intel microprocessors as opposed to custom circuitry like the larger vendors, Nokia was able to develop a digital switch (DX 200 system) that required only 1000 engineering hours to develop, or one-tenth the resources that were reportedly used by the large vendors such as Ericsson and Siemens.[27] The use of microprocessors makes Nokia's system more flexible and scalable than other systems and this has also helped Nokia succeed with new carriers who want to add capacity in an incremental manner.

Firms struggle to strengthen their committee- and market-based capabilities

Ericsson, Nokia, and to some extent Motorola were able to develop strong expertise in GSM through many initial orders. Ericsson's and to some extent Motorola's success came through their ability to translate committee-based competitiveness into market-based competitiveness. They used their analog orders and their strength in the standard-setting process to develop strong products in cooperation with these service-providers. Ericsson has continued to be the leading supplier of GSM-based infrastructure, both switching equipment and base stations.

Motorola's problem in GSM (and other standards as described below) has been its lack of switch capability and its inability to form an effective alliance with switch vendors. Its share of new GSM orders has declined sharply since Siemens developed its own base station and began looking for orders on its own in 1995. Since this time, Motorola has received very few orders from new operators worldwide and only one order from a new operator in Europe[28] since its May 1996 order from Radiomobil, the second Czech operator.

This lack of switch capability highlights an additional aspect of committee-based competition in mobile infrastructure. In this industry, the continuity in vendor–customer relationships extends across multiple products in that many service-providers increasingly desire a single vendor or at the minimum two firms who work closely together. Motorola has not been able to create a mutually beneficial sole source alliance with a switch provider in a number of mobile communication standards.

Nokia has largely succeeded through market-based competition. It did not have the committee-based strength at least in terms of previous analog customers, but it was able to innovate in terms of market-based competition. It was probably able to do this better than the traditional wireline switch suppliers such as Alcatel, Siemens, PKI, and Matra since it had (like Ericsson and Motorola) never depended as much on its national PTT for telecommunication orders and cooperative development work as Alcatel, Siemens, PKI, and Matra.

These latter four infrastructure suppliers were slow to recognize the need to translate their committee-based strength into market-based strength. Alcatel, Siemens, PKI, and Matra were able to obtain some orders through continuity in customer–supplier relations and preferences for national suppliers. However, these orders were not sufficient to develop the necessary expertise in GSM infrastructure. In particular, initially Alcatel and Siemens did not even bother developing base stations or the technologies necessary for them. They focused on switches and primarily used Motorola, Nokia, PKI, and Matra base stations in their orders. This slow move to develop base stations is reflected in their shares of the base station market even as of 1998.

PKI developed some capabilities in base stations since Deutsche Telekom DeT Mobile's parent company, had designated it as the base station supplier in the analog C-Netz system in the early 1980s (Siemens was the switch supplier). It then used this and related analog (that is, committee-based competition) orders to obtain GSM orders from several service-providers. However, it was unable to translate this committee-based competitiveness into market-based competitiveness and this prevented it from receiving contract renewals from any service provider (for example, Mannessmann, Luxembourg PTT, TMN in Portugal, Comvik in Sweden, and Telefónica in Spain) except Deutsche Telekom. Instead, its poor performance in base stations caused its switch partner, Siemens, to work more closely with Motorola before Siemens developed its own base stations. In some cases, PKI's equipment was replaced by Motorola equipment (for example, Sweden, Portugal, and Spain) and later Siemens delivered its own as opposed to Motorola base stations to these service-providers in subsequent orders.

PKI had difficulty translating its committee-based competitiveness into market-based competitiveness for the same reasons as Alcatel and Siemens. All three had been focused too heavily on a single service provider in both their wireline and mobile businesses. In PKI's case, this is clear from its even worse performance in its non-mobile businesses such as the wireline, office communication, Newscable and related businesses that had caused PKI to have major losses as early as 1989.[29] In particular, PKI was still receiving about three-quarters of its infrastructure orders from Deutsche Telekom in 1993.[30]

Matra was not doing much better than PKI although its problems reflected weaknesses in committee-more than market-based competition. Its lack of previous wireline experience and the fact that it had had only one analog order meant that it only received one major initial contract, which was from France Télécom. This meant that in spite of investing 500 million French francs (about $100 million) in mobile communication between the early 1980s and July 1992, its profitability worsened in 1991 and 1992. After making 68 million French francs in 1990, it lost 9 million francs in 1991 and 150–200 million francs in 1992. This caused Matra to begin looking for an international partner in the fall of 1991, which it eventually would find in Nortel.

Initially, Nortel and Lucent were even bigger losers than Matra and PKI in GSM due to their even weaker committee-based competitiveness. They did not receive any early orders for GSM systems because unlike Motorola, they had not sold any TACS equipment (nor wireline equipment) in Europe and they did not have a European development center that would have enabled them to participate in the GSM standard-setting process. And their failure to obtain any initial GSM orders forced them to purchase the necessary committee- (carrier connections) and market-based capabilities (GSM base stations).

Nortel created a joint venture with Matra[31] that enabled it to obtain GSM base station capability and more importantly customer contacts. One of the conditions for Nortel purchasing Matra was a commitment to orders by French service-providers. This accelerated in the fall of 1994[32] with an order from Bouygues Télécom which was one of the first 1800 GSM service-providers. Bouygues Telecom has grown quickly and it has bought a lot of equipment from the old Matra (that is, base stations) and very little from the old Nortel (that is, switches). Subsequently, Nortel-Matra has received four orders for 1800 systems from either France Télécom or a service provider in which France Télécom has made an investment. These four orders represent more than 40% of Nortel-Matra's nine total orders for 1800 systems as of mid-1999 and more than two-thirds in terms of current sales. Further, Nortel's French sales represent more than 80% of its European sales.

Lucent (at that time it was AT&T) was slower to recognize its need for a stronger GSM presence and the committee-based capabilities needed to compete in the GSM market. Thus, it was forced to work with PKI which was clearly weaker than Matra both technologically and in terms of carrier connections.[33] Lucent began offering GSM equipment in 1993 after it completed an Original Equipment Manufacturing wing (OEM) agreement with PKI where Lucent switches were sold with PKI base stations. In 1995, Lucent acquired PKI and it moved more than 3000 of PKI's 12,000 employees to Lucent.[34] In the following years, Lucent was able to acquire a few orders from carriers in Taiwan, Hong Kong, Malaysia, and India.

Nevertheless, DeT Mobile is still Lucent's best GSM customer and it is generally believed that Lucent is losing money in GSM infrastructure. Its lack of committee-based capabilities prevented it from creating market-based capabilities and the acquisition of PKI has not helped much in either area. Thus, it has only been able to obtain orders from new service-providers except when it has set very low prices. Further, it has also sold some switching equipment to existing service-providers, but in this case it must sell at a low price in order to compensate the service provider for switching vendors (that is, its switching costs). Lucent also pursued this low cost strategy in the US digital infrastructure market where its subsidization of loans has lead to significant financial problems.

The result of Nokia's market-based competitiveness, Motorola's lack of a switch, and Nortel's acquisition of Matra, which increased Nortel's market-and committee-based competitiveness, caused their shares to change with the second and third service-providers. This is shown in the European GSM 1800 infrastructure market in 1997 (see Table 4.11); many of the second and third service-providers used the

Table 4.11   Base station and switching shares in the European GSM 1800 market in 1997

Vendor	Base station share (percent)	Switch share (percent)
Nokia	55	53
Nortel	30	9
Ericsson	11	36
Motorola	3	
Siemens	1	2

1800 as opposed to the 900 frequency band. Further, since this market lags the 900 market by a few years, sales in this segment are primarily for providers that started services after 1994. Lucent, Motorola, and Siemens had none or few shipments of 1800 equipment in 1997. On the other hand, Nortel's success with Bouygues Télécom and Nokia's overall success with new carriers is reflected in their relatively high market shares for 1800 base stations and switches in Europe. Nokia still dominated this market in 1997 while Nortel was second in base stations and Ericsson was second in switches. Nortel's stronger performance in base stations than in switches reflects Bouygues Télécom's commitment to the old Matra.

It took several years for Ericsson to begin focusing more on market-based competition and to create the necessary tiger teams for obtaining orders from new carriers. However, in the first eight months of 1998, Ericsson captured more than 50% of the capital expenditures (switching, base station, and transmission) for the ten newly licenced GSM operators in Europe. It was the major supplier of equipment for five out of the ten new 1800 licencees announced in Europe in 1998.[35] As for the other vendors, only Nokia received orders from three or more of the new licencees while Siemens and Nortel each received two, Alcatel and Lucent each received one, and Motorola received none. Therefore, it can probably be said that Nortel's acquisition of Matra and its customer contacts have helped it move to the number three spot in the GSM market behind Nokia and Ericsson.

Committee-based competition outside Europe

Committee-based competition also played a strong role in competition for orders from those service-providers outside Europe who were the first firms to start GSM services in their respective countries. Thus, it appears that the change from committee-based to market-based competition that we saw in Europe in the last two sections has more to do with the appearance of second and third service-providers than with the general maturing of the market. Although as the uncertainties in GSM decreased, it became easier for service-providers to compare vendors and thus service provider–vendor relations became less important, many service-providers still preferred their analog suppliers. Of 24 service-providers outside of Europe who had provided both analog and GSM services as of late 1999, thirteen bought the GSM equipment from their analog vendor.[36] Further, although this analysis excludes China due to a lack of data on all of the regional Chinese

Table 4.12   Analog and GSM suppliers to Middle Eastern
countries (for service start dates through 1996)

Country	Service provider	Analog supplier	Initial GSM supplier	GSM start date
Bahrain	Batelco	NEC	Ericsson	May 1995
Egypt	Arento	Alcatel	Alcatel	1996
Kuwait	PTT	Ericsson	Motorola/ Siemens	November 1994
Morocco	PTT	Ericsson	Motorola/ Siemens	April 1994
Oman	GTO	Ericsson	Motorola/ Siemens	1996
Qatar	Q-tel	Alcatel	Motorola/ Siemens	February 1994
Saudi Arabia	PTT	Ericsson	Lucent	January 1996
Turkey	PTT	Ericsson	Ericsson	1994
Turkey	Telsim		Motorola/ Siemens	April 1994
UAE	PTT	Ericsson	Lucent/ Motorola/ Siemens	1994

carriers, Motorola and Ericsson have more than 80% of the GSM
market in China, which is due to their success in the TACS market.

There are two interesting aspects of this committee-based competition outside Europe. First, some of this committee-based competition
involves old-fashioned politics and the US used its political strength to
obtain orders for US firms. For example, of the eleven (24 − 13)
service-providers who did not purchase equipment from their analog
supplier, seven of the eleven are in the Middle East. As shown in Table
4.12, many Middle Eastern countries had installed NMT or TACS
systems that were supplied by Ericsson or in one case by NEC. Although NEC's lack of participation in GSM would have led to a new
supplier, most of the other countries would probably have purchased
their GSM equipment from Ericsson if the Gulf War had not occurred
in 1991, just as many countries had begun thinking about digital
systems.

The US-led recovery of Kuwait from Iraq and gentle pressure from
the US government caused many Middle Eastern countries that are
friendly to the US to change from Ericsson to US suppliers like Lucent

or Motorola/Siemens (see Table 4.12). Then President George Bush Sr sent letters to many Middle Eastern countries urging them to work with US firms. In the most prominent example, Lucent received a $4 billion order from Saudi Arabia for a mobile and fixed line system and Lucent was paid almost three times the going rate on a per subscriber basis. Nevertheless, Lucent's somewhat poor performance enabled Motorola and Siemens to also eventually become suppliers to Saudi Arabia. These Middle Eastern orders suggest that if the Gulf War had not occurred, the degree of continuity outside Europe would have been much stronger. Probably 20 of the 24 service-providers outside Europe who have provided both analog and GSM services would have purchased their GSM equipment from their analog supplier.

The second interesting aspect of the committee-based competition for orders outside Europe is the role that some service-providers have played when they have made an early investment[37] in an applicant for a new licence. Many of the service-providers who have done this like Millicom (described earlier), Vodafone, Cable & Wireless, the Scandinavian carriers, DeT Mobile, and France Télécom have apparently influenced the vendor selection process since the investing service provider often has little time to evaluate multiple vendors while trying to meet deadlines for licence applications.

There is typically about one year between the call for applications and the announcement of the award and negotiations between carriers and vendors can often take six months. The licence applications are very long and complicated and they often include 100 pages of technical questions that the vendors are more capable of answering. Negotiations concerning price, maintenance, training and other topics can also be time-consuming. Thus, service-providers not only often buy multiple generations of equipment from the same vendor or vendors; they also often favor certain vendors when they invest in new service-providers. This is another example of the strength of committee-based competition in products that display the characteristics of complex products and systems (CoPS).

As shown in Table 4.13, when service-providers have made early and significant investments in another service provider, the majority of these service-providers have purchased the equipment from a specific vendor. Ericsson's early order from Vodafone in the UK led to several other orders. Ericsson has received orders from seven of the nine carriers in which Vodafone provided early, large (>25%) and direct investments (five were GSM orders).[38]

Table 4.13 Leading vendors for selected service-providers when the service-providers have made *early* investments in other service-providers

Carrier	Number of early investments	Primary supplier	Number of orders	Secondary supplier	Number of orders	Exceptions
Millicent	24	Motorola	15	Ericsson	7	3
Vodafone	9	Ericsson	7			2
Scandinavian carriers	14	Ericsson	8	Nokia	6	2
France Télécom	15	Alcatel	7	Nortel-Matra	6	4
DeT Mobile	12	Siemens	11			1
Bell South	9	Motorola	3			6
US West	9	Ericsson	5			4
Airtouch	6	Ericsson	4			2
Cable & Wireless	16	Ericsson	8	NEC	3	6

Scandinavian national carriers favored Scandinavian vendors, particularly in Europe. Telia (Sweden), Telecom Finland, Tel Danmark, and Telenor (Norway) almost always gave their equipment orders to Scandinavian suppliers.[39] All of the service-providers in which Telia was an investor purchased equipment from Ericsson as a sole vendor except when Telecom Finland was also an investor. In these cases, there appears to have been agreement to give half the orders to Ericsson and the other half to Nokia.[40] In the eight service-providers in whom combinations of Telia, Telecom Finland, Telenor and Tele Danmark were investors, seven contracts were awarded to Nokia and one contract was awarded to Ericsson. This preference for Nokia by these investors may be due to the fact that Ericsson had supplied the first licencee in six of these eight countries.

DeT Mobile and France Télécom have favored German and French manufacturers respectively. For DeT Mobile, the only exception was an 1800 system order in Italy that was awarded to Ericsson. France Télécom has given French manufacturers most of the equipment orders for the three systems that it operates in France plus the overseas service-providers in whom it was an early investor. The majority of exceptions are for 1800 systems, which are the more recent investments by France Télécom.[41] The awarding of the most recent contracts to non-French and non-German manufacturers suggests that both DeT Mobile and France Télécom may be supporting German and French manufacturers less than they used to do.

The US market, however is slightly different and this brings us back to the earlier discussion of the relative importance of committee-versus market-based competition in the US. It was argued earlier that market-based competition has been more important in the US than in other countries due to the large number of licences awarded and thus the fragmentation of the market. This along with the subsequent merger and acquisition activity caused the US service-providers to develop the capabilities necessary to work with multiple vendors. As shown by the data for Airtouch,[42] Bell South,[43] and US West[44] in Table 4.13, it appears that the US service-providers have taken these capabilities abroad and thus have not favored any single vendor to the extent that the European vendors have favored.[45]

For example, the former Airtouch,[46] Bell South,[47] and US West,[48] Ameritech, Bell Atlantic, McCaw Cellular, Nynex, and Southwestern Bell have made many investments in foreign service operators. Ameritech, Bell Atlantic, McCaw Cellular (now AT&T), Nynex, and Southwestern Bell made too few investments to draw any conclusions about their preferences for a specific vendor. With the others, however, it is safe to say that they have not favored any single vendor to the extent that the European vendors have. This is probably to be expected given the lack of focus on a single vendor by US service-providers in the US both within analog and between analog and digital. Further, Lucent was the major supplier to the Baby Bells and it was very slow to move overseas.

Committee-based competition in the form of investor effects may be weakening as service-providers become more sophisticated. Initially, service-providers needed a great deal of help from vendors to file for licences and they had little time to evaluate multiple vendors. But there is a growing group of sophisticated service-providers who understand the licensing process and much of the technology. Carriers like Cable & Wireless,[49] Bell South, US West, and Airtouch moved overseas early and developed a great deal of experience. Their early moves overseas coupled with their early experience with multiple vendors (primarily in the US) has probably made them much more sophisticated as regards handling the licensing process and multiple vendors than other carriers. Further, as service-providers like France Télécom and DeT Mobile have developed experience, they also appear to be moving towards a multiple vendor model. As mergers and acquisitions spread among these and other carriers (such as, the Scandinavian carriers), the multiple vendor model will most likely increase.

INFRASTRUCTURE COMPETITION IN THE US DIGITAL STANDARDS

Committee-based competition in the form of strong vendor–customer relationships has played a weaker role in the US infrastructure market than in other markets both in analog and digital technology. However, in spite of this lower level of continuity in vendor–customer relationships in the US as compared to Europe and the rest of the world, the suppliers of the US market based many of their digital development decisions on which systems they thought their largest analog customers would install. They realized that switching costs were high and thus there would be some continuity in customer–supplier relationship particularly since there was a strong desire by the service-providers to use part of their AMPS switching and network management systems in their digital systems.

Thus, the US market shows the necessity and difficulties of predicting the relative importance of committee-versus market-based competition. While there has been some continuity in vendor–customer relationships from AMPS to DAMPS and AMPS to cdmaOne in the US (see Table 4.5) and even to a greater extent in the rest of the world, the suppliers to the US market actually overestimated the importance of this committee-based competition. The result is that in some cases firms did not make the best development decisions.

As described in Chapter 3, three major digital standards are used in the US: cdmaOne, DAMPS, and GSM 1900. The analog service-providers upgraded their AMPS systems using cdmaOne or DAMPS while all three digital standards have been implemented by at least one of the new service-providers (who purchased spectrum for Personal Communications Services). The following two subsections describe the expected and actual continuity in vendor–customer relationships in these technological changes.

Expected committee-based competition: the expected continuity in customer relationships and their effect on development decisions

Lucent developed both cdmaOne and DAMPS[50] equipment since its major customers included carriers who planned to implement one or the other technology. Lucent's major analog customers included AT&T, SW Bell, and Centennial Cellular who planned to introduce DAMPS and Bell Atlantic, Nynex, Ameritech, GTE, PrimeCo,[51] and to some extent Airtouch who planned to introduce cdmaOne. Nynex, Bell Atlantic and to some extent PacTel have been major Lucent customers since the beginning of analog services. Thus, it was natural that Lucent would develop both DAMPS and cdmaOne. Lucent became a major supplier of DAMPS equipment to AT&T and a major supplier of cdmaOne equipment to BA/Nynex, PrimeCo (partly through its Bell Atlantic and Nynex connections), Ameritech, Frontier (a joint venture with Bell Atlantic), and GTE.[52]

Motorola's analog major customers were GTE, Bell Atlantic (through its acquisition of Metro Mobile), Airtouch (through PacTel), and 360 Communications and they all intended to introduce cdmaOne. This fact caused Motorola to stop its DAMPS development activities in the early 1990s to focus on cdmaOne.[53] Motorola has become the major supplier of cdmaOne equipment to GTE[54] and 360 Communications and the second-leading supplier to PrimeCo[55] and Airtouch.

Ericsson's focus on DAMPS can also be explained in terms of its customers and its early work on DAMPS. For years Ericsson claimed that it did not develop cdmaOne equipment due to technical and licensing problems with cdmaOne. While there was some truth to the licensing costs as was discussed in Chapter 3, it was clear that Ericsson saw very few technical problems with CDMA as it developed and subsequently promoted CDMA as a third generation system. In reality, Ericsson needed to make this argument since Ericsson was not a supplier of cdmaOne equipment.

The real reason why Ericsson did not develop cdmaOne equipment is that its major customers were not planning to introduce cdmaOne in the US or elsewhere. In North America, Ericsson's major analog customers were McCaw Cellular, Rogers Cantel and to some extent Bell South and they were only intending to introduce DAMPS. Ericsson had also not sold analog equipment to cdmaOne's other early adopter, Korea. This meant there were no service-providers for Ericsson to work out the initial problems with cdmaOne that exist in any standard.

Thus, it is natural that Ericsson focused on DAMPS since its major US customers planned to adopt DAMPS. Further, Ericsson along with Nortel had been the strongest supporter of DAMPS when the US CTIA had chosen the underlying technology of DAMPS called TDMA over FDMA in 1989.[56] Ericsson had established a development center in Texas in 1984 and it did its first testing of TDMA-based DAMPS systems with LA Cellular in 1990.[57] LA Cellular, which was jointly owned by McCaw Cellular and Bell South, provided Ericsson with its first DAMPS order in 1991, Rogers Cantel was the first carrier to start services based on DAMPS, and Ericsson later also became a supplier of DAMPS to Bell South.

Nortel's major analog customers were US West, Cellular Communications (part of Airtouch), US Cellular, and a number of smaller service-providers.[58] Almost all of these service-providers adopted cdmaOne so it was natural that Nortel developed cdmaOne infrastructure. Nortel became a supplier of cdmaOne infrastructure to Sprint (a new entrant to the US mobile field), Airtouch (through both the US West and Cellular Communications connection), Telezone (a joint venture between Bell Atlantic and Airtouch in Canada), and others.[59] The Sprint order came through Nortel's success with Sprint in the wireline field in the 1980s since at that time Sprint did not want to buy from Lucent and Lucent's parent at that time was AT&T, a competitor of Sprint.

Nortel probably developed DAMPS more for market-than committee-based reasons. Nortel along with Ericsson was one of the early supporters of TDMA-based DAMPS and few of its analog customers adopted DAMPS. It had a few analog orders from the major service-providers who adopted DAMPS such as McCaw Cellular and Bell South. As of early 2000, Nortel only supplied some DAMPS infrastructure to one major US carrier, Bell South, and several foreign carriers.

The decision by equipment vendors to develop GSM 1900 equipment was clearly based more on market-than committee-based factors since most of the GSM 1900 operators were new entrants that had not offered analog services. Ericsson, Nortel, Nokia, Motorola, and Siemens all developed 1900 equipment due to their relative success in the GSM market. However, Nokia, Motorola, and Siemens initially only developed base stations and not switches (the US market required a different switch from the rest of the world) which prevented them from obtaining many orders. As discussed earlier, many service-providers desire a single vendor or at the minimum a close alliance between the base station and switch provider. For Nokia, it had never developed a switch for the US mobile communications market and thus saw it as being too large an investment. Its lack of sales in the analog market also meant that it was relatively unknown in the US market.

For Motorola, it was partly bad timing but the underlying problem was a lack of switch capability or a close relationship with a switch supplier. When many of the equipment tenders were released in 1995, it was in the process of changing switch partners from Siemens to Alcatel. Further, this change in switch partners had followed problems with its previous switch supplier, DSC Communications, in the early 1990s,[60] and a failed agreement with Nortel in 1993. The agreement with Nortel was cancelled in 1993 only two years after it was first made due to Motorola's sole interest in cdmaOne; Nortel wanted to also sell DAMPS equipment since at that time Nortel was focused on DAMPS. As a result of this and its very strong belief in cdmaOne, Motorola did not offer GSM 1900 equipment until mid-1997.

The result was that Ericsson and Nortel became the leading suppliers of GSM 1900 equipment in the US market. Both Ericsson and Nortel were helped by their success both in the European GSM and US analog market. Ericsson has more than 50% of the US GSM 1900 market while Nortel has more than 30% of the market.[61]

Actual committee-based competition: the actual continuity in orders

The actual amount of committee-based competition was much less than expected. Many vendors made their initial digital development decisions based on expectations that committee-based competition in the form of continuity in vendor–customer relations would dominate the overall competition. However, in the end there was much less continuity in vendor–customer relationships than in the European or other GSM markets. As shown in Table 4.5, eight of eleven digital service-providers (73%) used one of their initial analog service-providers versus 93% in the case of GSM (of the 27 service-providers who offered both analog and digital service). Of the first twenty services started by GSM operators the difference is even more striking in that only two service-providers actually replaced vendors (10%) as opposed to 27% of the US service-providers.

On the other hand, committee-based competition did play a strong role in the US digital standards *outside* the US where there was a great deal of continuity in vendor–customer relations. As of mid-1998, DAMPS was being used in 35 countries and all of these service-providers bought the DAMPS equipment from their AMPS suppliers. With cdmaOne, of the eighteen countries outside the US who had ordered cdmaOne equipment and had previously installed AMPS equipment, the carriers in fifteen of those countries ordered from their analog suppliers. This continuity has given Motorola and Ericsson a strong advantage in the non-US market for cdmaOne and DAMPS respectively.

Motorola is the leading supplier of cdmaOne equipment outside of the US since it has a larger global customer base than Lucent or Nortel. Of the fourteen countries outside of the US in which Motorola has received cdmaOne orders, Motorola had previously supplied equipment (all AMPS) to the carriers in twelve of these fourteen countries, making it very difficult for Lucent, Nortel,[62] or even the Korean firms in the cdmaOne market. Although Korean firms were initially the leading suppliers of cdmaOne equipment through the early start of cdmaOne services by Korean carriers in 1996, their lack of previous orders outside of Korea has made it very difficult for the Korean vendors to succeed outside Korea.

Ericsson has done much better than Nortel and Lucent[63] in DAMPS equipment outside of the US for similar reasons. Ericsson has almost 60% of the worldwide DAMPS market (including the US) and more than 90% outside the US. Ericsson has installed DAMPS in 33 countries outside the US and Canada. None of Ericsson's DAMPS customers have bought their AMPS equipment from another vendor and none of Ericsson's AMPS customers have bought DAMPS equipment from another vendor.

The strong continuity in vendor–customer relationships for US digital technologies outside of the US again shows the importance of

Table 4.14   US infrastructure shares in 1997

Vendor	Share (percent)
Lucent	35
Nortel	20
Ericsson	17
Motorola	15
Nokia	4

market fragmentation on the relative effect of committee-versus market-based competition. The differences in continuity between the US and non-US markets for the same technology suggests that market fragmentation is driving the relative importance of committee-versus market-based competition. This was found to be also the case in the US analog market and in the case of US service-providers who were early investors in GSM service-providers. In both cases, US service-providers favored the same vendor less than non-US service-providers and thus there was more market-than committee-based competition.

Differences in expected and actual committee-based competition

The US digital standards also show the necessity and difficulties of predicting the relative importance of committee-versus market-based competition. While the actual committee-based competition was less than expected in the US market, it was as high or higher than expected outside of the US. Although in this case, the US market is larger than the non-US market due to the relative lack of success of both cdmaOne and DAMPS outside the US, this may not have been the case if cdmaOne had succeeded to the extent that many people have believed that it would.

Nevertheless, despite the fact that the US ended up being a larger market for these technologies than outside the US and there was less continuity in vendor–customer relationships than expected, it can be said that some vendors made development errors. For example, Ericsson's initial failure to develop cdmaOne and Motorola's initial failure to develop DAMPS and GSM 1900 equipment has severely impacted on their market shares. For example, as orders for cdmaOne systems increased as a percentage of total infrastructure orders in the US between 1995 and 1997, Ericsson's share of the US market dropped from 28% in 1995 to 17% in 1997 (see Table 4.14). Motorola's share is

Table 4.15   Japan's service-providers, service start dates,
and infrastructure suppliers

Service provider	Standard	Start date	Major initial investors	Major base station supplier	Major switch suppliers
NTT	NTT	1979	NTT	NEC	NEC, Fujitsu
Docomo	PDC	1993		NEC, Ericsson, Mitsubishi, Fujitsu	NEC Fujitsu
IDO	NTT	1988	Toyota	NEC	NEC, Fujitsu
	TACS	1991		Motorola	NEC
	PDC	1995		NEC, Fujitsu	Fujitsu, NEC
	cdmaOne	1999		Motorola	NEC
Cellular	TACS	1989	DDI	Motorola	NEC
Group	PDC	1994		Motorola	NEC
	cdmaOne	1998		Motorola	NEC
J-Phone	PDC	1994	Japan Telecom	Ericsson	Ericsson
Tsuka Cellular	PDC	1994	Tokai and Tokyo: DDI	Motorola	NEC
			Kansai: Nissan	NEC	NEC
Digital Tsuka	PDC	1996	Japan Telecom and Nissan	Ericsson, NEC	Ericsson, NEC

also significantly lower than it may have been if it had developed DAMPS and GSM 1900 equipment. In 1997, cdmaOne infrastructure sales represented more than half of total sales while DAMPS represented about 30% and GSM 1900 represented about 20%.

INFRASTRUCTURE COMPETITION IN JAPAN'S TOC MARKET

At one level, the relative importance of committee-versus market-based competition in Japan is similar to that in Europe. As shown in Table 4.15, there has been a great deal of continuity between suppliers and customers and the second and third carriers have mostly bought from different vendors than the first carrier did. At another level, however, there are much greater levels of committee-than market-based competition in Japan than in the US or Europe.

First, NTT Docomo is currently much more involved with the development and design of its infrastructure (both wireline and fixed) than other service-providers in the world, which leads to greater committee-based competition. While most wireline and mobile service-providers leave the design and implementation of their systems to the vendors, NTT Docomo created an unique wireline and mobile systems[64] and it is now creating the Japanese version of W-CDMA with various manufacturers[65] as subcontractors. NTT's adoption of a an unique wireline system forced Japanese firms to develop a completely different kind of wireline switch for the foreign market. This has made it harder for foreign and Japanese firms to sell switches in Japan and overseas respectively, and in the mobile world, it has caused there to be more continuity in switch providers than in base station providers not only across generations but also across different service-providers than with base stations (see Table 4.15).

Motorola enters the market through committee-based competition

Second, Motorola entered the Japanese market primarily through committee-based competition through help from the US government and through the desire by a new service provider, DDI Cellular, to differentiate itself from Docomo. Pressure in the mid-1980s from foreign governments, notably the US, caused Japan's Ministry of Posts and Telecommunications to give one licence to a firm that promised to implement a foreign standard and buy from a US company. DDI, whose major owner is Kyocera, is the major investor in the Cellular Group. It wanted to use a different technology from Docomo in order to differentiate itself from Docomo. It started a TACS service in early 1989 using Motorola equipment, which later led to PDC and cdmaOne orders for Motorola from the Cellular Group.

Subsequently, Motorola also obtained TACS orders from IDO through committee-based competition in the form of help from the US government. As discussed in Chapter 3, IDO initially adopted the NTT standard. However, through pressure from the Cellular Group, who wanted nationwide roaming, from Toyota, who did not want to endanger its second largest market, and from the US government, IDO also adopted and gradually implemented TACS. Subsequently, IDO purchased PDC and cdmaOne equipment from Motorola. In April 1999, IDO started services based on cdmaOne thus achieving a nationwide service in partnership with DDI Cellular that resulted in their merger into KDDI in late 2000.

Of course, market-based capabilities also played a role in Motorola's success in Japan. Motorola was one of the two leading providers of

TACS equipment in the world along with Ericsson. But it was the committee-based capabilities that enabled it as opposed to Ericsson to obtain the orders from DDI Cellular and IDO. Further, since the newly merged entity KDDI is the leading service provider in terms of introducing new cdmaOne technologies, Motorola's work with KDDI is expected to help Motorola develop market-based capabilities in cdmaOne and its successor cdma2000. Thus, this is a good example of the reinforcing nature of committee-and market-based capabilities.

Committee-based competition helps Motorola and Ericsson in digital systems

Motorola and Ericsson also used committee-based competition to succeed in the Japanese digital market, although here foreign governments only played an indirect role. As described in Chapter 3, NTT Docomo had originally planned to base PDC on FDMA technology, which it had been working on since the mid-1980s. However, in order to avoid further trade friction with the US concerning telecommunications, it ended up basing PDC on TDMA technology and selecting Motorola's coding and decoding technology as part of Japan's full-rate digital system.

This adoption of foreign technology provided Motorola and Ericsson with opportunities in the Japanese digital market. The relative success of these two firms is largely a function of continuity in vendor–customer relationships and the desire of service-providers to differentiate themselves from their competitors. Motorola became the leading supplier of PDC equipment to its analog customer the Cellular Group and to Tsuka Cellular Tokyo and Tsuka Cellular Tokai, of whom DDI was and still is the major investor (see Table 4.15). However, DDI was not an initial investor in Tsuka Kansai since it already owned at that time another service provider in Kansai that is part of its Cellular Group. Thus, the Cellular Group was against Motorola supplying equipment to its competitor, Tsuka Kansai. Similarly, IDO also wanted a vendor that was not supplying Tsuka Tokyo and Tokai so this prevented Motorola from supplying IDO with PDC equipment. Therefore, both Tsuka Kansai and IDO bought from NEC, who had previously supplied IDO with analog equipment that was based on the NTT standard.

Ericsson became the leading supplier of equipment to J-Phone and Digital Tsuka, and a small supplier to Docomo.[66] Ericsson was helped by the desire of J-Phone to differentiate itself from the other service-providers and the influence of investors on vendor selection. The other service-providers were purchasing base stations either from NEC, Fujitsu, or Motorola, thus providing Ericsson with an opportunity to help J-Phone differentiate itself from the other service-providers. With Digital Tsuka, Ericsson supplied half of the regions and NEC supplied the other half through an agreement to split the orders. Digital Tsuka's two major investors were Japan Telecom (also an investor in J-Phone) and Nissan (also an investor in Tsuka Kansai and a purchaser of NEC base stations).

Although Ericsson only supplied one portion of Docomo's PDC system, this work with Docomo is a major reason why it was able to convince Docomo to adopt the evolution of the network interface of GSM in W-CDMA and why it is now working closely with Docomo on W-CDMA development. Ericsson's PDC order from Docomo was a result of a number of factors including the NTT Procurement Agreement, Docomo's declining share in the analog market, Ericsson's strength in TDMA technology, and the organizational capability that it established in Japan. As part of the NTT Procurement Agreement, which was part of the 1985 US–Japanese Telecommunications Agreement, NTT agreed to purchase 20% of its equipment from foreign suppliers. In the early 1990s, Docomo's share of the analog market was declining and it felt that foreign suppliers had a technical advantage over NEC and Fujitsu since they had been working on TDMA-based systems (GSM and DAMPS) for much longer than NEC and Fujitsu. NEC and Fujitsu had been focused on FDMA until Docomo switched its efforts to TDMA in 1990.

Docomo also realized that Ericsson was the leading supplier of TDMA technology. It had been much more involved with the development of TDMA technology for the US DAMPS standard and also for GSM than any other firms. It had played a major role in the creation of both GSM and DAMPS standards and it was the leading supplier of equipment in both standards.

Finally Ericsson had been making organizational investments for many years, including the establishment of a development center in Japan. Ericsson established a technical office in 1985 called Nippon Ericsson. In 1989, it was invited to develop one part of a base station prototype called a transreceiver with NEC and Mitsubishi. In this project, it learned about Docomo's method of evaluating proposals and setting prices. In 1991, it established Nippon Ericsson KK and in 1992, it established Ericsson Toshiba KK. The partnership with Toshiba was created as Ericsson was receiving its first orders for mobile infrastructure from Japanese carriers. It established the relationship with Toshiba in order to both demonstrate its commitment to the Japanese market and to have Toshiba provide servicing of the equipment.

SUMMARY AND DISCUSSION

Committee-based competition and the interaction between these committee- and market-based competitions have played a stronger role in overall competition than just market-based competition by itself. The successful firms participate in standard-setting committees while they simultaneously develop technology in cooperation with a service provider. These early orders for test and commercial systems are necessary to develop experience as is shown by the similarities between the shares of the early orders and the eventual breakdown of shares.

Traditional wireline switching equipment suppliers like Alcatel, Siemens, PKI, Lucent, and NEC were the slowest to develop capabilities in market-based competition. They remained focused on committee-based competition and did not move overseas in analog, took a long time to develop base station capabilities in GSM, and in general remained focused on existing relationships with service-providers. It is argued that this was the same strategy they used in the wireline market, unlike Ericsson, Nokia, and Nortel who were not dependent on a single service provider even in the wireline market.

Some firms did try to develop market- and committee-based capabilities within a single generation through acquisitions. In GSM, Nortel acquired Matra and Lucent acquired PKI. Nortel's acquisition was more successful since Matra had stronger base station capabilities and the French government made sure that Nortel-Matra would obtain some early orders from a French carrier.

The relative importance of committee- versus market-based competition

Overall, market-based competition played a stronger role in obtaining orders from *new* service-providers while committee-based competition played a stronger role in obtaining orders from existing service-providers. However, this distinction did not appear to be a function of pricing, as the literature on switching costs often argues (Farrell and Satoner, 1988a). Firms were able to discriminate between customers and thus were able to set different prices for existing and new customers.

Committee-based competition played a stronger role than market competition in the mobile infrastructure market since existing service-providers tended to place the earliest orders for a new generation of infrastructure. This committee-based competition primarily manifested itself in high switching costs and strong continuity in the relationships between infrastructure and service-providers. This continuity appeared to be independent of the maturity of the technology as the strong continuity in GSM and non-US orders for digital infrastructure demonstrated. However, this committee-based competition often manifested itself in odd ways as the US government's role in obtaining orders for US firms from the Gulf States shows.

Of greater interest, the relative importance of committee-versus market-based competition was more a function of the degree of market fragmentation than the level of change in technology. In spite of the smaller technological discontinuity and greater compatibility between first and second generation systems in the US than elsewhere, the US market exhibited less continuity in vendor–customer relationships within the analog market, between the analog and digital markets, and in the activities of US service-providers when they invested in foreign service-providers.

Committee-based competition extends across multiple products

Motorola suffered from the lack of a switch provider, which is a necessary part of committee-based competition in the mobile infrastructure market. Just as service-providers like long-term multi-generation relationships with infrastructure providers, they also prefer to work with one infrastructure provider or two closely aligned infrastructure providers.

Motorola worked with DSC Communications in the US in spite of numerous switching problems and also with Nortel, Siemens, and most recently Alcatel. The agreement with Nortel was cancelled in 1993 only two years after it was first made due to Motorola's sole interest in cdmaOne; Nortel wanted to also sell DAMPS equipment since at that time Nortel was focused on DAMPS. Almost immediately, Nortel purchased Matra and subsequently its share of the worldwide market has grown through sales of GSM, DAMPS, and IS95 equipment. With Siemens, although Motorola was initially successful in the European GSM market, after Siemens began selling its own GSM base stations in 1995, Motorola's sales of GSM equipment have plummeted. Motorola is now trying to work with Alcatel as a switch provider in both the

GSM and cdmaOne market. But the change from Siemens to Alcatel in the mid-1990s made it difficult to obtain early orders in the GSM 1900 markets since these markets started during this time period. Thus, it will be very difficult for Motorola to stop the slide in its share of the GSM infrastructure market.

For years Motorola argued that its lack of switch capability enabled it to work with a greater variety of switch suppliers and thus provide more flexible solutions to service-providers. In fact, as late as 1998 Motorola was telling its investors at its Global Wireless Industry Alliance Forum that it had alliances with all of the mobile switch suppliers. In the network industries where compatibility is critical, continuity exists in the relationships between customers and suppliers, and single systems vendors are desired, a broad product line or at the minimum a tight strategic alliance with the appropriate suppliers is necessary.

A corollary to this is that customers in the network industries want a single contact point from suppliers since compatibility between products is so important. Motorola was the last firm to provide a single contact for its customers. Instead, as part of its "warring tribes" philosophy, multiple Motorola divisions would approach customers and try to sell them various forms of infrastructure. This was something that Motorola's customers did not appreciate and Motorola was accused of doing this until as late as 1998.

Competing in the subsequent generation of technology

In the subsequent generation of technology, it is important to translate capabilities in market-based competition into capabilities for committee-based competition. Firms must participate in standard-setting committees while they simultaneously develop technology in cooperation with a service-provider, who most likely is an existing service provider with existing suppliers. This is of course problematic given the high switching costs and continuity in vendor–customer relationships and changing sources of each generation of technology.

Therefore, in order to succeed in a subsequent generation of technology, firms need to acquire the relevant capabilities in committee-based competition in a foreign country before the next generation of technology begins. Ericsson and to some extent Motorola have done this through the early creation of global customer relationships (that is, relationships with service-providers all over the world) and by using these global relationships to acquire early orders in both second (including GSM) and third generation standards. Global development capabilities and participation in foreign standard-setting processes were necessary parts of these global relationships with service-providers.

Both Ericsson and Motorola responded more quickly to requests from Great Britain on the creation of the first TACS standard and created these and other key global relationships in the US, Europe, and Japan. These key global relationships include Ericsson's relationships with Vodafone, McCaw Cellular, and NTT Docomo and Motorola's relationships with Millicom, Cellnet, and DDI. These key relationships and in the case of GSM alliances enabled Ericsson and Motorola to obtain early orders, which were critical for creating capabilities in market-based competition. They also created the global development capability necessary to participate in foreign standard-setting bodies. Ericsson's development center in Texas supported its participation in the DAMPS standard-setting process while Motorola's development center in England (Swindon) supported its participation in the GSM standard-setting process. Both firms also created similar capabilities in the Japanese market.

Other vendors moved much more slowly to create the necessary global relationships and development capabilities and participate in foreign standard-setting processes. These firms believed that it was sufficient to work with one service provider, which always happened to be their domestic service provider, on the development of new technology, and focus on domestic standards since this was the model they used in the wireline field.

As we shall see in Chapter 6, Ericsson's large global customer base basically guarantees them success in third generation systems due to the earlier start of these services in Europe and Asia where Ericsson has a large customer base and service provider–vendor relationships are fairly strong. Further, Ericsson will also benefit from the fact that there will probably be smaller technological discontinuities in the move from second to third generation services than there was in the move from first to second generation services. Most GSM service-providers plan to introduce third generation services in a very incremental manner.

These results suggest that firms must be careful not to focus too much on their domestic markets. As new technology and standards come from an increasingly larger number of nations, it becomes increasingly important in a large variety of industries for firms to create global customer relations, participate in foreign standard-setting activities, and create foreign development capabilities to support these activities. For example, many of the standards in mobile computing, mobile Internet access, and to some extent digital television are coming from outside the US. And it is not clear that US firms are doing the things necessary to succeed in such foreign standards.

Notes

1.   Farrell and Shapiro (1988) argue that firms will be unwilling to cut their prices for new customers when they cannot discriminate between them and new customers. In this case, however, the infrastructure providers can to some extent discriminate between existing and new customers.
2.   Similar situations are described in Klemperer (1995) and Klemperer and Padilla (1995).
3.   All of the investments by a service provider in a foreign service provider that are mentioned in this book are for early investments when the investor can influence the vendor selection. Data on the timing and extent of these investments was found in Garrard (1998).
4.   Lucent was spun off from AT&T in 1996 after had been merged with AT&T in 1983 (previously it was Western Electric).
5.   For example, the Baby Bells had demanded that Western Electric help Nortel develop a wireline digital switch in the late 1970s in order to reduce their dependence on AT&T.
6.   See S. Adams and O. Butler, *Manufacturing the Future: A History of Western Electric*, Oxford University Press, 1999. For example, Bell South gave ten of its twelve orders to Motorola and US West gave six of eight orders to Nortel in the largest 90 markets. Bell South purchased equipment for its small markets from Astronet, which was a joint venture between Mitsubishi and the UK's GEC Plessey.
7.   Motorola obtained all fourteen of the GTE initial orders although it later lost several of these orders to Nortel. Motorola was also strong with United Telespectrum and Centel while Lucent was only strong with SNET.
8.   Motorola's major customers included Metro Mobile, General Communications Industries, and Metromedia, Ericsson's major customers included Graphic Scanning and RAM Broadcasting, while Lucent and Nortel's major customers were limited to Contel Cellular and Cellular Communications respectively.
9.   The main reason for this change in shares is that Lucent received a large number of orders from the former wireline operators and they were the first service-providers to receive the licences in their markets. Ericsson was much stronger with the RCCs (radio-common carriers) who received their licences much later than the former wireline operators did.
10.   On the average, 76% of their regions that are in the top 90 US markets used equipment from the same vendor.

11.   Garrard (1998).
12.   This includes carriers purchased from MCI, Maxcell Telecom Plus, Charisma Communications and the Washington Post.
13.   Ericsson's 45% and Lucent's 35% share of McCaw's markets in the top 90 US markets is far higher than their overall share of the non-wireline carrier markets (26% and 19% respectively). Subsequently, Lucent's share of McCaw's markets increased after McCaw Cellular was acquired by AT&T and AT&T acquired SNET.
14.   In the largest 180 markets, PacTel replaced Lucent equipment in three and NEC equipment in four markets all with Motorola equipment. Ericsson had supplied all of RAM Broadcasting's equipment (seven markets that are in the largest 90 markets) while Motorola had supplied General Communications (it had two of the largest 90 markets).
15.   Cellular Communications had used Nortel equipment in eight of its ten markets that were in the largest 180 markets in 1992. In 1996, PacTel acquired Cellular Communications, half of the joint venture.
16.   Some of Motorola's equipment was later replaced with Lucent equipment in order to solve compatibility problems.
17.   Contel bought only from Lucent in its fourteen markets that are in the largest 180 US markets. Nevertheless, Motorola remained GTE's leading supplier.
18.   It was subsequently acquired by Sprint in 1993 and spun off as 360 Communications in 1996.
19.   For example, Mexico was divided into eight regional markets where Iusacell operated services in several markets and purchased analog equipment from multiple vendors and in some cases changed vendors for digital equipment. Indonesia was divided into six analog markets where the PTT was a majority investor in each regional operator. Some of these regional operators implemented NMT with Ericsson or Nokia and others implemented AMPS with Motorola. It became more complex with digital systems when new licences were awarded to consortiums that included foreign firms. The three analog equipment suppliers plus Siemens and Alcatel supply digital equipment.
20.   *Financial Times*, 17/8/1983, p. 5, Swedish equipment likely for Racal; *Financial Times*, 20/9/1983, p. 8, Motorola set for BT/Securicor radio contract.
21.   Further, both firms also worked hard to accommodate governmental and carrier requests in the area of local manufacturing. For example, Ericsson agreed to allow Racal Electronics (Vodafone's major investor) to make base stations under licence in Great Britain. *Financial Times*, 17/8/1983, Swedish equipment likely for Racal. *Financial Times*, 15/5/1984, p. 18: market set for wide expansion. Racal has had a long-term plan to enter the equipment market and one of the reasons it received the licence was because it promised to create manufacturing jobs in the UK (*Financial Times*, 15/5/1984, p. 18: Market set for wide expansion; Meurling and Jeans, 1994). Ericsson's work with local Italian manufacturers (Italtel and Telettra) helped it obtain an even larger order in 1989 from Italy's national carrier SIP in competition with Motorola. Ericsson supplied the switches and management system while Italtel and Telettra

supplied base stations under licence from Ericsson (Meurling and Jeans, 1994).

22. Further, three of the orders that it did not receive were for NMT equipment of which Motorola did not provide and two orders were in cases where Motorola had previously invested and supplied another service provider in the same country.

23. NEC has obtained a small number of AMPS and TACS orders. Two of them were from Hong Kong and Singapore Telecom who had previously bought very small NTT systems. Several other systems in the Middle East were the result of government subsidies; the Middle East is the Japanese government's largest destination for overseas assistance. However, more than 90% of the subscribers who are connected to NEC's TACS and AMPS equipment in the world are in Brazil. These orders were obtained through second generation Japanese living in Brazil, which says a great deal about the challenges NEC faces in trying to create a global customer base.

24. It is generally agreed that most of the ideas for the air interface came from Ericsson followed by Nokia, Motorola, and Matra while most of the ideas for the network interface came from Siemens and Alcatel. In terms of patents it is generally agreed that Motorola has been more aggressive than the other firms and it probably has as many patents as Ericsson and Nokia. Nevertheless, other than patent income, neither the volume of technology that a firm was able to contribute towards the standard nor the number of patents appears to have had much effect on competition.

25. The cases where the suppliers were not exactly the same were where both national suppliers were allowed to supply equipment (France Télécom and SFR), Motorola was replaced only as a switch supplier (Spain and Austria), or new suppliers were added (in Portugal, Sweden and Norway) in the GSM order.

26. Other exceptions include Nokia's involvement with both Finnish carriers and the orders from Mobistar where Motorola–Alcatel received the order through France Télécom's part ownership of Mobistar and Alcatel's close contacts with France Télécom. On the other hand, the second Dutch (Libertel), Greek (Telestet), and Spanish (Airtel) carriers along with One-2–One were exceptions in that they ordered equipment from vendors who had previously supplied other service-providers in the same country.

27. This system was first installed in Finland in 1983 and it is still the basis for Nokia's wireline and mobile telecommunication systems. *Financial Times*, 19/8/1983, p. 21, Telenokia finds fresh two-way connection, by Hilary Barnes.

28. This order was from Portugal's Optimus in 1998 although Ericsson is the major supplier to Optimus.

29. *Handelsblatt*, 16/5/1990, Philips Kommunikations Industrie AG, p. 27.

30. The losses incurred in 1989 continued and in 1993, PKI had record losses of 348 million marks ($188 million) that required a capital infusion of 300 million marks by its parent company Philips to write off further losses. The rising losses were in both wireline and wireless and they were

in spite of the increasing orders from Deutsche Telekom in the former East Germany where a completely new telecommunications infrastructure needed to be created, *Handelsblatt*, 20/6/1994, PKI/Van der Waal Kündigt offensive auf Auslandsmärkten, p. 13.

31. Matra had received offers from a number of prospective partners such as PKI, Siemens, and Lucent all of whom where considered preferable to Nortel by Matra's key customer, France Télécom. However, Matra chose Nortel due to its plan for combining the two firm's capabilities. Nortel invested 1.36 billion French Francs in Matra Communications in July, 1992 giving them a 20% stake with a commitment to increase this share to 49% in 1995. *Financial Times*, 3/7/1992, p. 19, Northern Telecom invests in Matra, by Alice Rawathorn and Bernard Simon. In 1994, Nortel doubled its stake in Matra thus raising its total investment in Matra to about US$430m. The venture used the new cash to recruit extra 150 engineers for its French-based research center. *Financial Times*, 26/7/1994, p. 23b, Nortel strengthens Matra ties.

32. Previous to this order, its major orders were from Taiwan's and Tunisia's PTTs and the US's Omnipoint.

33. It also chose PKI partly since Lucent has worked with PKI in the telecommunications field since 1983.

34. *Financial Times*, 28/7/1995, p. 23. AT&T deal changes Philips focus.

35. These include Orange in Belgium, Optimus in Portugal, WIND in Italy, Retrovision in Spain, and Telfort in the Netherlands.

36. This excludes China, Russia, and Brazil where good data were not available when the analysis was carried out. Each of these countries has a large number of regional operators and it is difficult to sort out the geographical and operator complexities.

37. All of the investments by a service provider in a foreign service provider that are mentioned in this book are for early investments when the investor can influence the vendor selection.

38. In one of the exceptions, the first carrier, South Africa's PTT (51%) owned more of the second carrier (Vodacom) than Vodafone (35%) and Vodacom awarded the order to the PTT's previous vendor (Siemens). In cases where Vodafone only provided small initial investments such as in Sweden's Europolitan (initially 10%), Denmark's Sonofon (4%), and Germany's E-Plus (16%), Ericsson has also not received the awards.

39. The only two exceptions were in Lebanon where Libancel (Telecom Finland owned 14%) gave the order to Motorola and Siemens and in Ireland where Esat Digifone (Telenor owned 40%) gave the order to Nortel.

40. For example, Eesti Mobiltelefon gave its NMT and GSM orders to Ericsson and Latvia's Mobilais Telephone gave its NMT and GSM orders to Nokia.

41. For example, Mobistar claims that it had no choice but to give the order to Alcatel. As for some of the exceptions, in Greece Vodafone owned a much larger percentage of Panafon than France Télécom and awarded the contract to its favorite supplier, Ericsson. The other exceptions are Italy, Portugal, and Denmark, which are 1800 systems.

42.   Ericsson's success with Mannesmann in Germany, who initially received investments from Airtouch may have lead to a number of orders from companies in whom Airtouch was also a major investor (> 15%). This includes Telecel in Portugal, Airtel in Spain, and Connex in Romania. The two cases where Ericsson was not a supplier to an Airtouch-affiliated service provider were in Belgacom (Belgium) and Plus GSM in Poland where it is believed that Belgacom favored local suppliers (described earlier) and Ericsson supplied the previous service provider in Poland, EraGSM.

43.   Bell South has made early and significant (>20%) investments in at least nine foreign carriers (primarily in South America) but no one vendor has received more than three orders. Motorola, which was Bell South's leading supplier in the US, also received three orders from Bell South outside the US.

44.   The overseas service-providers in which US West has made early and significant (>20%) investments have given more than 50% of their orders to Ericsson probably since US West first focused on Eastern Europe when NMT systems were being installed.

45.   Although Ameritech, Bell Atlantic, McCaw, Nynex, and Southwestern Bell have also made many investments in foreign service-providers, they made too few investments to draw any conclusions about their preferences for a specific vendor.

46.   See n. 42.

47.   See n. 43.

48.   See n. 44.

49.   Cable & Wireless (C&W) is more difficult to analyze since its initial vendor (NEC) received very few subsequent orders from anyone and many of C&W's investments have been in very small carriers. Carriers that have received significant (>20%) investments from Cable & Wireless (C&W) have not favored any one supplier probably since C&W's first investment was in Hong Kong Telecom who first purchased NTT and later TACS equipment from NEC in the early 1980s. Subsequently, C&W affiliated carriers did not buy much equipment from NEC since it did not become a strong supplier of TACS or AMPS equipment. Instead, these carriers awarded about half of their orders to Ericsson. However, the sixteen investments included in Table 4.12 do not include the cases where C&W invested in very small carriers (such as in the Caribbean) that may be using only one or two base stations. In these countries, a US firm Plexys, that specializes in small systems, has supplied most of these systems to the Caribbean countries.

50.   Lucent developed DAMPS in spite of the fact that it initially supported FDMA when the CTIA was debating the relative merits of FDMA and TDMA for DAMPS.

51.   PrimeCo was initially a joint venture between Airtouch, US West, Bell Atlantic, and Nynex. Airtouch contains operations from both US West and PacTel.

52.   It had some sales to Airtouch, which also was supplied by Nortel and to some extent Motorola. Further, it is the major supplier to Sprint PCS

with Nortel supplying 25% and Motorola supplying 20% of the equipment (*Wireless Week*, 3/2/1998, Sprint Staying With Motorola).
53. The US CTIA's decision to use TDMA instead of FDMA technology also encouraged Motorola to focus on cdmaOne.
54. Keller, J.J., "Motorola Beats AT&T to get GTE Order of Wireless Gear for up to $800 billion," *Wall Street Journal*, 18/9/1995, Sec: A p: 3.
55. Technology Brief, "PCS PrimeCo: DSC, Motorola to Supply Gear for $1 Billion Project," *Wall Street Journal*, 5/9/1995, Sec: B, p: 2).
56. Sizzling markets speed vendors in drive to digital cellular. *Electronics* 2/1/1989.
57. See n. 56.
58. This includes Vanguard, Alltel (acquired by 360 Communications), CMS St. Cloud, and Century Cellunet.
59. This includes CMS St. Cloud, Cellcom, and South Central Utah.
60. There were problems with Motorola analog equipment in networks managed by GTE, SW Bell, Bell South, and Metro One in the early 1990s and most recently with its cdmaOne equipment in PrimeCo in 1996. Airtouch Might Replace Motorola Gear in Pivotal Los Angeles Cellular Market, Quentin Hardy, *Wall Street Journal*, 23/10/1996. PrimeCo won't rip out network but future Motorola work inperil, LynetteLuna, *RCR Wireless News*, 3/6/1998.
61. Ericsson supplies APC, Omnipoint, Airadaigm, Powertel and Microcell (in Canada), Nortel supplies Omnipoint, Western Wireless, APC/Sprint, Conestoga Wireless, NPI Wireless, and Bell South Mobility, and Nokia supplies Western Wireless and Aerial Communications. Nokia's orders from Aerial Communications and Western Wireless were helped by Sonera's (a Finnish carrier supplied by both Ericsson and Nokia) 30% investment in Aerial Communications and Orange's (supplied by Nokia in the UK) investment in Western Wireless respectively.
62. Nortel has only received orders from carriers outside North America in China and Guatemala.
63. Nortel has sold to AMPS customers like Antel in Uruguay and Telemig in Brazil and new customers like Cellcom in Israel and Uzdonrobita in Uzbekistan who had never installed AMPS. Lucent has only sold one DAMPS system outside the US to a carrier in Costa Rica who had previously bought an AMPS equipment from it.
64. NTT Docomo has historically requested detailed proposals for each subsystem including detailed cost estimates for various portions of each subsystem. It has then compared each firm's cost estimates, identified the lowest-cost proposals for each portion of the subsystem, and asked each firm to reduce the proposed cost for each portion of these subsystems to the level of the lowest-cost proposal. Once Docomo had done this, it has allowed each firm to increase its cost estimate by about 10% in order to obtain a profit. NTT Docomo also takes full responsibility for site planning and selection and installation of base stations whereas the equipment suppliers provide very little input in these analyses. The installation of the base stations is also carried out by Docomo construction subsidiaries that contain a number of former NTT executives. These construction subsidiaries contain a number of former NTT

executives through *amakudari*. *Amukudari* literally means descent from heaven and is a common means of controlling subsidiary and other companies. Even NEC contains a few former NTT executives. And site preparation, installation of base stations, and site maintenance are critical activities in Japan's market; they represent 70% of the total installation cost for base stations versus 30% for the cost of the base station itself.

65. NEC became the major supplier of analog and subsequently digital base stations to Docomo through its success in private mobile radio systems while both NEC and Fujitsu became the major suppliers of switches through their success in the wireline switch business.

66. Docomo bought equipment for its 1500 MHz systems, which represent a minority of Docomo's frequency spectrum. J-Phone and Tsuka Cellular only use the 1500 MHz frequency band.

5 Committee and *Particularly* Market Competition in the Mobile Phone Market

This chapter describes the role of committee- and market-based competition in the mobile phone market. As in the mobile infrastructure market, firms need to participate in committees in order to understand the standards and to develop products that are based on the standard. And to some extent firms compete to have their technology included in the standard and earn licensing fees while they simultaneously use their superior knowledge of this specific technology to develop superior products.

For example, some firms failed in markets because they did not participate in the relevant standard-setting committees like the Japanese firms did in the European digital standard, GSM. By not participating in the relevant GSM committees, they did not simultaneously develop the necessary technology and thus were forced to pay rather high licensing fees for critical patents.

Also, some firms succeeded, at least initially, through their strength in committees. For example, Oki Electric had a great deal of early success in the US analog standard AMPS through its early work with AT&T, Nokia and Ericsson's success in the Scandinavian analog standard NMT was helped by their early work in the standard, and Qualcomm and Sony were able to dominant the early years of the cdmaOne market through their domination of this standard-setting process.

However, the best example of committee-based competition can be found in Japan where NTT DoCoMo and its semi-exclusive suppliers used their domination of the Japanese digital standard, PDC, to develop better phones than the other manufacturers. These lighter phones enabled DoCoMo to dominate the Japanese digital phone market for many years and caused two of its competitors, DDI Cellular and IDO (since merged into KDDI), to implement cdmaOne before they had even recovered their investment in PDC.

However, in general, market-based competition has played a more important role than committee-based competition in the overall mobile phone competition due to the high levels of openness in the standards and the relative simplicity of the product, at least as compared to mobile infrastructure. The global standards AMPS and GSM and other standards such as NMT and DAMPS were created in open standard-setting processes, thus preventing any one firm from developing a significant competitive advantage from their domination of the standard-setting process. The greater simplicity of phones as compared to infrastructure has meant that relationships with service-providers are much less important than with infrastructure. The result is that competition has largely focused on competition between products and their features and costs.

For example, in the US analog market, Oki Electric's share of the market quickly dropped due to superior products from Motorola and other Japanese firms and eventually Motorola dominated the market due to its superior product line strategy. In the Scandinavian standard, NMT, Motorola also became the leading supplier through its superior products and other forms of market competition. In GSM, Motorola, Ericsson, and Nokia emerged as the leaders through market competition. In the US digital phone market, as cdmaOne became more open, Motorola, Nokia and Samsung (through its early success in the Korean market) became the leaders, thus causing Qualcomm and Sony actually to exit the mobile phone business within one year of being the market leaders. Even in the Japanese digital (PDC) phone market, the non-DoCoMo phone suppliers eventually eliminated the weight advantage of the DoCoMo suppliers as information about the PDC standard diffused in the marketplace and market competition asserted itself.

In this market competition, the appropriate product line and platform management has changed as the industry has evolved from a small-scale regional-based industry to a global industry and there are still important regional differences. Figure 5.1 summarizes the evolution of volumes, unit costs, and the successful product line/platform management strategies in the mobile phone industry. The change in unit costs reflects changes in the ratio of operating to fixed costs (and thus marginal costs), which declined greatly between 1985 and the late 1990s.

These changes in volumes and costs have caused the appropriate product line/platform management strategy to change and also market leadership to change from the Japanese firms to Motorola and later to

147

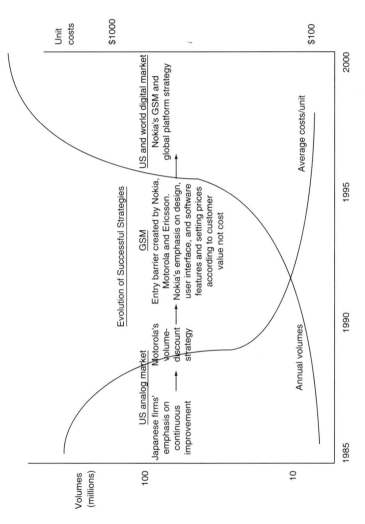

Figure 5.1   The evolution of successful product line strategies, volumes, and unit costs in the mobile phone industry

Nokia. Motorola overtook the Japanese firms by introducing a strategy of volume discounts and rapid price decreases in the late 1980s, introducing this strategy just as costs began to drop dramatically and the environment began changing from a business to a personal market. Motorola, Nokia, and Ericsson initially dominated the GSM market by rapidly reducing prices as the environment changed. Their subsidization of low-end models while making profits at the high end of the market enabled them to overtake the Japanese firms, but it was Nokia that became the leader through its superior performamce, focusing more on aesthetic design, user interface, and software features in its product line and platform management approach than on weight and costs as Motorola and Ericsson have done respectively. It has coupled this with setting prices in terms of customer value and not product costs. This has provided Nokia with an advantage as aesthetic design, user interface, and software features have become more important than phone weight and size. Nokia has also implemented its strategy more effectively than both Motorola and Ericsson who have experienced several implementation problems.

Further, Nokia has used its GSM phones as global platforms to create phones for the US (DAMPS) and Japanese (PDC) digital markets, which were slower to begin growing than the GSM market. These global platforms enable it to introduce more digital phones for the same development costs than other firms do. A development cost comparison between Nokia, Motorola, Ericsson, and the Japanese firms at a *global* level shows that Nokia is able to introduce more than twice as many digital phones for the same development costs as Motorola and the Japanese firms (with a slightly smaller advantage over Ericsson). The rest of this chapter describes the evolution of these regional differences and the appropriate product line/ platform strategy in the context of market- and committee-based competition.

THE US ANALOG MARKET (AMPS): THE EARLY SUCCESS OF JAPANESE FIRMS AND MOTOROLA'S EVENTUAL DOMINATION

Japanese firms and Motorola were the early leaders in the US market as they were expected to be. Japanese firms already dominated the worldwide consumer electronics market and cellular phones appeared to be their next victory. They had and still have the shortest development times and probably the highest development efficiencies at the mobile phone development project level.

Oki Electric was the first Japanese firm to enter the US market since it had been working with AT&T on mobile phones since the mid-1970s. This committee-based strength enabled it to be an early provider to the Baby Bells when they started their services in 1983 and 1984. It had the highest share of the market in 1984 and 1985 when cellular phone sales were fairly low[1] followed by other Japanese firms due to their superior quality. For example, dealers initially complained that 25% of Motorola's phones did not work as compared to 1% of Oki Electric's phones. Even in late 1985, dealers claimed that Motorola's failure rate was still 5% more or more than three times that of Oki Electric.[2]

But Oki Electric's success was fairly short-lived. Other Japanese firms, in particular those that had sold private mobile radio systems in Japan such as Panasonic, Toshiba,[3] Mitsubishi, Fujitsu, and NEC, were only a little behind Oki Electric in entering the US market. They and to a lesser extent Motorola quickly eliminated these quality differences as they became adept in the AMPS standard and Motorola implemented its six-sigma quality improvement program. This caused any advantages that Oki Electric had had in committee-based capabilities to disappear and by 1986 it had lost the top spot and its share never stopped declining as market-based competition, where Oki Electric was weak, determined the winners.

Oki Electric's overemphasis on committee-based competition could be seen in its response to Nokia's marketing agreement with Tandy, which was the owner of the Radio Shack stores. When it was announced in May 1984, Oki downplayed Nokia and Tandy's agreement "as we're not selling portable radios and CDs."[4] Clearly, Oki Electric did not see mobile phones as a consumer electronics product where mass production and mass-market outlets would be important. Tandy had 1100 Radio Shack stores in the US in 1984 and it was the first major retail outlet to sign agreements with mobile phone carriers.[5] By 1985 Tandy was selling phones from Nokia and other manufacturers in the top 30 US markets and in most major cities and by 1988, it was selling phones in most of its 4850 Radio Shack outlets in the US.[6]

The Japanese firms recover from dumping charges

The Japanese firms successfully used their continuous improvement capabilities to dominate the US mobile phone market in the mid- to late 1980s. As in many other industries, they combined these continuous improvement activities with aggressive reductions in prices. These aggressive price reductions caused Motorola in late 1984 to bring dumping charges against nine Japanese firms since they were selling these phones for about half the price that they sold phones in Japan.[7] The Japanese manufacturers countered that a comparison between Japanese and North American prices was unfair since they are two different systems and the Japanese system was of a higher quality than the North American system.[8] The Japanese manufacturers were right that the systems were different and thus comparisons were difficult. However, by constantly claiming that Japanese products were of a higher quality than the US and everyone else's product in a variety of industries, there was very little credibility left in this argument, particularly when not a single country adopted the Japanese NTT system. The real problem was the lack of competition in the Japanese market, which enabled the high mobile phone prices to exist. This problem of course still exists in many Japanese industries.

The US International Trade Commission ruled against the Japanese firms and calculated the dumping charges by comparing North American prices with prices paid by NTT to the Japanese phone suppliers. The result was that dumping charges were leveled against Matsushita (106.6%), NEC (95.57%), Mitsubishi (87.83%), Oki Electric (9.7%) and Hitachi (2.99%). Toshiba was unaffected since it did not sell phones to NTT.

However, there was actually very little impact on the shares of the Japanese firms since many of the other Japanese firms began making phones in the US by the time dumping charges began to take effect in late 1985.[9] By 1990, all of the Japanese firms were making phones in the US and many of them had expanded production capacity several times.[10] The largest direct effect of the dumping charges was that Toshiba's share rose and it held the top share in the US market for several years.

The low cost of production of phones and in some cases of parts in the US enabled Japanese firms to be the market leaders. As shown in Figure 5.2, Japanese firms had between 77% and 81% of the top ten US markets for non-portable phones (car and transportable phones) between 1986 and 1989. Although Motorola was the leader with a 16.1% share in 1989, Matsushita, Mitsubishi, and Toshiba also had shares over 10% followed by Uniden, NEC, JRC, Oki Electric, NEC, Shintom, and Fujitsu.

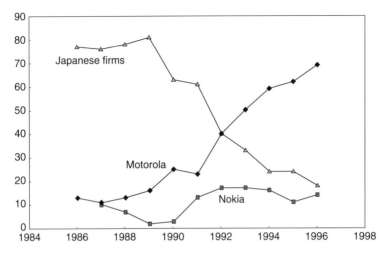

Figure 5.2   Shares of US analog mobile phone market

Motorola's strategy of volume discounts and rapid price decreases

The market began changing from a business to a personal market in the late 1980s. The wholesale and retail prices of phones were dropping dramatically due to technological progress in the semiconductor industry and these low prices began driving a rapid increase in subscribers, particularly non-business subscribers. Evidence from other industries[11] shows that when this occurs, there is a synergy of rising volumes and cost and price reductions that cause the competition to change from performance to price. Motorola was the first firm to notice this change and create the appropriate strategy not only in the AMPS but also in the TACS (Great Britain was the biggest user) and NMT (Scandinavian) markets. Naturally, the similarities between the AMPS and TACS standards allowed large economies of scale between the two standards.

In addition to encouraging service-providers to increase the activation commissions they were paying retail outlets to sign up subscribers,[12] Motorola began giving volume discounts to service-providers and extracting volume discounts from suppliers. It set low prices on the expectation of these volume discounts and it used the increasing volumes to rapidly reduce its costs. The volume discounts it received from suppliers often reached more than 10% for the five- to ten-volume increases that Motorola was offering (see Figure 5.3).

152

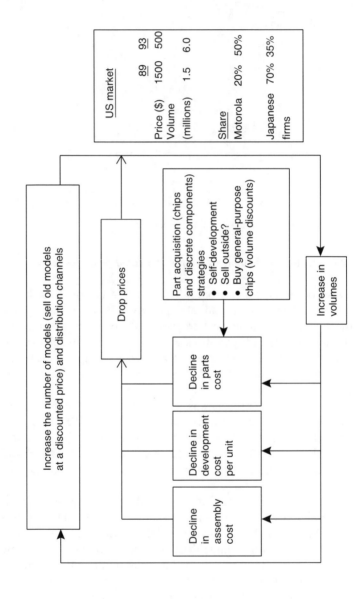

Figure 5.3   Positive feedback between price and volumes in the US analog market

The service-providers did their part by increasing their activation commissions and signing up large stores such as Sears, Macy & Co., and Tops Appliance as exclusive distributors. In early 1990, the activation commissions were about $300, thus making it possible to obtain in some cases a phone and contract for less than $70.[13] The phone prices continued to drop such that by 1994, the average retail phone prices were $300 for mobile phones and $568 for portable phones. These lower prices caused the number of subscribers to quintuple between 1989 and 1994.[14]

Simultaneously with its giving and receiving of volume discounts, Motorola began selling its new and old phones simultaneously in different price segments. In some cases the older phones were slightly modified for the lower end of the market using cheaper discrete components. This strategy enabled Motorola better to meet a wider variety of consumer needs while the costs were kept down through the large number of common parts. Further, it set particularly low prices for the low-end phones where it did not expect to make money. Instead, it made its profits on the high-end phones.

For example, Motorola's shares had always been higher in the portable than in the non-portable market due to Motorola's early emphasis on this market (see Figure 5.4). And Motorola's share of this market began rising after 1989 by introducing the smallest phones

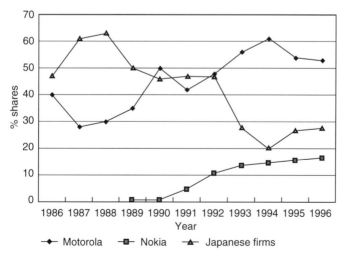

Figure 5.4   Percentage shares of US analog portable phone market

and then modifying them to expand its product variety. It introduced four models based on its successful Microtac (first introduced in early 1989) between August 1990 and August 1991. After releasing the Microtac Lite in August 1991 and the Microtac Ultralite in September 1992, its four portable phones covered the price range from a few hundred dollars to more than $2000 while most of its Japanese competitors only sold one or two phones during this time period.[15] By 1992, Motorola had 48% of the portable phone market and portable phones represented 33% of the total market. Motorola had already won the battle since its share and thus volumes were about six times higher than NEC, which was the Japanese firm with the highest share in the portable phone market. By 1994, Motorola had 61% of the portable phone market and portable phones represented 50% of the total market.

At this point, there was very little the Japanese firms could do since they had severe volume disadvantages. Even though several Japanese firms did begin widening their product lines in late 1992, they could not generate the necessary volumes for the phones. For example, both NEC and Fujitsu were selling portable phones in three price segments in 1993 but their already low shares in both portable and other phones (<5%) and thus lack of presence in distribution outlets in 1992 made it difficult for it to expand their share.

Motorola also created a volume advantage in the Scandinavian NMT market although acquisitions played a more important role in this market than in the AMPS market. Motorola's share began to increase in 1988 due to its acquisition of three Scandinavian manufacturers, Storno, Esselte, and Talkline, in the mid-1980s and the substantial volume discounts that it began to offer to carriers in 1988. Almost overnight, the price of its phones dropped by 30%. Ericsson was forced to lose money in order to maintain its market share.[16] By early 1991, Motorola had achieved the top share of 26% when the shares for its acquisitions are included. Nokia Mobira was second with 24.4% (including Technophone's 5.6%), followed by Ericsson with 20.1% (including the 6% from its joint venture with Panasonic), Philips (9.9%) and Mitsubishi (5.6%).[17]

The rising share of Nokia in AMPS and TACS

Nokia had been doing very well in the Scandinavian NMT market through its committee-based strength in the creation of the NMT standard. Its early involvement and success in NMT also caused it to enter both the AMPS and TACS markets early. But it was not until the 1990s that its share began to rise in the AMPS and TACS markets by using a similar strategy to Motorola. It offered volume discounts to service-providers and received them for part suppliers. While it did not emphasize small phones as much as Motorola, it did emphasize the use of general-purpose parts and production in Korea that enabled it to offer the lowest-price phones. It also used its relationship with Tandy to obtain dedicated space for its phones in Radio Shack.

But Nokia's biggest decision was the acquisition of the British firm Technophone in February 1991. At that time, Great Britain had the largest phone market for TACS, which is of course a derivative of the US analog standard, AMPS. Several firms including Japanese firms had tried to acquire Technophone but Technophone agreed to a Nokia buyout because it believed that Nokia would allow them greater opportunities than a buyout from other firms, particularly a Japanese firm.[18] The successful acquisition of Technophone caused Nokia to instantly become the third largest provider of phones in the US and the second largest provider in Europe. Although one of the announced reasons for the acquisition was access to a manufacturing plant in the European Community (Finland was not in the EC), the acquisition of Technophone enabled Nokia to create greater economies of scale both in production and procurement for AMPS- and TACS-based phones. Further, in a move that would eventually enable it to become the leading producer of phones in the world, it began creating global platforms that could be used to develop phones for multiple standards. For example, in March 1992, it released its best-selling 101 series in the AMPS, TACS, and NMT standards.[19]

Why were the Japanese firms so slow to notice the changes in the US market?

One question remains as to why the Japanese firms were initially slow to respond to the changes that began to occur in the analog market in the late 1980s. The basic problem was that the market changes required a strategy that was very different from the strategy used successfully by Japanese firms in the past. And these differences show some of the problems with the conventional wisdom concerning the strengths and weaknesses of Japanese firms. Japanese firms are strong in high *variety* assembly industries where JIT (just in time) manufacturing and continuous improvement are most useful. They work closely with a dedicated set of suppliers and often emphasize the use of their own parts. They expand from the low end into the high end of the market and they are able to produce a variety of cars, consumer electronics, and machinery at costs that are similar to the costs of a low-variety mass production facility.

Japanese firms are not strong in the real high-volume manufacturing industries as their lack of success in continuous flow manufacturing (for example, toiletries, pharmaceuticals and chemicals), personal computers and cellular phones shows. Japanese firms do not understand the fundamental advantages of high volume. This is why they have not created the high-volume capabilities through mergers and acquisitions that are needed in these and other industries. For example, in spite of the existence of between five and ten producers of most consumer electronics products in the late 1990s, there have been almost no mergers or acquisitions in this field. The same holds for the Japanese mobile phone market where there are more than fifteen producers of cellular and more than ten producers of PHS phones in Japan and yet mergers and acquisitions are not occurring.

This was also true in the US market in the 1980s when there were more than ten Japanese producers of cellular phones, many of whom placed a strong emphasis on the use of internal parts. This internal production made it difficult to generate economies of scale in parts and made it even more difficult to overcome Motorola's initial share advantages.[20] This was exacerbated by Japan's unique standard and the low growth in the Japanese market. These problems have continued to hurt them in the GSM market where Nokia, Motorola, and Ericsson use their economies of scale as entry barriers and the Japanese firms continue to only compete in the low end of the market.

Second, Japanese firms were slow to understand the changes that were occurring in the US market since most decisions are made in Japan. Most Japanese firms in this and other industries[21] do not like to delegate responsibility to foreign managers and their lack of English-language skills makes it hard for managers in Japan to work closely with foreign managers. And managers in Japan were heavily influenced by the slow growth in Japan, the lack of price competition, and the one-segment cellular phone market that continues to exist even now in Japan.

They are also heavily influenced by the government's concern about trade friction. In fact, it is not an exaggeration to say that the globalization of Japanese firms in the 1980s was almost entirely driven by concerns about trade friction. The cellular phone dumping charges successfully levied against them in the US and unsuccessfully in Europe (in 1987[22]) convinced many Japanese managers that they could not compete aggressively on price in the analog cellular phone market in the late 1980s and early 1990s when Motorola was implementing its volume discounts. The government's concern about trade friction and its opposition to imports is another example of how the strong Japanese companies (that is, those who can compete overseas) must bend over backwards to help protect the weak Japanese firms who only participate in the protected, overregulated Japanese economy.[23]

THE SUCCESS OF NOKIA, MOTOROLA AND ERICSSON IN GSM

Market competition also played a much larger role in GSM phone competition than committee-based competition although it could be said that success in the latter was a prerequisite to participation in the former. The best example of this can be found with the Japanese firms. As discussed in Chapter 3, they did not participate in the creation of GSM since they did not have development centers in Europe nor did they have the inclination to participate in the standard-setting process partly since their globalization strategies still revolved around concerns about dumping charges. Further, they underestimated the trends towards increasing patent protection in the US and Europe. Therefore, they did not simultaneously develop products while participating in the standard-setting process and thus they did not have any patents to exchange with Motorola and the European manufacturers. They were forced to pay licensing fees of between 6% and 10% as a percentage of sales. These patent negotiations caused Mitsubishi, Matsushita and other Japanese firms to delay their entry into the GSM market.[24]

Outside the Japanese firms, however, it may be said that market competition in the form of product line and platform management played a more important role in the GSM phone market than committee-based competition. Further, this was true to even a greater extent than in the US AMPS market. The reason is that volumes rose much more quickly in GSM than in the analog AMPS market. While it took almost five and eleven years for the number of annual AMPS phone sales to pass the one million and ten million marks respectively, it took less than $1\frac{1}{2}$ and $3\frac{1}{2}$ years respectively for the number of GSM phone sales to pass these marks. These quickly rising volumes made market-based competition, rather than committee-based competition, more important in GSM than it was in AMPS.

Further, these quickly rising volumes made it even more important for manufacturers to use volume discounts and quickly introduce products into multiple countries and multiple price segments more than was the case in the US AMPS market. Motorola, Nokia, and Ericsson implemented this appropriate product line and platform management strategy much more quickly than other firms did due to their optimistic forecasts about the GSM market. As shown in Figures 5.5, 5.6, and 5.7, they were introducing products into multiple price segments by late 1994 while Alcatel and Siemens (not shown in the figures) did not do this for all of Europe until the latter half of 1996 and the Japanese firms had still not done so as of late 1999. Motorola, Nokia, and Ericsson were from countries that had experienced rapid growth in their domestic markets and their executives were greatly influenced by these high growth rates. Other manufacturers such as Siemens, Alcatel, and Philips were from countries that had experienced very little growth in the analog market. They depended on consulting forecasts that predicted a slow move from analog to digital GSM services.

Further, it may be said that many of the other European firms over emphasized committee-based competition and this prevented them from implementing the appropriate product line and platform man-

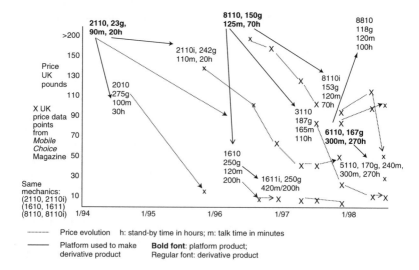

Figure 5.5   Evolution of Nokia's GSM 900 MHz phone line

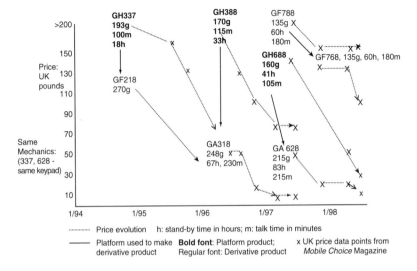

Figure 5.6   Evolution of Ericsson's GSM 900 MHz phone line

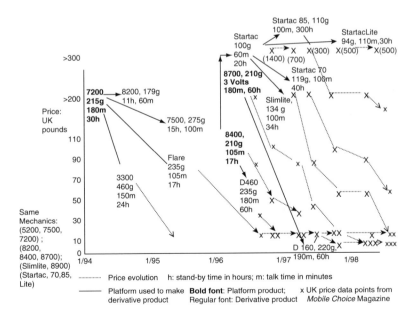

Figure 5.7   Evolution of Motorola's GSM 900 MHz phone line

agement strategies. Firms like Dancall, Hagenuk, Ascom[25] and even to some extent Siemens, Alcatel, and Philips were from countries where analog phone and even to some extent wireline phone competition was based on committee-based competition where exclusive relationships between manufacturers and service-providers largely determined the winners. These firms were ill-prepared for regional, much less global, competition and their narrow perceptions of the market prevented them from making the necessary investments in technology, products, and manufacturing capacity. For example, although Siemens released its first GSM product at about the same time as Nokia and Ericsson, it initially focused on Germany. It did not begin selling phones until 1996 in Asia or the UK although the UK was the second largest GSM phone market in the world in 1996.

The slow moves by these firms to expand their product lines has made it difficult for them to succeed in the GSM market since Motorola, Nokia, and Ericsson have used their product line/platform management strategies as an entry barrier against these firms. Further, as is described later, differences in both the strategies and implementation of their product line/platform managements led to differences in market share between Motorola, Nokia, and Ericsson.

Platform Management as a Barrier to Entry

Motorola, Nokia, and Ericsson's early expansion and their pricing strategies act as a barrier to entry to other firms as Motorola's strategy did in the AMPS market. They use a large number of common parts in multiple segments and they subsidize their low-end phones, which makes it very difficult for firms to first succeed in the low end of the market and then move to the high end of the market. Most firms admit that they either lose money or barely break even in the low end of the market while the high end of the market is where Nokia and to some extent Motorola and Ericsson make their profits. These three firms quickly created a strong brand image in the high end of the market and thus have been able to differentiate themselves from the other manufacturers in this market. The low-end phones from Motorola, Nokia, and Ericsson merely provide the volumes necessary to have low costs in both the low-end and high-end phones and reduce the amount of price erosion in the high-end phones. Further, the brand image they have created in the high-end segments has to some extent subsequently carried over into the low-end segment and this brand image has enabled them to charge slightly higher prices than the other manufacturers in the low-end segment.

This strategy makes it difficult for firms to gradually move from the low end to the high end of the market as the Japanese did in a variety of industries such as automobiles and consumer electronics during the 1970s. This is the major reason why Sony quit its joint venture with Siemens in the GSM market where neither Siemens itself or both together were able to crack the entry barrier created by Nokia, Motorola and Ericsson.[26]

Thus, in order to be profitable, firms must compete in all segments and they must do so from the point at which these segments begin to appear. In the GSM phone market, some late entrants have attempted to enter all segments simultaneously and there have been disastrous results of which the best example is Philips. After Philips stopped development in 1994 and sold Nokia's 2110 as an OEM for several years, it reentered the market in 1996 with an ex-Motorola manager, Mike McTighe, as the general manager. McTighe brought Motorola's method of platform management to Philips, including the realization that success required participation in multiple segments. Philips released products in the low (Fizz) and high (Genie) ends of the market and a third product (Spark) between them from June 1996 to July 1997. Lucent's agreement to merge its consumer phone unit with that of Philips in mid-1997 gave Philips the opportunity to also compete in other standards like AMPS and cdmaOne.[27] Mike McTighe predicted that the new company would increase its 1996 GSM share of 1.6% to 5% in 1997 and it would be in the top three manufacturers in the world by the year 2000.

The results have been disastrous, however. The joint venture lost about $500 million on sales of $2.5 billion in 1998[28] and the joint venture between Philips and Lucent was dissolved. Although Philips blamed Lucent for problems in the cdmaOne market,[29] it was clear that Philips could not break through the entry barrier that Motorola, Nokia, and Ericsson had created in the GSM market. Philips did not have the brand image to acquire a strong share in the middle or high-end markets nor was it able to achieve the necessary market share needed in the low end of the market to reduce costs. In spite of price reductions, the Spark and Genie (400,000 units were reportedly sold in 1997) achieved lower-than-expected market shares in the middle and high ends of the market. The Fizz had production problems and it was only able to obtain a 4% share of the low-end market.

Differences in product line/platform management and the rise of Nokia

Differences in product line and platform management also explain the differences in performance between Nokia, Motorola, and Ericsson in the GSM phone market. These include differences in strategy and implementation. The strategic differences include the ratio of platform to derivative products and the method of product differentiation. Nokia has focused more on aesthetic design, user interface, and software features in its product line and platform management approach than on weight and costs as Motorola and Ericsson have respectively done. This has enabled Nokia to set prices more in terms of customer value than product costs.

These strategic and implementation differences explain the falling shares of Motorola and Ericsson and the rise of Nokia. Initially, it was Motorola that was the most optimistic of all of the firms and this caused it to introduce more products and distribution channels than the other firms. This enabled it to capture about 28% of the market in 1993 and 1994. On the other hand, Ericsson's failures in the personal computer market in the 1980s caused it to initially question its involvement in the handset business and thus invest less than Motorola and Nokia. However, as shown in Figure 5.8, Motorola's share dropped to around 20% by 1996 where it has remained since then while Nokia's share had risen to about 32% by 1998.

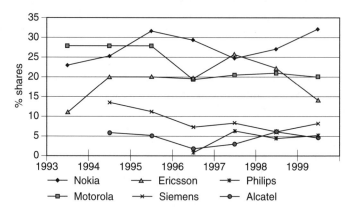

Figure 5.8   GSM handset shares

Table 5.1   A comparison of GSM 900 platform management strategies for Nokia, Motorola, and Ericsson between 1994 and 1997

Item	Nokia	Motorola	Ericsson
Number of platform products	3	3	3
Number of derivative products	8	10	5
Ratio of derivative to platform products	2.7	3.3	1.7
Total development costs[1]	4.29	4.80	3.50
Development costs/product	0.39	0.36	0.44

[1]Units are in "standard development projects" where a standard development project includes a phone with a new architecture, baseband chips, discrete components, printed circuit board(s), mechanics, and software.

Strategic differences

The first strategic difference between the three firms is that Motorola and Nokia introduced substantially far more products than Ericsson between 1994 and early 1998 (see Table 5.1). The reason is that both Motorola and Nokia introduced derivative products both simultaneously and subsequently to the introduction of a platform product while Ericsson only did the former. This enabled Motorola and Nokia to more effectively cover the various price segments in the market (see Figures 5.5, 5.6 and 5.7) while maintaining a lower development cost per product than Ericsson.

Platform and derivative projects can be defined in terms of the degree of change in the product. This requires a brief explanation of phone designs. Phone designs can be divided into baseband designs, which are largely a function of the standard, radio frequency designs, which are a function of the frequency band used, along with printed circuit board, mechanical and software designs. The integrated circuits and discrete components that make up the baseband and radio frequency designs are mounted on printed circuit boards. The software is stored in various memory chips and it handles a variety of functions such as the user interface.

A platform product is defined as a new product that contains a new architecture or at the minimum a new baseband or radio frequency design. For example, the change from a 5-volt to either a 4- or 3-volt design required a new product architecture and all of the platform products shown in Figures 5.5, 5.6, and 5.7 contain all new baseband or radio frequency designs. The derivative products use either existing or modified baseband and radio frequency designs. The degree of newness in the printed circuit board, mechanical and software designs varies by project.

The overall development costs (in units of standard development projects) for Motorola, Nokia, and Ericsson can be compared using data on the degree of newness in each phone for the architecture, baseband, radio frequency, printed circuit board layout, mechanical, and software design. This was done through interviews with platform management managers although with software the costs were assumed to be the same.[30] Motorola's and Nokia's greater use of derivative projects enabled them to reuse architecture, baseband, radio frequency, board layout, mechanical, and software design more effectively than Ericsson and thus have lower development costs per product (including both platform and derivative products) than Ericsson.

The second strategic difference involves the method of product differentiation. Motorola has primarily emphasized the development of very light phones for the high end of the GSM market while Nokia has emphasized aesthetic design, user interface, and software features and Ericsson has emphasized low cost. As shown in Figures 5.5, 5.6 and 5.7, Motorola has consistently introduced lighter phones than the other manufacturers. Its 8200 was the first sub-200 gram phone, its Startac series included the first sub-100 gram phones and its Slimlite was also the lightest mid-range phone in 1997. Motorola has also devoted considerable resources to maintaining the top spot for the Startac series. The Startac 70 and 85, which were less expensive versions of the original Startac, were introduced since the original Startac was too expensive for the market. The Startac Lite was released in response to Philips' release of the Genie, which became the lightest GSM phone on the market for a very short time.

Ericsson has placed more emphasis on product cost than Motorola or Nokia. This is one reason why it has primarily released derivative products simultaneously with the release of the platform product as opposed to Motorola's and Nokia's strategy of both simultaneous and subsequent introductions of derivative products. This was part of Ericsson's strategy to cost-minimize each platform design from the beginning whereas Nokia often reduces the cost in the subsequent derivative products. Ericsson changed its strategy slightly in 1997 when it used the highly successful 688 platform to develop the 788, 768 and 628 derivative products. However, in these derivative projects Ericsson primarily focused on changing the mechanical and software portions of the design without modifications to the discrete components and board layout. Further, this change in strategy partly led to some of the implementation problems that Ericsson experienced in 1998 and 1999 (see below).

Nokia has placed more emphasis on aesthetic design, user interfaces, and software features than on weight or costs and these three factors have become much more important than they were in the analog era. Designs with rounded edges, good proportions, interesting colors, and high quality mechanical components such as higher resolution and sometimes larger displays, hardtop as opposed to rubber keys, and magnesium as opposed to plastic housings have become key features in the high-end phones. Further, the increasing importance of message and data services, memory dialing, answering services, caller notification, vibration notification, and the control of everything from display strength, button and ringing volume, ring tone and melody, clock and alarm, to security features has increased the importance of both user interfaces and software features.

Nokia has received the best reviews for its designs and user interfaces largely due to its large emphasis on these factors. For example, Nokia's highly successful 2110 phone had an award-winning design and a very successful user interface, which has subsequently become an industry norm. As shown in Figure 5.5, Nokia has used the 2110 platform and other platforms to create a large number of derivative products.[31] Nokia released a new platform (8110) with an award-winning design in early 1996 for the high end of the market from which three derivatives were developed. Further, the 8110 and one of its derivatives, the 1610, were subsequently redesigned in the form of the 8110i and the 1611i. The talk and stand-by times were extended in the 1611i, new software features were added in the 8110i, and a substantially cheaper version of the 8110 was created in the 3110. The 3110 was Nokia's first product to contain soft keys and in particular the Navi key which have become standard items on its subsequent phones; these functions are a major reason why Nokia's phones are considered to have the best user interfaces. In late 1997 and early 1998, Nokia introduced the 6110 (a new platform) for the middle market and from the 6110 platform the 8810 was developed for the high-end market. As with the 2110 and subsequent products, Nokia has created distinctive styling for both phones. The 8810 is light, metallic, and small while the 6110 series uses different materials and chameleon colors.

The success of the 2110 along with the brand image campaign, which Nokia had started before other firms in 1992, dramatically increased user awareness of Nokia. Nokia had begun building its brand image from 1992 through advertisements on television and other media. Subsequently it has continued to improve its image through interesting products that contain new functions (Nokia Communicator), materials, and innovative colors. This brand image has enabled Nokia's phones to sell at a higher price to consumers than the phones from the other manufacturers while their phones are also receiving a higher activation commission from the carriers than the other manufacturers.

Nokia's emphasis on design, user interface, software features, and brand image is a good example of how Nokia has set prices based more on customer value than on cost. Many of its high-end products have costs that are very similar to those of its low-end products. The larger difference between the high-end and low-end products is in customer value. The high-end products have better aesthetic designs, user interfaces, and software features. In many cases, Nokia has only included these software features in the high-end phones in spite of the fact that it is actually more expensive to do this than to include them in all phones.

Problems with implementation – Motorola

Motorola and Ericsson have also had many more implementation problems than Nokia. These problems are major reasons why Motorola's share dropped in 1996 and 1997 and Ericsson's share dropped in 1998 and 1999. First, Motorola's three platform projects were not evenly spaced between 1994 and 1998 and thus technology was not used as effectively as it could have. Motorola had planned to introduce its 8400 in 1995 and its 8700 platform in 1996. The 8400 phone was expected to include a new radio frequency design while the 8700 phone was expected to include the new radio frequency design along with a new baseband design. However, delays in the radio frequency design caused the platforms to be introduced almost simultaneously. The ideal timing of platform products depends on a number of technical and market factors including the technological progress in semiconductors and discrete components. For example, since new generations of semiconductors with more narrow line widths appear about every one to two years, ideally, new platform products are also released on a similar schedule.

Second, Motorola allowed a large gap to appear in the mid-price segment of the 900 phone market, which Nokia was able to dominate with its 3110, 8110i, 6110, and 5110 phones between 1996 and 1998. The reason is that Motorola thought that the 1800 market was ready to take off in 1998 and thus was the first firm to introduce a dual-mode phone (for the 900 and 1800 markets), called the 8900, which was also a platform product for Motorola. Although now there are almost no cost or performance disadvantages to a dual-mode over a single-mode phone (and thus almost all phones were dual-mode by 1999), this was not so in 1997 and 1998. This problem was exacerbated by Motorola's emphasis on the high-end market, which was mentioned above (that is, the Startac). The result was that after Motorola introduced the 8400 in June 1996, it did not introduce another phone that was developed specifically for the middle 900 market until it introduced the d520 in May 1998.

The lack of a new 900 MHz phone for Motorola in the mid-price segment caused Motorola to dramatically drop the prices of its higher-end phones in 1997 and early 1998 in order to fill the vacant price segment. Further, Motorola's lack of a strong brand image in terms of aesthetic design, user interfaces, and software features created additional downward pressure on the prices of these phones. For example, as shown in Figure 5.7, the price of the Slimlite, Startac 70 and 8700 dropped from an initial price to the user of greater than £200 to £50 for the Startac 70 and £10 for the Slimlite and 8700 by early 1998. At the end of 1997, Motorola was selling the D160, D170, D460, and 8700 all for £5 or £10 along with the Slimlite and three Startac phones. At the same time, Nokia was selling the 1611, 2110i, the 3110, and the 8110i with only the 1611 being sold for £5. Ericsson was also selling two with one of them being sold in the bottom market (£20).

This strategy of aggressive price reductions that Motorola had successfully used in the AMPS market was much less successful in the GSM market due not only to changes in the customer needs (mentioned earlier) but also to the cost and weight drivers in mobile phones. Whereas in the analog market, semiconductor chips and discrete components drove weight and costs, mechanical components such as plastic housings, liquid crystal displays, printed circuit boards, keypads, shields, and antennas have gradually become a larger percentageage of total phone weight and cost. And as they have become a larger percentage of phone weight, it has become more important to use the most expensive mechanical components in the high-end phones in order to reduce the weight and improve the styling of the phones. These components include higher resolution and sometimes larger displays, hard-top as opposed to rubber keys, magnesium as opposed to plastic housings, and the latest printed circuit board technology. However, the cost of these mechanical components does not drop anywhere near as fast as the cost of semiconductor chips and discrete components do.

Thus, the high-end phones need to be redesigned using less expensive mechanical components before they are sold in the lower-price segments.

Problems with implementation – Ericsson

Ericsson stumbled heavily in 1998 and 1999 when it tried to change its method of product line and platform management. This included an attempt to introduce more derivative projects (mentioned previously), the change from 4-volt to 3-volt technology, an attempt to integrate Orbitel's development efforts with its own, and most importantly its attempt to redefine the market segments. Ericsson has had problems with integrating its efforts with Orbitel, in which it acquired a 50% interest from Racal Electronics in 1991. In 1996, Ericsson purchased Racal Electronics' remaining shares in Orbitel thus making Orbitel a 100%-owned Ericsson subsidiary. However, Ericsson did not integrate Orbitel's development efforts with its own until 1998 after Orbitel had released several products that competed directly with its own products. Contrast this acquisition with Nokia's acquisition of Technophone also in 1991 and it is clear that Nokia has handled its acquisition better. Interestingly, in an independent comparison of the Technophone and Orbitel acquisitions, the managers at Technophone felt they played a much larger role in Nokia than the Orbitel managers felt they played in Ericsson.[32]

Ericsson has also struggled to redefine the market segments in the mobile phone market. Previously, the market segments (that is, price) were primarily determined by weight and to some extent design/user interface. The former was primarily Motorola's strategy with Nokia emphasizing the latter beginning in 1994 with the 2110. Since 1998, Ericsson has been defining the market in terms of entry level, design-intensive, and functional phones. The design-intensive phones will emphasize weight and size while the functional phones will emphasize large displays and data capabilities. While Ericsson's new definition of the market may eventually result in a higher share, the change in platform strategy along with the change from 4-volt to 3-volt technology and the integration of Orbitel efforts hurt it badly in 1998 and 1999. No new phones appeared between the end of 1997 and early 1999, thus causing its share price to drop dramatically.

The lack of new phones caused major problems for Ericsson as a whole and it was one of the reasons why Sven-Christer Nilsson was forced to resign as chief executive in July 1999 after just fifteen months in the position. Until late 1998, few people saw Ericsson's lack of new phones or lack of strength in data networking, Internet protocol and other Internet-related technologies as major problems. After all it had seen its sales triple between 1992 and 1997 while pretax profits climbed fourteenfold to $2.2 billion. Mobile phones accounted for 25% of its sales[33] and gross margins were 41.7% in 1997 just before Nilsson was made the new CEO in January 1998.[34]

The lack of phones and the lack of strength in data networking, Internet protocol and other Internet-related technologies began to be noticed in mid-1998 by the stock market when second quarter mobile phone sales showed no growth and subsequently Ericsson began announcing profit warnings.[35] These problems continued in the third quarter of 1998 as Nokia's 8810 was released and Ericsson's mobile phone sales fell 2% while Motorola's rose 9% and Nokia's surged 94%.[36] The release of the T28 in January and the T18 in March 1999 and an announcement that a phone aimed at cost-conscious clients with prepaid cards (the A118) would be available by mid-year did little to change the stock market.[37] In July 1999 pressure from shareholders and financial markets drove Ericsson to ask for chief executive Sven-Christer Nilsson's resignation.[38]

THE US DIGITAL PHONE MARKET AND NOKIA'S GLOBAL PLATFORMS

Market-based competition also played a more important role in the US digital phone market than committee-based competition although some firms managed to obtain high market shares for a short time period through their initial strength in committee-based competition. Examples of this are found in Ericsson's initial strength in DAMPS and the initial strength of Qualcomm and Sony in cdmaOne. This caused these firms to initially obtain reasonably high shares of the US digital phone market as shown in Table 5.2. Ericsson obtained a fairly high share of the US digital phone market through its strength in DAMPS and the overwhelming use of DAMPS as a digital standard in the US until 1998. Qualcomm's and Sony's shares began to rise as the cdmaOne handset market began to grow in 1997. While only 3% of the digital phones sold in 1996 were for cdmaOne, this rose to 33% in 1997 and 38% in 1998. Simultaneously, the percentage of new phones that were digital rose from 26% in 1996 to 50% in 1997 and 60% in 1998.

Table 5.2   Shares of the US digital phone market (percentage)

Company	1995	1996	1997	1998
Nokia	29	33	20	34
Ericsson	34	56	41	21
Motorola	36	8	6	12
Qualcomm		2.9	17	13
Sony			7	
Samsung			8	
Other		0.1	1	20

However, these were just initial advantages that disappeared as product line and platform management became the key factors in the market-based competition in the US digital phone market. In particular, differences in product line/platform management explain Nokia's success in this market. Nokia's GSM product line/platform strategy and its use of global platforms provide it with a large advantage over Motorola and Ericsson in the US and the global market for GSM and DAMPS phones. Although the effects of committee-based competition initially obscured this advantage, by 1998 Nokia's advantages had become completely clear as it become the leading producer of phones in both the US and the world. In particular, its use of global platforms enabled it to quickly and inexpensively modify its GSM phones for the US market. And as in the GSM market, Nokia's phones were perceived to have better aesthetic designs, user interfaces, and software features than those of the other manufacturers.

The DAMPS and GSM markets in the US

Motorola and Ericsson were the early leaders in the US digital phone market, which goes against the typical view of Motorola moving slowly into digital phones. Motorola has always been a leader in the GSM phone market, which is of course a digital technology. In the US market, however, the initial volumes were too small to be of consequence. The number of new digital subscribers as a percentage of the total new subscribers increased from 1.5% in 1993 to 7.5% in 1994 and 15% in 1995. Most of these digital phones were based on the initial versions of DAMPS called IS54. The existing analog service-providers sold these dual-mode phones, which were compatible with both digital and analog services, to increase calling capacity in highly populated areas.

As shown in Table 5.2, both Motorola and Ericsson were still the leading suppliers of these phones even as late as 1995. While Motorola's success was largely due to its overwhelming success in the US analog market, Ericsson's early success was largely through its committee-based strength in DAMPS. Since it had played a large role in convincing the US Cellular Telephone Association (CTIA) to adopt this standard (as discussed in Chapter 3), it made an early commitment to the development and production of these phones. It promised the US CTIA that it would begin volume production of these phones by January 1992 and did in fact show prototypes of these phones in December 1991[39] and receive FCC Type Certification in January 1992.[40]

Although Ericsson was able to maintain a large share of the US digital phone market for both committee- and market-based reasons, Motorola's share of the digital market dropped quickly in 1996 as the new personal communications services (PCSs) were started. As discussed in Chapter 3, the US began awarding new licences for digital services in 1995 and by 1996 many of these firms had started their digital services. Although more than 50% of these new licences were awarded to firms who elected to use cdmaOne (see below), cdmaOne services took longer to implement and thus most of the early digital services were based on DAMPS and GSM. Further, the start of PCSs caused many of the existing analog service-providers such as AT&T, Bell South, and Southwestern Bell aggressively to implement digital services in the form of an improved version of DAMPS called IS136.

The start of these digital services caused Ericsson's and Nokia's share of the US digital phone market to rise at the expense of Motorola which was slow to introduce products for the new version of DAMPS IS136 (in either phones or infrastructure). Instead, Motorola placed its emphasis on analog and cdmaOne phones. This was a mistake since IS136 phones represented about two-thirds of the market for digital phones in 1996 and about 50% in 1997.

In particular, Ericsson continued to benefit from its committee-based strength in 1996 and 1997 although here it was through its relationships with the service-providers. Ericsson was the major supplier of DAMPS and GSM 1900 infrastructure to these carriers.[41] It was able to use these relationships to make accurate predictions of demand and thus create adequate inventory for both DAMPS and GSM 1900 phones to satisfy the carriers' launch schedules. This enabled Ericsson to be the leading producer of these DAMPS and GSM phones in 1996 and 1997. While Nokia began to increase its share of the DAMPS and GSM 1900 phone markets in 1997 and 1998, Motorola had still not begun regaining share in the DAMPS market even as of late 1999. Motorola released a Startac version of DAMPS in late 1998 but it was only for the 800 band.[42] In early 1999, it released a 1900 band Startacs but still did not have the same number of models as Ericsson and Nokia in DAMPS, particularly for entry-level users.

The cdmaOne market

Like DAMPS, committee-based competition also played an important role in the early years of the cdmaOne market. Qualcomm through its joint venture with Sony called QPE (Qualcomm Personal Electronics), and Sony itself largely controlled this market until late 1998 due to their control of the cdmaOne standard and chip sets. Qualcomm set fairly high licensing fees for the standard and for its chip sets. The high licensing fees and the initially fairly slow growth in the cdmaOne market discouraged the large chip set suppliers like VLSI, LSI Logic and DSPC and the phone suppliers from developing cdmaOne chip sets. Qualcomm was still the only supplier of chip sets until the major chip set suppliers such as VLSI began shipping samples in June 1998 and large volumes in early 1999[43]: And Qualcomm's high prices for its chip sets discouraged the phone suppliers like Nokia, Ericsson, Motorola, and others from buying from Qualcomm since it was clear that these high prices would make it very difficult to make a profit on cdmaOne phones.

Sony became involved with CDMA technology in the late 1980s and with Qualcomm in 1992. Sony had previously worked with a Qualcomm competitor in the satellite field called Geostar. The combination of Sony's CDMA and design capability made Sony an appropriate partner for Qualcomm while a venture with Qualcomm gave Sony an opportunity to enter the mobile phone field where it had been largely unsuccessful. Cooperative work began in 1992 and in February 1994 QPE was created.

Samsung entered the US cdmaOne market relatively early (in 1997) since the Korean firms had struck a special deal with Qualcomm in return for Korea's wholesale adoption of cdmaOne. Samsung also benefited from Korea's weak currency and the high growth in their cdmaOne domestic market where it was the number one supplier. As discussed in Chapter 3, the US market for cdmaOne phones did not become larger than the Korean market until mid-1999 and these volumes have helped Samsung acquire a growing part of the US market in 1997, 1998, and 1999.

It was not until 1998 that other firms such as Nokia (April), Oki Electric (May) and Motorola (summer) introduced phones using their own cdmaOne chips. This was partly since Qualcomm had begun reducing the price of its chips and its patent fees in order to expand the market for cdmaOne and to compete with new entrants such as VLSI Technologies. The introduction of cdmaOne phones by Nokia and Motorola caused their shares of the US digital phone market to rise partly at the expense of Qualcomm and Sony but also Ericsson who had not released a cdmaOne phone even as of late 1999.

Motorola's share of the cdmaOne market continued to rise in 1999 due to its strong cdmaOne phones. A major event was an order from Bell Atlantic in May 1999,[44] which was one of the reasons why Motorola was able to become the leading supplier of cdmaOne phones by the second quarter of 1999. Moreover, this and the continuing growth of cdmaOne in the US caused Motorola to become the second largest supplier of digital phones overall in the US by the second quarter of 1999 with a 23% share of the market.[45] Although Nokia still had the largest share of the US digital phone market in the second quarter of 1999 with 32%, it had a much smaller share of the cdmaOne market than Motorola due its lack of emphasis on these phones.[46] This did not change until Nokia released its 6100 in early 1999.[47]

The rising share of Motorola and subsequently Nokia in the cdmaOne market reflected their greater strength than Sony and Qualcomm in market-based competition. As Motorola, Nokia, and others began to release phones in 1998 and 1999, prices began to plummet and both Sony's and Qualcomm's profits began to drop. Sony had already quit its joint venture with Siemens in the GSM market where neither Siemens itself nor both together were able to crack the entry barrier created by Nokia, Motorola, and Ericsson.[48] In the US, Sony had hoped that its early entry through the joint venture with Qualcomm would enable it to succeed in the US and provide a springboard to succeed elsewhere. But as in the GSM market, neither Sony nor Qualcomm had sufficient capabilities in market-based competition in phones. In particular, they did not have the global volumes to compete on costs, the manufacturing system to compete on quality, or the strong brand image to compete on design with Nokia or even Motorola.

For example, Sony had major quality problems in 1998 that badly tarnished its brand image in the mobile phone area. Sixty thousand phones were found to have defects in 1998. This along with the severe price competition caused Sony's US business to begin losing money in late 1998. Further, since Sony's US cellular phones represented 40% of its worldwide cellular phone sales (versus 20% in Europe and 40% in Japan), the losses in the US market caused it to lose money in its worldwide personal electronics business in the first and second quarter of 1999. This caused it to announce cutbacks in engineers and models in June 1999 and to announce it was quitting the US business altogether in July 1999 and move its development efforts to third generation phones.[49]

Qualcomm began coming to the same conclusions about its lack of capabilities in market-based competition in late 1999. It was finding it difficult to compete with Nokia and Motorola on costs and it was having problems obtaining enough parts due to a worldwide part shortage. Qualcomm and Sony sold their stakes to Kyocera in early 2000.

Motorola's slow move to digital

Although Motorola's rising share of the digital phone market signaled the start of a recovery for Motorola in early 1999, it was clear that Motorola would not dominate the US market like it had in previous years. In particular, although its 23% share in the second quarter of 1999 was a vast improvement over its 6% share in 1997, it is still a far cry from the almost 70% share that it boasted overall in the US market in 1995. As of mid-1999, it still had far fewer DAMPS and GSM 1900 phones than Nokia or even Ericsson. And Motorola's slow move to digital phones in the US is one reason that a $1.1 billion profit in 1997 became a loss of $1 billion in 1998.[50]

There are four reasons for Motorola's slow move to digital phones. First, Motorola ignored requests for digital phones to the extent that it was considered arrogant. For example, in February 1995, Ameritech, AT&T, Bell Atlantic, and others told Motorola they needed digital phones within a year. But Robert Weisshappel, Executive Vice President and General Manager of Motorola's Cellular Subscriber Group, believed the analog market would continue to grow due to the large size of digital phones and he thought the analog Startac would be a big winner. Even as late as February 1997 he joked that maybe Motorola should buy Qualcomm when asked by CEO Christopher Galvin why there were no digital phones.[51] And even when Motorola began paying attention to the requests from its customers it apparently did not listen to their needs enough. It developed cdmaOne phones with an 8Kbps transmission speed when service-providers wanted phones with rates of 13 Kbps in 1996. This further delayed Motorola's entry into the market.[52]

The analog Startac strategy was also flawed and demonstrated Motorola's arrogance. Introduced in January 1996, it was considered a great phone but far too expensive and its accompanying Signature campaign flopped. Motorola would only distribute the phone to carriers who bought 75% of their phones from Motorola and agreed to promote the phone's features in stand-alone displays.[53] Similar to what happened in the GSM market, the high price of the original Startac (still $1000 in January 1997) caused Motorola to release the Startac 6000 in January 1997. Although this phone retailed for about $500, it was still considered too expensive and the removal of key features such as the vibrating alert and two-line display caused it to not meet the original expectations.[54]

Second, Motorola's suppliers also believed that Motorola was arrogant. For years, Motorola used its high volumes to pressure part suppliers to reduce their prices and respond to large fluctuations in part volumes. And Motorola consistently had problems with managing its inventories as the US market grew rapidly in 1994, 1995, and 1996, particularly at the end of the year when there were large Christmas sales.[55] However, the angry suppliers had their chance for revenge when Motorola was struggling to create digital phones. The rising orders from Nokia and Ericsson not only made Motorola's purchases less important, their previous arrogance was well remembered.

Third, Motorola was slow to understand the difficulties of developing digital phones and create global platforms. It apparently took Weisshappel a long time to understand that digital phones required far more resources than analog phones due to their more complex software. Thus, even when Weisshappel was convinced that digital phones were needed in the US market, there were not enough resources to develop them. Interestingly, this misunderstanding was in spite of the fact that GSM phones were developed at the same complex as the US digital phones were developed; they were merely developed under a different vice president. Nevertheless, once Weisshappel's replacement recognized the need for digital engineers, Motorola quickly expanded the hiring of digital engineers[56] and purchased Lucent's consumer electronics business in NJ in 1998.[57]

Fourth, and most importantly, Motorola's regional organization has made it difficult for Motorola to create global platforms, which is Nokia's principal advantage. As described in the next section, Nokia can develop more than twice as many phones as Motorola and most other firms for the same level of development resources. This is why

Nokia was able to release a large number of phones in 1998 and 1999 while other firms struggled.

Nokia's global platforms

Nokia began developing global platforms in the analog era when it simultaneously introduced phones based on the AMPS, TACS, and NMT standards. Motorola also did this to some extent in the late 1980s and early 1990s when it used technology that was initially developed for AMPS phones in the TACS and GSM phones. However, while Nokia has continued to move towards a more integrated development process, Motorola gradually moved towards a regional organization where phone development decisions became very regionally independent. Further, Motorola had always moved technology from the US AMPS development group to the European GSM development group and thus found it difficult to reverse this flow when Motorola needed digital phones for the US market.

As shown in Figure 5.9, Nokia has used its three main GSM 900 platforms (2110, 8110, and 6110) to develop phones for the GSM 1800MHz and 1900MHz, DAMPS 800MHz and 1900MHz, and to some extent PDC 800MHz markets. GSM 900 and 1800 are used primarily in Europe and Asia while the 1900MHz band is used for

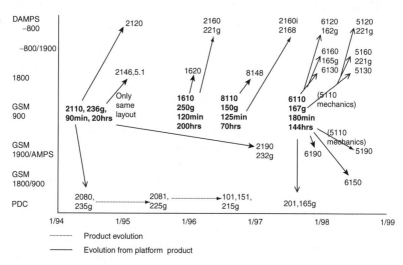

Figure 5.9   Evolution of Nokia's TDMA-based digital phone lines

Table 5.3   Percentage of common designs in Nokia's
digital phones by series (for different frequencies and standards)

Series	Architecture	BB	RF	Board layout	Mechanics	Software
2110	100	50	50	50	80	50
1610/8110	100	50	50	50	80	50
6110	100	50	50	50	100	50
5110	100	50	50	50	100	50

GSM in the US and South America. The US is the main market for DAMPS 800 and 1900MHz phones while Japan uses PDC. Naturally, Nokia's effective use of platforms in the GSM 900 market complements these global platforms. As discussed earlier, the 1610 is a derivative of the 8110 and both the 5110 and 8810 series are derivatives of the 6110.

Nokia's advantage gains in development efficiency from developing global platforms can be easily assessed using estimates on the percentage of product designs that are common within each series. Each firm provided information on the percentage of product designs that are common between different standards. As shown in Table 5.3, there are large amounts of commonality between standards for each of Nokia's product lines (this data only shows the percentage common among the GSM and DAMPS phones). Assuming that half of the non-common designs are unique for each phone, the number of equivalent projects needed to modify the GSM 900 platforms for the GSM 1800 and 1900, DAMPS 800 and 1900, and the PDC markets are shown in Table 5.4. For a total of 3.5 additional "equivalent" projects, Nokia was able to introduce seventeen new phones during these years.

Nokia also uses the GSM 900 platforms to develop cdmaOne phones. Although this is not shown in Figure 5.9, cdmaOne 2170 was developed from the 2110 GSM 900 platform and the cdmaOne 6100 was based on the GSM 900 6110. There is of course less commonality between the cdmaOne and GSM 900 phones than between the GSM, DAMPS, and PDC phones since the latter three standards are all based on TDMA technology. In general, the baseband designs are a function of the air interface standard while the RF designs are a function of the frequency band (for example, 800MHz). Nevertheless, there is still some level of commonality in all the design categories shown in Table 5.3 (at least half the figures shown in Table 5.4) with the greatest level of commonality in the mechanics.

Table 5.4   Amount of additional development resources
(units are equivalent development projects) needed to modify
Nokia's 900 platforms for the markets and phones shown in Figure 5.9

Series	Nokia	Motorola and the Japanese firms	Ericsson
2110	0.76	2.38	1.26
1610/8110	0.57	1.38	1.20
6110	1.31	2.66	1.75
5110	0.87	1.44	1.09
Total	3.51	7.86	5.30

Table 5.4 also contrasts Nokia's development numbers with those of
other firms. It estimates the amount of additional development resources (units are equivalent development projects) that would be
needed to modify Nokia's 900 platforms for the markets and phones
shown in Figure 5.9 if other firms attempted to do so.[58] Table 5.4 shows
that Motorola and the Japanese firms would have required almost twice
the level of development resources as Nokia to introduce the same
phones primarily since Motorola and the Japanese firms develop independent platforms for each standard and thus they use no common
designs *between* different standards. Since they do use some common
designs among the models within the same standard (for different
frequencies),[59] it is assumed that Motorola and the Japanese firms use
the same level of common designs as Nokia *within* the same standard
(for different frequencies). This probably underestimates Nokia's advantage since Ericsson and Motorola have not been able to implement
as effective a GSM 900 platform-method as the discussion of the GSM
market suggests that Nokia has for example, the 5110 is actually a
derivative of the 6110 whereas some of Nokia's competitors are not
developing derivative products from their platforms.

Ericsson fares slightly better in such a comparison as would be
expected by its stronger presence in the DAMPS market. It has used
its GSM 900 phones as a basis for developing DAMPS phones for
many years. Although there is almost no commonality between baseband chips, RF designs and board layouts, there is strong commonality in mechanics and to some extent in software. The interviews suggest
that if Ericsson were to have developed the same phones as Nokia, they
would have had the same commonality as Nokia in mechanics, three-
quarters the commonality in software, and half the commonality in
architecture. Using these estimates, Ericsson is about halfway between
Nokia and the other firms in terms of development efficiency.[60]

With this kind of difference in development efficiency, it is no wonder that Nokia was able to introduce many more new phones than Motorola, Ericsson and the Japanese firms in the US. For example, Nokia's 6100 and 5100 series were major hits in the second half of 1998 and the first half of 1999 respectively in the US. Their colors and features enabled Nokia to become the leading supplier of phones in the US and in the world in 1998 (see Table 1.2). Further, they enabled Nokia's sales to surge an additional 92% in the first quarter of 1999 while Ericsson's sales fell 12%. The new products and their trendy colors and features also enabled Nokia to get far better prices than Ericsson and Motorola while the larger amount of commonality reduced startup costs, which Ericsson claimed were very high. Meanwhile, in April 1999, one AT&T Wireless executive complained that Motorola had still not introduced a phone that is compatible with its latest technology.[61]

Nokia's use of common designs also enabled it to obtain greater economies of scale in purchasing components. An independent study carried out by a Japanese consulting firm found that Ericsson had 3% higher, Motorola had 13% higher, and Matsushita had 37% higher purchasing costs than Nokia. This is due to both Nokia's greater use of common designs and its procurement method, particularly with respect to Japanese components. Matsushita has the highest procurement costs since it buys primarily from other Matsushita companies who set very high internal prices. Ericsson and Motorola factories buy from local Japanese sales offices in Europe and the US; for Motorola, the decisions are made by each factory while for Ericsson, the decisions are made in a central European location (thus achieving some economies of scale).

Nokia buys many of its parts in Japan through its Nokia Japan office. Although individual factories buy standard parts on their own, Nokia Japan negotiates prices for semi-custom and strategic parts. The factories are only responsible for the shipment of these parts from a Japanese port to the factory. Nokia also asks for more detailed cost estimates than other firms do. For example, Nokia partly owns battery pack suppliers and uses this ownership to extract detailed cost estimates and negotiate lower prices on the parts within the modules (battery and control chips).

Why Nokia's global platform strategy is difficult to replicate

Firms in many industries have struggled to develop global platforms. The basic challenge is to integrate dispersed development centers or development groups that are within a single center. While one strategy is to centralize development in one location, this is becoming increasingly difficult as firms try to meet unique regional needs while they struggle to acquire sufficient development resources. The differences in needs and the understanding of these different needs require firms to create some level of development capability in key markets. This is certainly true in the cellular phone industry where Japanese firms failed in the US analog market because they failed to notice key changes in the US market. In the GSM market, Matsushita admits they underestimated the change from single-band to dual-band (both 900 and 1800) phones in the GSM market in 1999. And as is described in the next section, Nokia has had difficulties in the Japanese market because it took them so long to understand key differences between the Japanese and other markets.

A second reason why decentralization of development is becoming more important is the growing shortage of appropriate development resources in many industries. This is not just the case in cellular phones but in telecommunications in general, computing, and other high-technology industries. Firms must open development centers in various regions and countries in order to acquire the necessary engineers. This is a major reason why Nokia has handset development centers in Finland, England, the US, Denmark, and Germany.

Further, centralized development does not necessarily lead to the creation of global platforms. Nokia has the greatest amount of decentralization while Motorola has the least and they are at opposite sides of the spectrum in terms of using global platforms. The issue is more of process and communication. Nokia and to some extent Ericsson have created processes for identifying common technologies at the global level. The development plans for these common technologies are integrated with product development road maps that are also created at the global level. Other firms only have this process at the regional level. For example, Japanese firms do it within Japan while Motorola does it within each of their regional groups.

Communication between different organizations is necessary to identify common global technologies and designs. In particular, the large differences between different standards require a subtle understanding of these standards in order to identify potential common designs. Some firms, particularly the Japanese firms, have argued vigorously that it is impossible to develop baseband or radio frequency designs that have any form of commonality across standards. It is safe to say that within Japanese firms, there is basically not enough effective communication between the different regions to identify the commonality. This is unfortunate because the Japanese firms have developed the lightest phones in the world for their domestic market (discussed later) and they could potentially use these phones to enter and perhaps dominate the high end of the GSM phone market. They could then break through the entry barrier created by Nokia, Motorola, and Ericsson and potentially become leading producers of GSM phones.

Naturally, a common language is needed for effective communication. English is becoming the global language and it is the standard language within Nokia and Ericsson. All correspondence is written in English in these two companies as of course in the US companies. Other European firms such as Alcatel and Siemens have also come close to achieving this.

However, Japanese firms are still far behind in this area and this difference will continue for some time. Although the Japanese mobile phone businesses realize and admit that this is one of the major reasons for their inability effectively to integrate their US, European, and Japanese development centers, they have very little control over the basic English-language skills of Japanese citizens. For example, the scores of the Japanese in standard exams like TOEFEL are regularly lower than those in 90% of the Asian countries.

It will probably be very difficult for the Japanese firms and perhaps even Motorola and Ericsson to replicate Nokia's strategy. The problem is that process and communication are necessary to create the global platforms; and better process and communication will only be created when they realize they need and can benefit from global platforms. Motorola's digital stumble should have provided it with an incentive to create digital platforms. Instead, its concern for quickly releasing digital phones has prevented it from creating digital platforms. For the Japanese firms, the strategies they successfully used in the cellular phone and other industries in the 1980s and the unique aspects of their domestic market make it difficult for them to make significant changes.

For example, Mitsubishi is the Japanese firm which is most trapped by its existing strategy. In the early and mid-1990s, it was frequently said that Mitsubishi would have had the number one share in Japan if it had sufficient production capacity since it released very good phones. Mitsubishi's understanding of this problem and its desire to convince people that it was solving the problem led Mitsubishi to make frequent announcements about increased production capacity in both the domestic and foreign markets. Further, these announcements included forecasts of how the increased production capacity would lead to dramatically higher shares not only in the Japanese market but also in the GSM market where no one had argued that Mitsubishi's problem was a lack of production capacity. For example, such announcements were made in November 1994, August 1995, October 1996, and December 1996; the December announcement predicted Mitsubishi would be able to increase its share of the GSM market from the current 1% to 8%.[62] Needless to say its share of the GSM market in 1999 was still about 1%.

Beginning in 1997, Mitsubishi realized that it did not have enough phones on the market and began to make announcements about its increased number of development engineers. These increases and related announcements were first focused on the Japanese market but by mid-1998 it began to make similar announcements about the US and European markets. A major reason for these increases was that Mitsubishi (and other Japanese firms) were amazed by the number of phones that Nokia had released into the global market between 1996 and 1999[63] and Mitsubishi mistakenly believed that this was because Nokia merely used more engineers than other firms. Interestingly, Mitsubishi made these announcements while simultaneously implicitly admitting that production capacity was no longer important as it announced the sale of its US cellular phone factory in July 1998.[64]

Thus Mitsubishi was planning to increase the number of its engineers from 100 to 250 in the US and from 300 to 400 in Europe while increasing their number of GSM models from three to six. And similar to its previous announcements concerning increased production capacity, it believes that these additional engineers and phones will naturally lead to higher shares in the US, European, and world markets. It expected to increase its sales in the US and Europe from 7.5 million in fiscal 1999 to 12 million units in fiscal 2001. Mitsubishi had sales of 250 billion yen in cellular phones in fiscal 1998 and it expects 430 billion yen in sales in fiscal 2001. By 2003 it expects to achieve a 10% world share (up from a couple of percentage now) and it will increase the number of development personnel accordingly.[65]

However, it is clear that Mitsubishi does not believe that global platforms are an important part of its strategy. When asked why it does not develop global platforms or even use platforms to develop derivative products for the GSM market, it has no reply and politely says that it does not need to understand Nokia's method of platform management.

This confidence is also seen in their forecasts for Mitsubishi Electric in general. While the Western press wonders whether Mitsubishi can survive unless it quits money-losing businesses,[66] Mitsubishi claims that the recent improvement in DRAM (dynamic random access memory) prices will continue, thus leading to profitability in their DRAM business; that is, no changes are needed in this business. They have also announced in the Japanese press that increased sales and profits in their *overseas* cell phone businesses is the key to Mitsubishi's future and will be the way in which Mitsubishi Electric regains its profitability by 2001.[67]

THE JAPANESE MARKET

The Japanese market is the only major market in which committee-based competition and its relationship with market-based competition have been more important than pure market-based competition. There are two reasons for this. First, as discussed in Chapter 3, NTT DoCoMo has largely controlled the analog and digital standard-setting processes in Japan. This has enabled it to create a strong group of suppliers and maintain a large amount of control over them. Further, in some cases, the other service-providers have unintentionally strengthened DoCoMo's committee-based position by creating their own group of exclusive suppliers.

Second, the high activation commissions paid by the service-providers to retail outlets have prevented multiple price segments in the Japanese market from appearing. Japanese service-providers were paying retail outlets as much as 70,000 to 80,000 yen in early 1996[68] and about 30,000 to 40,000 yen in mid-2000 (there were 115 yen to the dollar at the end of 2000) to have retail outlets acquire subscribers. These high activation commissions caused the subsidized price to consumers of almost all handsets[69] to drop below 10,000 yen by early 1996 and by 1998 most phones were almost free. Further, the service-providers also began subsidizing *replacement* phones in 1998 in order to reduce cancellations and thus many replacement phones have also been obtainable for less than 10,000 yen since 1999. The result is that cost competition plays a much less important role than phone performance, which in Japan's case is phone weight and size.

Third, there is a large emphasis placed on weight and size in general in Japan. This and the high activation commissions have caused a single market segment to emerge where weight, size, and battery time are the key buying factors in the market-based competition. In fact, manufacturers with a large weight disadvantage (for example, 30% heavier) could not and still cannot give their phones away for *free* to the service-providers. This single market segment makes Nokia's GSM platform strategy inappropriate for the Japanese market and the importance of weight and size in the high activation commissions make it difficult for Nokia to modify its GSM phones for the Japanese market.

Committee- versus market-based competition in the analog market

As discussed in Chapter 3, NTT DoCoMo had a monopoly of the Japanese mobile phone market until 1989 when IDO and DDI Cellular (since merged into KDDI) introduced services based on two different standards. IDO adopted the NTT standard, which was controlled by NTT DoCoMo (then a division of NTT) and DDI Cellular adopted TACS, an open global standard. In this case, the market-based competition available in TACS handsets caused more TACS than NTT phones to appear in the market and this enabled DDI Cellular to do far better than IDO and even NTT DoCoMo. DoCoMo's share of the analog market was steadily falling and in the early 1990s it was expected to and did continue to decline for several years due to the DDI Cellular Group's superior technology and the entry of two new carriers. These (Tsuka Cellular and Digital Phone[70]) started digital services in Tokyo, Kansai, Kyushu, and Tokai in mid-1994. This additional competition caused NTT's cumulative share of subscribers to reach a minimum of 48% in March 1996.[71]

NTT's phone suppliers (Matsushita, NEC, Fujitsu, Mitsubishi) were also concerned with the success of the open TACS standard. Since they had been discouraged by NTT to sell TACS phones to the Cellular Group, the success of the Cellular Group meant that their shares were also dropping. Motorola, Oki Electric, Toshiba, Kyocera, and Sony were the major suppliers of TACS phones. In 1993, NTT's four phone suppliers only had 72% of the total phone market versus 85% in 1988 before the DDI Cellular Group and IDO started services.[72] Further, in early 1994 it was widely expected that the shares of the NTT suppliers would continue to drop due to both the liberalization of the phone market (the rental system was eliminated) in April 1994 and the entry of new carriers who were planning to buy phones from a number of suppliers.[73] In reality, their shares did drop to a level between 47% and 53% between 1994 and 1997.

NTT DoCoMo refines its committee-based strategy

As discussed in Chapter 3, NTT DoCoMo could have adopted an open standard like GSM and encouraged the creation of market-based competition in the Japanese digital phone market. It did not do this. It chose to refine its committee-based strategy in a way that has been very successful in the Japanese market. Although Japan's MPT required NTT to open its digital standard, PDC, for free to other service-providers, the standard initially contained far less documentation than open standards like GSM. This has enabled NTT DoCoMo to use its early development of PDC, initially by itself and subsequently in cooperation with key phone manufacturers, to create a strong committee-based advantage in PDC.

NTT DoCoMo's parent NTT developed PDC when DoCoMo was still a division within NTT. When NTT DoCoMo was spun off from NTT in 1992 (NTT is still NTT DoCoMo's largest investor), most of the engineers who had been developing PDC were sent to NTT DoCoMo. As of mid-1996, there were about 500 engineers in NTT DoCoMo of which the vast majority were responsible for the development of the PDC standard.

These engineers also worked closely with engineers at Matsushita, NEC, Mitsubishi, and Fujitsu to develop and implement the PDC standard both in phones and infrastructure. In particular, DoCoMo has provided these four phone suppliers with preferential information about the PDC standard in return for their delay in sales of PDC phones to other service-providers. An example of this kind of preferential information can be found in the early development of PDC. NEC was the primary supplier of base stations during 1992 and 1993 when NTT DoCoMo was building its PDC system. The sole participation by NEC and NTT DoCoMo in these tests meant that information was primarily shared among the DoCoMo suppliers.[74] This type of preferential information was considered essential to quickly solving various air interface problems when phones were first being developed for the PDC standard.

DoCoMo's four suppliers have continued to receive preferential information about the PDC standard through DoCoMo's monopoly on PDC development work and its domination of Japan's standard-setting body, the Association for Radio Industry Business (ARIB). Each time DoCoMo proposes an update to the PDC standard, NTT DoCoMo and its phone suppliers do not release the details of the changes until the revised standard has been officially accepted by the ARIB.

The access to this preferential information enables DoCoMo's four phone suppliers to obtain almost 100% of DoCoMo's phone market and puts the other service-providers at a distinct disadvantage with respect to DoCoMo.[75]

In return for this type of preferential information, Matsushita, NEC, Mitsubishi, and Fujitsu agreed to not sell phones to other service-providers until six months after they were made available to NTT DoCoMo. And when they do sell these phones to other service-providers, they must pay DoCoMo a licensing fee since DoCoMo technology is in the phones. This is because DoCoMo has used its early and continuous development of PDC and its market power to require the handset manufacturers to use its technology in the phones. For example, DoCoMo created the basic call functions for the phones using about seventy of the 500 engineers it had assigned to the PDC standard. DoCoMo requires its four phone suppliers to use this technology in their phones and charges them a licensing fee (about 3.5% of the sales) when they do sell the phones to other carriers. And the proceeds from the sale of these handsets to other carriers easily cover the cost of the seventy engineers that DoCoMo had assigned to the PDC handsets.

DoCoMo's four phone suppliers develop lighter phones

DoCoMo's four phone suppliers used their committee-based advantages in PDC in the form of preferential access to information about the PDC standard to develop lighter phones than the other phone suppliers. They did this in two ways. First, they used the preferential information to make better design tradeoffs between parts with respect to weight, size, and battery time.

Second, they used the preferential information to obtain more co-operation from parts suppliers than the other phone suppliers. In the early years of PDC, development cooperation between phone and parts manufacturers was important due to the low volumes, undefined PDC standard, and thus lack of standard parts. These development projects contained non-disclosure agreements where the part suppliers agreed not to disclose the contents of the development project or sell the developed component to other phone suppliers for a given time period – it was typically six months in the mid-1990s.[76] The preferential information that the DoCoMo suppliers obtained from DoCoMo enabled them to obtain more cooperation from these part suppliers.

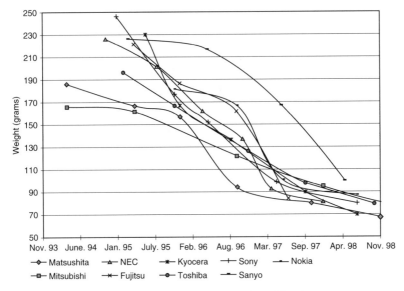

Figure 5.10   Weights (grams) of Japanese digital mobile phones

This greater cooperation and better design tradeoffs enabled them to develop lighter phones than the other phone manufacturers in the early years of the PDC market. As shown in Figure 5.10, two DoCoMo suppliers, Matsushita and Mitsubishi, offered far lighter phones than the other manufacturers and their advantages had largely disappeared by late 1998. This change in the weight advantages of the DoCoMo suppliers appears even larger when one considers that the DoCoMo suppliers were slow to release phones that contained lithium ion batteries. Matsushita, NEC, and Fujitsu were the last three major manufacturers to release phones in the Japanese market (in 1996) that contained lithium ion batteries. Other firms such as Kyocera, Toshiba, Kenwood, and Sony released phones that contained lithium ion batteries in some cases more than two years before Matsushita did. Matsushita and to a lesser extent NEC were late adopters primarily due to their concerns about the higher cost of lithium ion batteries and in particular whether their adoption of the lithium ion battery might cause prices to rise dramatically.[77]

The late adoption of the lithium ion battery by Matsushita, NEC and to a lesser extent Fujitsu concealed their true design advantages in non-battery parts of the phone in 1994 and 1995 and the fact that these

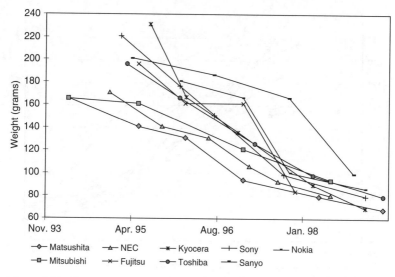

Figure 5.11   "Imputed" weight of Japanese digital mobile phones

advantages have slowly declined since 1995. Further, NEC's emphasis
on folding phones, which are fundamentally heavier than regular
phones, also concealed its true design advantage. The change in the
true design capability of the DoCoMo suppliers can be estimated by
subtracting between 20 and 30 grams from all phones that did not
contain lithium ion batteries and between 30 and 40 grams from
folding phones.[78] This assumes that all of the firms adopted a lithium
ion battery at the same time and that they all produced regular, non-
folding phones.

Figure 5.11 shows how the DoCoMo suppliers' imputed weight
advantage has dropped considerably since between 1994 and 1998.
First, Matsushita and NEC had far lighter phones than the non-
DoCoMo suppliers did until the end of 1997 while Mitsubishi's phones
were also much lighter than the non-DoCoMo suppliers' were until the
end of 1996. Second, Fujitsu's phones were for the most part in the top
five through 1997.[79] Third, the difference between the heaviest and
lightest phones of the eight leading suppliers dropped from 68% in
April, 1995 to 25% by late 1998.

The results of DoCoMo's committee-based strategy

NTT DoCoMo's advantage in handsets caused its share and the shares of its phone suppliers to rise dramatically beginning in late 1996. This occurred for two reasons. First, the other service-providers reduced their activation commissions in 1996 in response to their rising cancellation rates.[80] Although the higher cancellation rates of the non-DoCoMo carriers were also partly due to their weaker coverage than DoCoMo, another reason was the superior handsets from DoCoMo.[81] The other service-providers found that they were not able to retain their subscribers long enough to justify the high activation commissions.

The second reason is the introduction of the first sub-100 gram phone in October 1996 by Matsushita. Although Matsushita had always produced lighter phones than the other manufacturers, its use of the lithium ion battery enabled it to release a phone that was more than 40 grams smaller than the smallest non-DoCoMo phone. Subsequently, NEC and Fujitsu also used lithium ion batteries and thus were able to release even smaller phones in the summer of 1997 followed by Matsushita's second sub-100 gram phone in October 1997.

The lower activation commissions and sub-100 gram phones caused DoCoMo's share of new subscribers to rise dramatically following the introduction of Matsushita's first sub-100 gram phone. On a monthly basis, DoCoMo's share of new subscribers rose from 48% in August 1996 to over 60% in October and it stayed over 60% throughout 1997 and most of 1998.[82] Matsushita, NEC, and Fujitsu also benefited from their early release of sub-100 gram phones. As shown in Figure 5.12, Matsushita's share rose from 20% to 29% between 1995 and 1997; and NEC's share rose from 11% to 15%, and Fujitsu's share rose from 7% to 12% between 1996 and 1997.

This total domination of the market by DoCoMo and its four phone suppliers caused the Cellular Group and IDO to decide in the spring of 1997 to start services based on cdmaOne. This system would be the third and fourth cellular system for the Cellular Group and IDO respectively. These two service-providers believed that they could not compete with DoCoMo due to its superior committee-based capabilities and the resulting lighter phones. The Cellular Group started cdmaOne services in the Kansai and Kyushu regions in July 1997 and the Cellular Group and IDO achieved a nationwide service in April 1998. Ironically, Kyocera released the smallest PDC phone in July 1997 just as its subsidiary Kansai Cellular started cdmaOne services.

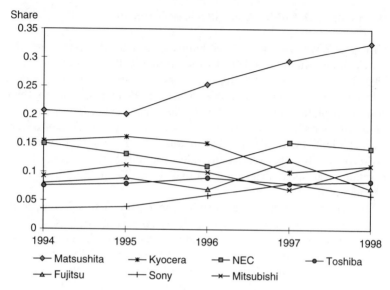

Figure 5.12   Market shares for cellular phones in Japan

In other words, just as it was starting services based on cdmaOne, the original reason for starting these services disappeared.

Nevertheless, the strong brand image created by NTT DoCoMo has enabled it to continue its domination of the Japanese cellular phone market. In spite of the disappearance of its weight advantage, it continued to obtain more than 50% of the new subscribers in 1998 and 1999. Interestingly, the Digital Phone Group (also called J-Phone) was also acquiring a larger percentageage of the new subscribers than the Cellular Group in 1998 and 1999 due to its popular message service and advertisements that emphasize voice quality.[83]

Market-based competition becomes stronger

As discussed above, the weight gap between DoCoMo and the non-DoCoMo phones had largely disappeared by the end of 1998. The reason for the disappearance in the weight advantages of the DoCoMo suppliers is that the competition changed from committee- to market-based competition. This occurred in three ways. First, the non-DoCoMo phone suppliers began copying the phone designs used by the DoCoMo suppliers as soon as they noticed the large weight differences. In particular, Matsushita's design became the dominant design at most levels in the phone design and other phone suppliers were forced to copy its design in order to obtain access to the best parts.[84] At the same time, discrete component suppliers who were not supplying DoCoMo suppliers were forced to make their parts match the DoCoMo "dominant design" in order to sell components.

Second, information about the PDC standard diffused throughout the market thus eliminating the information advantages initially held by the DoCoMo suppliers. This combined with the emergence of the DoCoMo dominant design caused the performance differences between phone and between discrete component suppliers to become smaller.

Third, phone production volumes grew dramatically. The production of phones increased from about 3 million in 1994 to more than 20 million in 1998. For digital phones, the percentageage increase is even larger. In 1994, about 35% of the phones were digital phones while in 1998 more than 90% of the phones were digital phones. Thus, there was about a 20–fold increase in the production of digital phones between 1994 and 1998.

These changes in production volumes caused the market for discrete components to change from a low-volume and high-variety market to a high-volume and low-variety market. Whereas in 1994 most parts were produced on special production lines, by 1997 the discrete component suppliers wanted to produce all parts on the same high-volume production line which dramatically increased the price differential between the standard high-volume and custom low-volume parts. Further, when phone suppliers still demanded custom-developed parts, they were willing to accept a shorter delay (from six to three months) in selling parts to other phone suppliers in order to receive price discounts in the parts. The result was that by 1997 most phone suppliers were using the same parts, which caused the weight differences between phone suppliers to disappear.[85] Further, as the information differences narrowed between the various parts suppliers, their weight differences also narrowed.[86]

Committee-based competition and foreign manufacturers

Japan's committee-based competition and the related weight competition have also made it difficult for foreign manufacturers like Ericsson, Motorola, and Nokia to compete in Japan. None of these firms worked with DoCoMo on the development of PDC phones and none of them has been able to become a preferential supplier to DoCoMo like Matsushita, NEC, Mitsubishi, and Fujitsu.

Further, all of them took a long time to recognize the importance of weight and size and develop an appropriate product line strategy. Ericsson did not release a phone for the Japanese market until early 1999 and it did not break the sub-100 gram barrier until late 1999. Motorola has never released a sub-100 gram phone for the PDC market and it has squandered its early advantages in the Japanese TACS market. In spite of receiving help from the US government to sell its TACS infrastructure in Japan, it has never made a strong effort in the TACS phone market. It never released as many TACS phones in Japan as in other countries due to the small Japanese market (at least until 1995), the large number of strong domestic firms, and slight differences in the Japanese and European TACS standards. This caused its share of the Japanese analog phone market to drop from 45% in 1990 to below 20% in fiscal 1994 and below 10% in fiscal 1995.

As described earlier, Nokia has released a number of phones for the Japanese market that are based on its GSM 900 platforms. This enabled its phones to be far cheaper than the phones produced by the Japanese manufacturers. Nokia spent years trying to convince many service-providers to create a new business model that would enable Nokia to utilize this cost advantage. Nokia argued that it would supply cheaper phones that would enable the service-providers to substantially reduce their activation commissions and still provide inexpensive phones to the users. Since a significant fraction of the costs for the service-providers are activation commissions, the service-providers could have used these lower activation commissions to reduce their monthly and air time charges and thus create a new business model. Unfortunately for Nokia, the Japanese service-providers believed that Japanese consumers would value weight and size more than cost.

This is why Nokia did not release a sub-100 gram phone until mid-1998, about twenty months after Matsushita released its first sub-100 gram phone. Although this and subsequent PDC phones are still based on the GSM 900 platform, it has developed special mechanics for the Japanese market in order to create a very light phone, albeit a phone that is still about 20% heavier than its major Japanese competitors. However, Nokia's biggest problem as of mid-2000 is the same problem that all Japanese manufacturers except Matsushita, NEC, Mitsubishi, and Fujitsu have: they are not a major supplier to NTT DoCoMo and thus are not privy to the same information as these four suppliers are.

Market-based competition in Japan's PHS phone market

As mentioned earlier, Japan is the only major mobile phone market in which committee-based competition has played a larger role than market-based competition. Some people might argue that this is a characteristic unique to Japan. However, other proprietary standards have exhibited this type of committee-based competition and more interestingly, committee-based competition did not play a strong role in another Japanese mobile phone standard, PHS.

Because there are many similar attributes of the PHS and PDC markets, it would be expected that committee-based competition would also play a major role in the PHS phone market. PHS is also a Japanese standard, services were started shortly after services based on PDC were started, many suppliers collaborate closely with a single service provider, NTT carried out the original development work on the standard, one of the PHS service-providers was created by NTT and NTT DoCoMo (and now owned by NTT DoCoMo), and DoCoMo's handset suppliers also delay the sale of their PHS phones to the other two service-providers. The only difference in term of manufacturers is that NTT replaced Fujitsu with a much stronger consumer electronics producer, Sharp. Thus, one would expect that NTT Personal (now a wholly owned subsidiary of NTT DoCoMo) and its suppliers would have been able to dominate the PHS market through committee-based competition.

However, the critical difference between PHS and PDC is that Japan's MPT and the manufacturers were responsible for the creation of and modifications to the PHS standard. The MPT opened the standard to all interested Japanese firms in 1993 (it was not opened to foreign firms until early 1996) and no one firm controls the stand-ard-setting process. Further, many firms pushed for a well-defined standard in order to reduce phone and part costs.[87]

The result of this more open standard is that NTT Personal's four suppliers were not able to create a large initial weight advantage in PHS phones as they were able to do in PDC phones. Sharp was able to develop the first sub-100 gram phone by convincing part suppliers to develop very light and small discrete components for it; Sharp argued that it would place a great deal of emphasis on PHS and thus war-ranted the preferential cooperation. However, its temporary advantage (and temporary high market share) quickly disappeared as all of the PHS phone suppliers began focusing on the development of small and light phones and similar discrete components became available from all of the part suppliers. By mid-1996, the smallest phones were available from Toshiba and Sanyo. By 1998, Matsushita's and Sharp's phones were the only phones produced by an NTT Personal supplier that were in the top eight lightest phones. As the DoCoMo suppliers had originally worried when the PDC standard was being created, new firms like Sanyo, Denso, Kenwood, and Casio have become major suppliers of PHS handsets. The main four NTT Personal suppliers had less than 25% of the PHS handset market in 1997 and the largest share was held by Sharp. Sharp was not one of DoCoMo's four PDC phone suppliers and it was actually one of the suppliers whom Matsushita, Mitsubishi, NEC, and Fujitsu were worried about when they were creating their strategy for PDC with NTT DoCoMo in the early 1990s.

Finally, NTT Personal has also not done well in PHS. It had 23% of the subscribers as compared to 60% for DDI Pocket and 17% for Astel as of early 2000. DDI Pocket is primarily owned by DDI (the major investor in the Cellular Group) while power companies and Japan Telecom are the primary investors in Astel. DDI Pocket has succeeded through its introduction of a larger base station than the other two carriers, which enabled it to expand coverage faster than the other two carriers. The success of DDI in long-distance, the Cellular Group in analog cellular, and DDI Pocket in PHS shows how many of Japan's traditional companies such as NTT-related companies cannot compete with new companies in an unregulated environment unless they maintain some form of control over the standard-setting processes or the regulatory agencies. NTT's high local phone charges are also holding back Japan; they are a major reason why Japan still has much lower Internet usage than the US, Great Britain, or Scandinavia.

SUMMARY AND DISCUSSION

This chapter describes the role of committee-and market-based competition in the mobile phone market. Committee-based competition played a strong role during the early years of most standards. Some firms were unable to compete due to their lack of participation in a standard-setting process while others obtained initially high shares through their strength in committee-based competition. Within the major markets, only in the Japanese market did committee-based competition play a long-term role and even here, brand image was playing a larger role than committee-based competition in 1998 and 1999.

Market-based competition has played a much more important role than committee-based competition in the global mobile phone competition due to the high levels of openness in the key standards and the relative simplicity of the product, at least as compared to mobile infrastructure. Market-based competition determined the winners in the global standards AMPS and GSM and even in other standards such as NMT, DAMPS, and cdmaOne.

In this market competition, product line and platform management has been the critical method of competition. The evolution of the successful strategies over time in the mobile phone industry suggests that volumes, costs, and the diversity of user needs impact on the appropriate product line and platform management strategy. When volumes and costs are not changing rapidly, competition often focuses on quality, cost, and performance. This is how, in the 1980s, the Japanese firms dominated the US AMPS market while Motorola, Nokia, and Ericsson dominated the NMT markets.

However, when markets change from a business to personal market, there is often a synergistic effect between rising volumes and falling prices. The general literature on technology management describes this phenomenon primarily in terms of the emergence of a dominant design or standard, their effect on costs, and a change in competition from performance to price. This chapter finds that a more complex phenomenon exists.

This chapter finds that the length of the transition period (from a business to personal market), the relative importance of volume-sensitive parts to phone cost and weight, the amount of activation commissions, and the diversity of users, needs are key variables that impact on the appropriate product line and platform strategy. When the transition from a business to a personal market takes place over a number of years (about five years in the US) and volume-sensitive parts represent a large percentageage of phone costs, the winner is often the firm who can turn the volume wheel the fastest. This was how Motorola came to dominate the AMPS and to some extent the NMT markets. It gave volume discounts to increase volumes and thus received volume discounts from suppliers. This was particularly effective since volume-sensitive parts such as semiconductor devices represented a large percentageage of the product cost.

In GSM, the transition from a business to a personal market happened so quickly that the market had evolved into a second stage of multiple segments before one firm could win the volume discount battle. Further, the key drivers of cost and performance had changed from very volume-sensitive parts such as semiconductors to less volume-sensitive parts such as mechanical parts. Both of these factors meant that Motorola's volume discount strategy was much less effective in the GSM than in the AMPS markets.

Rising volumes and falling phone prices (for the manufacturers) also had a different effect in the Japanese market on the appropriate product line and platform strategy. Here, the transition from a business to a personal market also happened quickly. However, the high activation commissions coupled with the low diversity of user needs caused a one-segment market to appear where weight and size determined the market winners. Through their committee-based strength, NTT DoCoMo and its four suppliers were able to produce the lightest phones until the rising volumes caused market-based competition to emerge.

Without the high activation commissions and low diversity of user needs, the Japanese market would probably have evolved in different ways. For example, without the high activation commissions, multiple segments would probably have appeared as they did in the AMPS and GSM markets. And if this was coupled with a low diversity in customer needs, the Japanese market may have resembled the US AMPS market where price was primarily related to weight. On the other hand, if there were low activation commissions and a higher diversity of customer needs, the Japanese market may have resembled the GSM market with its emphasis on multiple segments.

The multiple-price-segment GSM market is probably typical of the emerging network economy where there are high fixed and low marginal costs. The spread of these high fixed and rapidly declining marginal costs from the service side to the manufacturing side of the network economy is changing the way manufacturers carry out product line/platform management. The platform products used by Motorola, Ericsson and Nokia to develop derivative products represent the high fixed costs of the network economy. These high fixed costs of course require large volumes and thus these three firms subsidize the low-end phones in order to obtain high volumes. Further, these high fixed costs and their required high volumes represent a barrier to entry for other firms.

These three firms, particularly Nokia, make money at the high end of the market by creating a strong brand image. Nokia has created a stronger brand image than the other firms by focusing on aesthetic design, user interfaces, and software features. Its success in these areas enables it to set prices that are based more on customer value than on cost.

Global platforms represent the ultimate platform strategy and as most industries globalize, this strategy will become even more prevalent and important to success. Global platforms enable firms to create global economies of scale in development, manufacturing, and purchasing. Firms with this global development capability can change the competition from competition within a single standard, including its relevant committees and markets, to competition at the global level. However, global platforms raise the level of technical and in particular organizational complexity. Development processes for both technologies and products must be globalized and effective communication is needed to support global development.

Nokia's failure in the Japanese market illuminates some of these challenges. Nokia was able to succeed in the GSM and DAMPS markets but not in the PDC market in spite of similarities in the underlying technology (PDC) for these standards. But it was critical differences in both committee-and market-based competition that caused Nokia's strategy to fail in Japan. The different relationships with service-providers, the high activation commissions, and the resulting high emphasis on weight and size required Nokia to develop different phones for the Japanese market than for the other markets. Although theoretically this can be done using global platforms, the identification of commonalities and differences between Japan and the other markets requires better processes and communication than Nokia had in early 2001.

Notes

1. Only 132,000 and 234,000 phones were sold in 1984 and 1985 respectively. Herschel Shosteck Associates, *The Retail Market of Cellular Telephones*, June, 1997, Figure 7.2.
2. Motorola also angered the distributors by selling both through carrier-approved dealers (name or logo goes on the phone) and through its own sales force (*Fortune*, 20/1/1986. A Phone war that jolted Motorola, pp. 43+: Motorola has small share of market).
3. Toshiba signed an exclusive US distribution deal with Audiovox, which was a distributor of car accessories including stereos for Toshiba and other firms (*Forbes*, 11/7/1988: Trouble on the Line).
4. *Wall Street Journal*, 11/5/1984, Tandy to make and sell cellular phones under agreements with three concerns, p. 13.
5. For example, it signed agreements with SW Bell Mobile Systems and Metroplex Telephones in late 1984. *Business Week* 12/10/1984, Tandy sets accords on cellular phones with two concerns).
6. *Wall Street Journal*, 7/2/1985, Tandy will provide cellular phone gear to 4 more companies. (*Wall Street Journal*, 8/12/1988, Tandy corp. fights hard to shake radio shack image, p. b4)

198   *Global Competition Between and Within Standards*

7. The wholesale price of a standard phone fell from about $1700 early in
    1984 to about $1300 six months later while the retail price fell from
    $3000 to $2500. *Fortune*, 20/1/1986. A Phone war that jolted Motorola,
    pp. 43+: Motorola has small share of market. (*Nikkei*, 28/10/1985,
    Genchi seisan ni isso hakusha, beishomusho ga jidosha denwa de nihon-
    sei danpingu seishiki. The US government's dumping charges against car
    telephone manufacturers is leading to greater local production.)
8. *Nikkei*, 6/7/85, Jidousha Dennwa mehkah Taibei senryaku neri-
    naoshimo-Danpingu "Kuro" Karikettei. Car telephone manufacturers
    urge the US to reconsider their implementation of dumping charges.
9. Oki Electric began assembling phones in the US in 1984 and gradually
    increased its procurement of parts from North American sources. The
    Matsushita Group established America Matsushita Communications
    Industries and America Matsushita Electronic Parts and it began
    making phones in Illinois and parts in Tennessee in April 1985. (*Nikkei
    Industrial*, 16/4/1985, Matsushita Guruhpu beikokuni 2genchihohjin
    setsuritsu-Jidohshadenwa shea kakudai nerau. Matsushita group estab-
    lished two local manufacturing facilities – it is aiming for a higher share
    of the car telephone market.) Mitsubishi also began making car phones
    in its Georgia factory in 1985. (*Nikkei Industrial*, 20/12/1985, Mitsubishi-
    denki Bei Giorgia no shinkohjoh kensetsu ni chakushu. Mitsubishi
    Electric started constructing a new factory in Georgia in US.) NEC
    expected to start production in North America. While Uniden planned
    to begin making cell phones in Taiwan to sell in North America, both in
    1986. *Nikkei Industrial*, 15/5/1986, Yuniden Jidoshadenwa ni sannyu
    taiwan de seisan beikoku yushutsu atarashii hashirani ikusei. Yuniden
    is entering the car telephone market – it will manufacture them in
    Taiwan and export them to the US.
10. Matsushita closed its Chicago plant and opened a factory in Atlanta in
    1988 to increase its production capacity of car phones. By 1989 it was
    producing 20,000 phones a month with a 30%–40% increase planned in
    1990. *Nikkei Industrial*, 7/12/1989, Jidosha-keitaibei de zousan, OEM
    awse shea 8wari he – tsushinki mehka – ooze. The leading (Japanese)
    communication equipment producers have increased car and portable
    phone production – they have almost an 80% share of the US market.
    NEC's US subsidiary opened a factory in Hillsborough, Oregon, to
    produce car phones and other products in 1988. *Nikkei Industrial*, 23/
    4/1988. NEC Oregon koujou kikoushiki. NEC opens a factory in
    Oregon and in May 1990 it established a car phone factory in Mexico.
    The phones produced in its Mexican factory were sold in Mexico, the
    US, Canada, and South and Central America. *Nikkei Industrial*, 19/12/
    1989, Nichiden mekishiko de jidohsha denwa wo seisan. Nichiden pro-
    duces car phones in Mexico. Mitsubishi completed its second production
    line in its Georgia factory in 1988. It planned to make 10,000 phones a
    month. *Nikkei Industrial*, 26/1/1988, Bei no jidosha yoh denwaki Mitu-
    bishiden gessan 1man dai ni – Dai 2ji kohjoh zousetsu wo kentoh.
    Mitsubishi Electric's car phone production monthly output reaches
    10,000 – it is considering the construction of a second factory. Oki
    Electric continued to increase its production capacity in its Georgia

factory. It produced 150,000 phones in its Atlanta factory in 1989 and it expected to double that by 1991. *Nikkei Industrial*, 25/1/1990, Atlanta ga kawaru Nihon kigyoh Rasshu (Shita) Kininaru rohmu – "Shinshutu shisugi" no koe. Japanese companies will (or will not) change Atlanta, concern over labor issues – the voice of too much. Toshiba and Fujitsu started producing phone in the US in 1989 and 1990 respectively. Toshiba produced 7–8 types of car phones in volumes of 10–12,000 phones a month in its Irvine, CA factory in 1989. *Nikkei Industrial*, 21/1/1989, Toshiba Bei muke jidohsha denwaki – Genchi seisan wo kaishi. Toshiba car telephones for the US market – it has started local manufacturing there. Fujitsu started producing phones in its Texas factory in October 1990 with a planned capacity of 100,000 phones per year *Nikkei Industrial*, 9/11/1990, Fujitsu amerika, bei de kogata keitai denwa hanbai – sekai saikeiryo no kishu. Fujitsu America has introduced the smallest phone in the world in America.

11. Abernathy and Utterback, 1978; Abernathy and Clark, 1985; Anderson and Tushman, 1990, Tushman and Anderson, 1986; Utterback, 1994.
12. Service providers pay retail outlets a specified amount of money to have the retail outlets sign up subscribers.
13. *Wall Street Journal* 5/14/1990, p. b1, Cellular marketing sees an edge through special offers and spying.
14. Herschel Shosteck Associates, *Data Flash Cellular Brand Sales*, Quarterly Survey, June 1996. Figures 7.2, 9.3, 12.3, 13.4, and 14.4.
15. Janet Farr, The Portable Jungle, *Cellular Business*, June 1993, pp. 24–58.
16. Meurling and Jeans, 1997.
17. Storno had 9.3%, Esselte had 3.8% and Talkline had 1.5% (Hulten and Molleryd, 1995).
18. *Financial Timer* 31/12/1991, p. 7. Importance of making the right connections, Barbara Benson
19. *Cellular Business*, 3/92, p. 70, New products: global portable phone.
20. Japanese firms did not begin abandoning their internal procurement policies until the volumes began to rise in their own market in 1994.
21. Hideki, Yoshihara, "Global Operations Managed by Japanese and in Japanese," *KobeUniversity, Research Institute for Economics and Business*, December 1999.
22. Motorola accused NEC, Matsushita, Mitsubishi, JRC, and Kokusai Electric of dumping TACS-based phones in UK and Ireland in September 1987. *Nikkei Industiral*, 4/9/1987, Nihondenki jidohsha denwaki hatu no ohshu seisan – raika medoni ei de yushutu kankyo akka ni taiou. NEC will produce by the summer car phones for the first time in Europe – it is responding to the worsening exporting environment.
23. The differences in competitiveness between the "global" and "domestic" Japanese firms are well summarized in "Two Japans: The gulf between corporate winners and losers is growing", *Business Week*, 27/1/1997, p. 35.
24. Mitsubishi had planned to begin selling GSM-based phones beginning in 1993 but was unable to come to terms with Motorola on patent negotiations. Matsushita began selling phones in 1993 but it only sold a few also due to patent negotiation problems. The risk of high royalties was

large so only a few phones were made. *Nikkei Industrial*, 13/9/1994, Dejitaru keitai denwa nihonzei ohshu sanyu ni deokure – tokkyo ru-ru ni bei motorohra nado hannpatsu. Japanese digital phone manufacturers had a late start in the European market – US Motorola and others against the patent rules.

25. For example, the Swiss producer Ascom had very little telecommunication experience outside Switzerland and thus was ill-prepared for the international GSM market. It has never made money in GSM phones and it quickly become a supplier of OEM phones *Handelsblatt*, 5/6/1993. Similarly, Hagenuk, a Danish producer for the German market believed it could survive as a small producer for Deutsche Telekom *Handelsblatt*, 5/6/1993, Ascom/Mit Ergebnisschätzung daneben getroffen, p. 16. *Handelsblatt*, 26/3/1992, Hagenuk/Umsatzsprung auf über 700 Mill. DM erwartet.)

26. Sony began developing and producing phones with Siemens in 1995 (3/1/1995), but found that it could not handle the price competition with Nokia so in late 1998 it decided to focus on high-end phones (12/11/1998, *Nikkei*, Sony Ohshu muke keitai denwa kohkinoh jisha kaihatuki shuryoku ni – kakaku kyousoh wo kaih. Sony develops high functional mobile phone for the European market to avoid price competition.)

27. J.J. Keller, *Wall Street Journal*, Lucent, Philips will Combine Phone-Production Operations: Dutch Electronics Concern to Control 60% of Phone Unit, 18/6/1997.

28. Martin Du Bois, Stephanie Mehta, and Gautam Naik, *Wall Street Journal*, 16/10/1998, "Philips, Lucent Prepare to End Their Struggling Joint Venture."

29. Martin Du Bois and Rebecca Blumenstein, *Wall Street Journal*, 16/10/1998, "Philips Electronics, Lucent will End Loss-Making Mobile-Phone Venture."

30. Firms agreed that the breakdown of development costs in 1994 was 15% for architectural, 15% for base band, 15% for radio frequency, 10% for board layout, 15% for mechanical, and 30% for software. Overall development costs had increased by 20% in 1997 of which software represented 40% and the contribution of architectural, base band, radio frequency, and board layout design down to 45%. Using estimates from firms on the degree of newness in each phone for each of these design categories, the number of "standard" development projects were estimated. Since it was difficult to identify differences in software platform management methods, software costs were assumed to be the same for each firm. It was assumed that each platform project required the full software contribution and the derivative projects required no software development.

31. Nokia used derivative projects and the 2110 platform to create both the 2110i for the middle part of the market and the 2010 for the low end of the market. Through the use of new mechanics and some new discrete components, the talk-time and standby time of the 2110 was extended for the 2110i and the cost was significantly reduced for the 2010.

32. *Financial Timer*, 31/12/1991, p. 7. Importance of making the right connections, Barbara Benson.

33. *Forbes*, 7/6/98. Mobile Mayhem by Richard Morais.
34. *Financial Timer*, 30/1/1998: Ericsson chooses surprise successor to Lars Ramqvist. P19.
35. These problems were exacerbated by reports that at least 20% of its GF788 and GH688 mobile-phone models were faulty (1/10/1998: Ericsson Unveils Overhaul, but Move May Do Little to Solve Its Problems By Almar Latour , Staff Reporter of *Wall Street Journal*.
36. Total Telecom, Ericsson Chairman Says Profit May Lag Forecast, By Linda Andersson at *Bloomberg News* 18/12/1998.
37. Search News Ericsson Warns First Quarter Profit Slipping, By Linda Andersson at *Bloomberg News*, 24/3/1999.
38. *Yahoo news*, 8/7/1999, Ericsson CEO Sacked Under Pressure-Papers, by Belinda Goldsmith, Stockholm Reuters.
39. 3/12/1991 ericsson press release.
40. 8/1/1992 ericcson press release.
41. In particular, it benefited from its shipment of entry-level phones for AT&T's low-priced nationwide digital cellular service that was very successful in 1996. Nokia was less successful since it emphasized mid-level handsets in 1996 *Twice*, 11/10/97, vol. 12, no. 26, p. 47. *Wall Street Journal* 25/2/1997 p. B6; Quentin, Hardy
42. "Motorola's Cell Phones On Hook By Andrew Zajac, *Chicago Tribune*, 21/7/1998, New York.
43. *Nikkei Industrial*, 18/6/1998, Bei VLSI tekunoroji-shinhoshiki keitai denwa no kinou, 1 chippu ni tosai – nihonmuke tounyu. The US firm VLSI technologies will introduce a chip for the new mobile phone system in Japan.
44. 27/5/1999, Motorola Wins Contract to Supply Bell Atlantic Unit With Headsets, by Quentin Hardy, *Wall Street Journal*.
45. cdmaOne phones represented 47% of digital phone sales in the second quarter of 1999 in the US versus 38% for DAMPS phones.
46. *Washington Post* Data Basics Digital Becoming Dominant, 4/11/1999; Page E06 , Digital wireless telephones continue to gain a greater share of the U.S. mobile market.
47. Throughout 1998, it only sold big clunky 2170 cdmaOne phone that contained old technology 10/11/1998, by Jennifer Files, *Dallas Morning News*. Service plan matters more than phone.
48. *Nikkei Industrial*, 26/6/1999, Ohbei no keitaidenwa jigyoh Sony tekoire – rainendono kurojika wo mezasu. Sony strengthens its mobile phone business in Europe – It is aiming to be profitable next year.
49. *Nikkei Industrial*, 8/7/1999, Sony Hokubei no keitai denwa tettai – jisedai houshiki kaihatuni shuhchuh. Sony withdraws from the North American mobile phone business – it will concentrate on next generation phones. Technology News, Mon, 11/10/1999, Qualcomm Says It's in Talks to Sell Phone-Making Business, to Cut Costs, By Erik Schatzker. Nikkei, 1/2/2000, *Bloomberg.com*. Technology News, 5/1/2000, Kyocera of Japan to Buy Qualcomm's Phone-Making Unit.
50. Motorola Rolls Itself Over: After a Bad Year, Almost Everything Is Coming Up Rosy, and Wireless, by David Barboza. *New York Times*, 19/7/1999.

51. *Business Week* "How Motorola lost its way". 4/5/1998
52. Crain's Chicago Business 25/11/1996 vol. 19, no. 48, p. 1; Joseph
     B. Cahill.
53. See n. 5.
54. 12/4/96, *Wall Street Journal*, Will Miniature Phones Ring Up Bigger
     Sales? By Quentin Hardy, p. b1. Mobile Computing & Communications
     (1/97) Vol. 8, No. 1, P. 27; Steven J. Handler.
55. Motorola Solves Inventory Woes; Profits Up 31% Earnings: Second
     quarter... *Los Angeles Times*, 12/7/1995, Motorola, Citing Swollen In-
     ventory Of Cellular Phones, Sees Damage to Net, *Wall Street Journal*,
     21/2/1995.
56. *Technology News*, 8/9/1999, Motorola to Hire 2,000 Workers for Digital
     Phone Unit to Meet Demand, by Andy Brooks.
57. "Consumer Phone Deal Seen Positive for Motorola, Lucent," *Dow
     Jones News Service*, 21/12/1998.
58. Naturally, Motorola and the other firms would not attempt to modify
     Nokia's 900 phones for the other markets. However, not only have
     Motorola and the Japanese firms not developed phones for all of the
     standards, for comparison purposes, it is more interesting to estimate
     how much commonality other firms would have if they developed the
     same phones as Nokia.
59. For example, Motorola and the Japanese firms use some common
     designs in their GSM 900, 1800, and 1900 phones.
60. Of course, the development problems that Ericsson had in the GSM 900
     market in late 1998 and early 1999 had a strong effect on Ericsson's use
     of global platforms and the DAMPS market and may have eliminated
     any benefits from its partial use of global platforms.
61. Total Telecom, Nokia's Advantage Over Ericsson Grows as Competition
     Heats Up by, Jonas Dromberg, *Bloomberg News*, 22/4/1999. 4/12/
     1998, *Wall Street Journal*, Digital Now Beats Analog In Sale of
     Cellular Phones, Scott Thurm, *Wall Street Journal*. Nokia latest to
     appear to lead cellular market, Jennifer Files, *Dallas Morning News*, 11/
     10/98.
62. 2,3 nennai medo, idou denwa seisan wo baizou, nichiou de nen 120
     mandai – mitsubishi denki. Mitsubishi Electric will double its mobile
     phone production to 12 million phone a year within 2–3 years. *Nikkei*
     10/11/1994. Mitsubishi denki buruta-nyu koujou – dejitaru de hanpatsu
     (nihon kigyou sekai ni ikiru). *Nikkei Industrial* 10/12/1996. Mitsubishi
     Electric's factory in Brittany, France is responding with digital (Japanese
     firms can succeed globally). *Nikkei Industrial* 7/8/1995. Keitai denwa no
     sekai seisan 200 mandai ni baizou, mitsubishiden, nichibeiou 3kyoten-
     toukatsu senta-mo shinsetsu Mitsubishi Electric will double its produc-
     tion of mobile phones to 20 million a year with its newly integrated
     production in Japan. *Nikkei* 15/10/1995. Oushu kikaku no dejitaru keitai
     denwa – mitsubishiden, NEC mo sannyu. Mitsubishi and NEC will enter
     the European digital phone market.
63. Keitai denwa Nokia sengyoh ni tennshin – chukakujigyoh top ni kiku
     Arafuta shi. Nokia made mobile phones its main business – interview
     with the top executive Mr Alafuta. *Nikkei* 28/8/1999.

64. Mitsubishi denki kaihatsu ni tokka bei de no keitai denwa wa seisan – sorekutoron ni itaku. Mitsubishi Electric outsources production production of mobile phones to Solectron. *Nikkei Industrial* 30/7/1998.
65. Mitsubishi denki keitaidenwa ohshu de gijutsusha zohkyoh – shea kakudai mezasu. Mitsubishi Electric adds development engineers to its European mobile phone business – it is aiming for a greater share of the market. *Nikkei* 12/8/1999.
66. B. Bremner, E. Thornton, and I. Kunii, "Fall of a Keiretsu," *Business Week*, 15/3/1999, pp. 35–40.
67. Mitsubishi denki, keitai denwa seisan 6bai ni, 2004, nendo, 7300 mandai ni – jiyou kakudai mikomi. Mitsubishi Electric expects to expand production of mobile phones by 6 times to 73 million phones by 2004. *Nikkei* 1/1/2000.
68. The four cellular phone service-providers chose to raise these activation commissions rather than further reduce their monthly and air-time charges. Monthly charges of 7500 yen and air-time charges of 50 yen per minute were the norm in early 1996 thus providing about 15,000 yen per month in revenue for Japanese service-providers versus $50 a month in the US.
69. The handsets produced by Matsushita and to some extent NEC, and Mitsubishi typically sell for about 20,000 in the first few months after they are released.
70. Digital Phone has subsequently changed its service name to J-Phone. Its major shareholder, Japan Telecom, has also acquired a controlling interest in Digital Tsuka, which operates in the other regions of Japan. These regional companies also use the brand name J-Phone.
71. See the market data section of *Telecommunication* magazine in the 1996 issues. Terekomyunike-shon, Tokyo: rikku terekomu.
72. Their share would have dropped even further if Motorola who had the other 15% of the NTT market in 1988 had not stopped supplying phones to NTT when it became the major supplier of TACS phones to the Cellular Group.
73. In particular, it was believed that Sanyo, Sharp, and Sony would dominate the cellular phone market just as they had come to dominate the cordless phone market after it was liberalized in 1985.
74. Further, these and subsequent generations of base stations are each very different thus requiring all handsets to be tested with most generations of base stations.
75. However, DoCoMo's control of these updates does not impact on competition between phones that are supplied to other service-providers and it does not impact on phone weight or size.
76. There are more than 100 suppliers of discrete components in Japan of which most firms deal regularly with about half of these suppliers. In the cases where the part suppliers are in a firm that also produces cellular phones, which is very common, the divisions are different and almost completely independent. The cellular phone divisions are not required to use the parts that are made by their discrete component divisions and the discrete component divisions are not required to sell exclusively to the cellular phone divisions.

77. NEC, Fujitsu and Matsushita were also influenced by DoCoMo's concerns about the safety of lithium ion batteries (there were some early cases of batteries exploding).

78. Matsushita claims that the adoption of the lithium ion battery saved 30 grams in 1996 and the performance of the lithium ion battery has improved faster than the performance of the previous generation of batteries (nickel-hydride). Therefore, 20, 25, and 30 grams are subtracted from all phones that did not contain a lithium ion battery in 1994, 1995, and 1996 respectively. Similarly, the NEC folding phone (105 grams) weighed 25 grams or was about 35% heavier than its regular counterpart (80 grams) in 1998. Therefore, 40, 40, 35, 30, and 25 grams are subtracted from folding phones that were released in 1994, 1995, 1996, 1997, and 1998 respectively.

79. The phone released in late 1996 by Fujitsu appears to have become heavier since Fujitsu increased the talk time of this phone substantially while it simultaneously adopted the lithium ion battery (thus 30 grams was subtracted from the phone released in October, 1995).

80. NTT DoCoMo had about one-third the cancellation rates of the other service-providers in 1996.

81. Many subscribers changed to DoCoMo to obtain these superior handsets. Unlike the US and other countries, the Japanese Ministry of Posts and Telecommunications (MPT) does not allow carriers to offer long-term contracts to subscribers. Therefore, it is very easy for subscribers to change service-providers and in the process receive a new phone for almost free given the high commissions paid by the service-providers. And because the retail outlets lose their commissions when subscribers cancel a contract within six months of signing the contract, the retail outlets do not want to sell phones that will result in early cancellations. Thus DoCoMo's superior handsets were a major reason for the cancellation rates of the non-DoCoMo suppliers and these higher cancellation rates increased the chances that a retail outlet would recommend DoCoMo phones in spite of DoCoMo's lower activation commissions.

82. See the market data section of *Telecommunication* magazine in the 1997 issues. Terekomyunike-shon, Tokyo: rikku terekomu.

83. NTT DoCoMo has the worst voice quality of all service-providers due to its large share and thus use of "half-rate" PDC where only 4800 as opposed to 9600 bits per second are used to send the voice signal. The Cellular Group's advertisements about its superior voice quality have inadvertently helped the other non-DoCoMo service-providers and the Digital Phone Group has been the biggest beneficiary due to its early use of commercials that emphasized its superior voice quality *vis-à-vis* DoCoMo.

84. The emergence of a Matsushita or even a DoCoMo dominant design be explained in terms of volumes. Matsushita has never obtained much more than 30% of the Japanese market and DoCoMo did not obtain more than 50% of the total digital subscribers until March, 1996, almost two years after the new entrants had started their digital service.

85. For example, most of the non-DoCoMo suppliers switched to DoCoMo parts (that is, firms that were supplying DoCoMo) in low noise regula-

tors (Toko), TCXO (temperature control exchange oscillators) parts (Toyo Communications and Japan Denpa), filters (Murata), modulators and phased-lock loop integrated circuits (suppliers shown in parentheses). Toko was the only supplier of the best low-noise regulator until the end of 1996. Toyo Communications (the top supplier) and Japan Denpa Industries (second leading supplier) were the only suppliers for the best TCXO parts until 1997. Murata, which is the world's leading supplier of filters with a share of more than 50%, produced far smaller and lighter filters than its competitors until 1997. Several firms produced modulators (Lucent, NEC, and Matsushita) and phased-lock loop integrated circuits (National Semiconductor, NEC, Matsushita, Fujitsu).

The most important design tradeoff involved power amplifiers, filters, and base band chips. Power amplifiers are critical because they have a very strong effect on a phone's power consumption through their connection with the voltages used in base band chips. And if the power consumption can be reduced, smaller and thus lighter batteries can be used in the phone. The DoCoMo suppliers used their preferential information about the PDC standard to make better design tradeoffs between these three types of parts. For example, base band chips are very standard specific and they are the most expensive chips in a phone. The DoCoMo suppliers, in particular Matsushita and to a lesser extent NEC, were able to produce far superior base band chips than either Toshiba (a non-DoCoMo supplier) or DSPC, an independent supplier of chips to the other non-DoCoMo suppliers. As the DoCoMo suppliers released phones that were designed with these superior design tradeoffs, their volumes of digital phones increased and the non-DoCoMo suppliers were forced to adopt the power amplifiers and filters that had been originally developed for the DoCoMo suppliers. For example, Toshiba was forced to stop its internal development of base band chips, power amplifiers, and filters and buy from DSPC, NEC, and Murata respectively.

86. For example, the differences between the base band chips produced by DSPC and the DoCoMo suppliers was reduced from about 30% to 10% in terms of power consumption between 1994 and 1998.

87. For example, the major manufacturers of TCXO parts (a type of crystal oscillator) defined standard packaging and other aspects of these parts in order to avoid the large amount of custom development that occurred in the PDC market. These manufacturers were forced to incur heavy development costs in PDC and they wanted to avoid this burden in PHS.

6 Third Generation and Mobile Internet Standards and Competition in Third Generation Infrastructure and Phones

This chapter shows how the hybrid model of committees and markets continues to explain standard setting in third generation and mobile Internet standards better than a model that only employs one or the other mechanism and it uses the hybrid model to also forecast competition between infrastructure and phone suppliers. As discussed in Chapter 3, the hybrid model of standard setting explains the choice of DoCoMo's W-CDMA technology by ETSI in January 1998. The subsequent patent disagreements and subsequent agreement between Ericsson and Qualcomm to license each other's patents along with the harmonization efforts can also be explained in terms of the hybrid model. On the surface, the patent disagreements between the two firms were largely played out in a committee-based battle both between the two firms and in the larger committees that are concerned with third generation standards. But the agreement was strongly affected by the market success of cdmaOne and Ericsson's growing realization that it needed a cdmaOne infrastructure business. Further, the rising expectations of market success for cdmaOne were strongly affected by committee-based competition in the form of the US government's pressure on China to adopt cdmaOne. The Chinese government's initial decision to adopt cdmaOne and its subsequent reversals also show the common thread of government involvement in the choice of mobile communication standards.

More interestingly, it is becoming increasingly clear that in third generation services, it is more than just the air and network interfaces that are important in terms of standards. There is a number of interfaces that are important to the successful development of the mobile Internet and also mobile computing where phones can be used to access the Internet or Intranets either directly or through other devices such as PDAs and laptop computers. And as discussed in Chapter 2, it is hypothesized that standard setting in the case of ill-defined interfaces will follow a different path than that for well-defined interfaces. The number and variety of committees and alliances increase since in addition to competition between various standards for each interface, there is competition between various interfaces and devices and thus between and within various committee and markets.

Committees and markets will also play a strong role in competition between firms in third generation infrastructure and phones. On the committee-based side, the choice of W-CDMA by the Japanese manufacturers and its two European supporters, Ericsson and Nokia, may help these firms to some extent, albeit not for the widely believed reasons. Although their early involvement in the standard setting committees is expected to help them understand this standard better than other firms do, the openness of the standard setting process will probably eliminate any of these committee-based advantages.

Instead, the expected and actual early start of services in Japan may provide Ericsson, Nokia, and the Japanese firms with an advantage in both the infrastructure and phone markets. For infrastructure, firms must simultaneously develop technology in cooperation with a service provider while they participate in standard setting committees due to the complexity of mobile communication standards and infrastructure. As of early 2001, the Japanese service providers had already given many of their orders for experimental third generation systems to their previous suppliers, which are basically the above-mentioned firms. These early orders will most likely lead to increased market-based capabilities and thus perhaps success in W-CDMA.

Further, as of early 2001, it appears that most of the third generation licenses will also be given to existing service providers in Europe and these existing GSM service providers were already giving many of their orders for enhanced versions of GSM systems and orders for experimental third generation systems to their previous GSM infrastructure suppliers as of early 2001. Thus, committee-based competition in the form of switching costs and continuity in customer–supplier relationships appears to be playing a strong role in third generation infrastructure.

For phones, market-based competition will probably play a larger role than committee-based competition due to the greater simplicity of phones as compared to infrastructure. Although some observers believe that the early start of Japanese services will provide Japanese manufacturers with an advantage, it appears that product line/

platform management and in particular global platform management will be the key factors to success. The relatively slow move by service providers to expand coverage means that it will be many years before the same phone can be used throughout Japan and Europe, much less the rest of the world. In other words, dual-mode phones will be the norm in Europe (W-CDMA and GSM) and Japan (W-CDMA and PDC) for many years. Further, there will most likely continue to be market differences between Japan and Europe such as those described in Chapter 5. These differences in phone standards and markets will require effective global platform management and Nokia is the only firm at the time of writing that displays this capability.

NEGOTIATIONS OVER THE THIRD GENERATION STANDARD

ETSI's decision in January 1998 to select W-CDMA as the European third generation standard made W-CDMA to all intents and purposes a global standard. Since GSM had already been adopted in more than 130 countries, the decision was made and thus reflected the desire by not just European but also Asian, African, and Oceanic service providers. Thus, it was a potentially major blow to supporters of other standards such as TDMA (the wide-band version of DAMPS) and cdma2000 (the wide-band version of cdmaOne). TDMA supporters quickly realized that they were badly outnumbered and largely through the efforts of Ericsson, agreed to adopt the evolution of the GSM network and air interfaces. Thus, TDMA operators were expected to implement and basically are implementing many of the GSM updates.[1]

The battle between Qualcomm and Ericsson

On the other hand, Qualcomm and other supporters of cdma2000 continued to fight for cdma2000 during 1998 and 1999 in various committees although it was the perceived market success of cdmaOne that enabled it to complete an agreement with Ericsson. In some ways these battles were similar to those that were fought over patents in the GSM standard-setting committees. As discussed in Chapter 3, operators wanted low patent charges in order to make money from service charges while manufacturers, particularly Motorola, wanted profits from both patent royalties and the sale of products. In the end, most manufacturers cross-licensed their technologies and made relatively little money from patent royalties. The low patent fee model was and still is particularly popular with Ericsson, Nokia, and other firms who believe they can compete along other dimensions such as product development, service, and relationships with service-providers.

The first difference between the GSM and W-CDMA cases is that unlike most other manufacturers, the majority of Qualcomm's profits comes from patents and thus they have little choice but to set relatively high patent fees and use all means to protect their intellectual rights.[2] A second difference is that Qualcomm probably holds a substantially larger number of patents than any other firm, while no one firm dominated GSM patents.[3] Third, Qualcomm has demanded changes in the third generation standard (that is, compatibility with cdmaOne[4]) in return for the use of their patents. This is very different from the GSM case where the dispute was only about the degree of patent charges.[5]

These differences have caused Qualcomm to strongly defend its W-CDMA patents in various committees and for these committees to see Qualcomm's patent charges as being excessive and as the bad guy in its negotiations with Ericsson. Qualcomm's hard line on patents was seen to be slowing down the implementation of third generation services by most observers in the US, Europe, and elsewhere.[6] In particular, the ITU (International Telecommunications Union) and its members were primarily pointing their fingers at Qualcomm when they threatened to throw out the cdma2000 and W-CDMA proposals in November 1998,[7] asked firms to make the proposed standards compatible in March 1999,[8] and throughout late 1998 and early 1999 asked Ericsson and Qualcomm to resolve their patent dispute and conform with the ITU patent policy.

Qualcomm was particularly disliked in Europe due to its criticisms of GSM[9] and these factors caused Qualcomm to have fewer supporters than Ericsson did during their patent battle. For example, Ericsson was able to count on Nokia for support when it proposed to reduce the W-CDMA chip rate from 4.096mcps (mega chips per second) to 3.840mcps in December 1998.[10] On the other hand, supporters of cdmaOne such as Nortel were fairly silent since they were concerned with angering their European customers. For example, in response to US claims that Europe's choice of a single standard is a trade barrier, Peter MacLaren, VP of business development with Nortel, disagreed, saying that "Nortel supports harmonization but claims that UMTS licensing has not created trade barriers."[11]

Ericsson–Qualcomm agreement

In the end, however, Qualcomm's poor image was not nearly as important as the growing pressure on Ericsson and more importantly the growing success of cdmaOne in the market. Ericsson was being pressured by its customers (service providers) to resolve its differences with Qualcomm while the growing installed base of cdmaOne made Ericsson realize that it needed to become a provider of cdmaOne infrastructure and phones. There were almost 35 million cdmaOne subscribers at the end of March 1999 up from nine million at the end of March 1998. While this was far less than the 300 million GSM subscribers at the end of March 1999, the number of cdmaOne subscribers had more than tripled in one year while the number of GSM subscribers had grown by about one-third. One consulting firm predicted in early 2000 that 180 million cdmaOne phones would be sold in 2004 as compared to 254 million GSM phones.

A big impact on forecasted installed base came from China's expected adoption of cdmaOne through lobbying from the US and Qualcomm. Qualcomm had been lobbying the US Congress and various federal offices including trade offices for years to provide support for its efforts to obtain backward compatibility for cdmaOne in the third generation standard. Although the US Congress's initial support for cdmaOne probably provided more damage than help,[12] at one point China reportedly decided to adopt cdmaOne in March 1999 in return for US government support in entering the World Trade Organization.[13] Since then China has changed its mind several times and its final decision is still uncertain.[14]

China is a particularly important market to Ericsson. It has been Ericsson's number one or number two market in the last 1990s and Ericsson has a 40% market share in China's mobile infrastructure market.[15] Further, China passed the US in 2001 to become the largest market in terms of mobile subscribers. Thus, China's initial decision to adopt cdmaOne increased Ericsson's desire for a presence in the cdmaOne market and Qualcomm could offer Ericsson help in this area.

An agreement between Ericsson and Qualcomm was announced in late March 1999 about the same time as cdmaOne's prospects looked the best in China and other countries. The Ericsson–Qualcomm agreement included: (1) the cross-licensing of patents; (2) Ericsson's purchase of Qualcomm's infrastructure business; and (3) both firms working towards a compromise in the third generation W-CDMA standard.

Following this agreement, Qualcomm's stock price rose more than 1800% in 1999 and continued to rise in early 2000 on the assumption that the agreement meant rising license fees for Qualcomm. As discussed earlier Qualcomm has been making money in cdmaOne through licensing fees for the technology and for the sale of the chips. It still had a large share of this chip market in mid-2000 since it knew the standard and the updates to the standard better than anyone else did. It has used this knowledge to release the first chips for the new revisions to the cdmaOne standard, which are periodically released primarily to enable faster data rates.

Some people believe that this situation will continue in third generation systems and chips. They believe that all third generation systems will use Qualcomm's technology and most third generation phones will use Qualcomm chips. This will probably depend on the extent to which W-CDMA utilizes Qualcomm's technology, the cross-licensing arrangements that are made by the manufacturers, and the extent to which Qualcomm will influence the standard-setting process and thus stay one step ahead of other chip manufacturers. A variety of ITU-related groups have been attempting to harmonize the cdma2000 and W-CDMA standards but the results have retained multiple paths and multiple modes. Further, little information has been released about the cross-licensing agreements although it is generally believed that Ericsson bought Qualcomm's patents. Thus, it is unclear how much W-CDMA will depend on Qualcomm technology. Nevertheless, it appears that Qualcomm is not in charge of the third generation standard-setting process and thus will have trouble staying ahead of the other chip manufacturers.[16]

W-CDMA versus 2G (second generation) enhancements

As discussed in Chapter 3, ETSI chose W-CDMA in January 1998 because it believed that W-CDMA offered far greater data transmission capabilities than GSM or an enhanced version of GSM and because W-CDMA included the evolution of the GSM network interface. While W-CDMA's performance advantages were most likely true at this time, several developments in GSM caused many GSM service providers to rethink their decision to implement W-CDMA. The first development was the finalization of the GPRS (General Packet Radio System) specification in early 1998. GPRS brings Internet Protocol (IP) into the GSM network and thus enables data to be sent in small packets, users to be charged for these small packets as opposed to connection times, and data transmission speeds up to 115 kilobits per second.[17]

The second major development, which was still underway as of early 2001, is called EDGE (enhanced data rates for GSM evolution). EDGE uses a new modulation scheme, which enables GSM networks to support data throughput speeds of up to 384 kilobits per second. This data rate is equivalent to the first phase of UMTS and some observers have pointed out that EDGE fulfils all the requirements laid down in the specification for IMT-2000. Thus, if a particular 3G (third generation) license does not mandate W-CDMA, then an operator could deploy EDGE as its third generation technology. Further, the GSM standards bodies as of early 2000 were also considering expanding the capability of EDGE to offer 2 megabits per second data capabilities for indoor applications. In other words, by early 2000 it was widely recognized that some GSM service providers might choose to merely incrementally improve their GSM systems as opposed to implementing a W-CDMA system.

Simultaneously, the TDMA (third generation version of DAMPS) industry group or UWCC (Universal Wireless Communications Consortium) had also elected to move in the same direction as GSM and adopt many of the GSM enhancements such as GPRS and EDGE. Ericsson has been a major proponent of these developments since this will make it easier for Ericsson to move its DAMPS customers to improved second generation and eventually to third generation services.[18] AT&T and other leading providers of DAMPS services expected to begin testing EDGE in 2000.[19]

These developments are best explained using the hybrid model of markets and committees. The market had demanded a cheaper alternative to W-CDMA and the committees had responded with GPRS and EDGE. Thus, by early 2000, they had begun to be seen as a potential third generation standard: one that would be far cheaper to implement than W-CDMA. Some people were predicting the demise of W-CDMA while many chip producers began putting third generation developments on the back-burner. For example, Texas Instruments removed "leadership in 3G" from a near-term goal for 2000 to a long-term goal since it believed that a true 3G market would not come until after 2003.[20]

As of early 2001, it appears that most service providers will adopt GPRS while few will adopt EDGE. As is discussed later, most GSM service providers will implement GPRS since Japan's success in the mobile Internet has demonstrated the importance of packet communications systems to the mobile Internet. The pessimism about EDGE is partly technical since W-CDMA increases the efficiency of the frequency spectrum while EDGE does not. But it is also since the use of W-CDMA is a prerequisite for obtaining a third generation license in most European countries. This means that the forecasted installed base for W-CDMA is much higher than that for EDGE.

This large forecasted installed base has even caused most of the TDMA (the third generation version of DAMPS) and some of the cdmaOne service providers to announce the adoption of W-CDMA. AT&T and its affiliates (including Rogers AT&T) announced the quitting of DAMPS and the adoption of GSM technology and its evolutionary pathway to W-CDMA on November 30, 2000.[21] Many people believe that Brazil will evolve from DAMPS to W-CDMA. And major cdmaOne and other users are also moving in the W-CDMA direction. All three South Korean carriers announced their intention to adopt W-CDMA in July 2000[22] while many believe that major US service providers like Cingular, Nextel, and VoiceStream will evolve towards W-CDMA. If this happens, the W-CDMA service providers would outnumber the cdma2000 service providers even in the US.[23]

However, the extent to which W-CDMA is actually implemented was still highly uncertain as of early 2001. Even though W-CDMA appeared to have beaten EDGE, there will still questions about whether high-speed data services (for example, 384 Kbps) are needed, be they from W-CDMA or EDGE (Kbps=Kilo-bits per second, where Kilo=1000). This is best seen in the lack of interest that third generation licenses received in Italy, Austria, and Switzerland. Following the huge bids made in Great Britain and Germany in early 2000, the number and amount of bids substantially dropped in the subsequent frequency auctions.[24] As of early 2001, there was a great deal of uncertainty surrounding the future of third generation services.

MOBILE INTERNET AND COMPUTING STANDARDS

The explosive growth in both the Internet (and Intranets) and mobile phones has caused many people to predict a convergence between the two. The mobile nature of people's lives both in work and in pleasure coupled with their increasing desire for information via the Internet suggests that a convergence between the Internet and mobile phones is one of the next huge markets. Of course, using mobile phones to connect to the Internet or Intranets requires a large number of standards to be created.

The battle to create the necessary mobile computing and mobile Internet standards is already following a very different path from the air and network interface standard battles described earlier. Although the battles can be effectively described using the hybrid model of committees and markets, unlike the air interface standard battles, governments have not been involved in defining the mobile Internet and computing standards. And their lack of involvement is only partially due to the lack of a historical role by governments in defining computer standards. Their lack of involvement and other differences between setting mobile Internet/computing and mobile air interface standards also exist because there are much lower levels of investment and much more undefined interfaces in mobile computing and the mobile Internet. The investments in third generation systems are much larger than the expected investments needed to create the products for linking mobile phones with corporate systems, e-mail or the Internet. While third generation investments by service providers are expected to exceed 10 billion US dollars for most service providers, mobile Internet services, contents, and handsets can be implemented for a fraction of this amount.

Competition between different interfaces

An even bigger difference with the air and network interface standard battles is the large number of interface standards and required compatibilities that are involved with making mobile computing and the mobile Internet a reality (see Figure 6.1). While the mobile phone standard battles have been solely about determining an air interface and to a lesser extent a network interface standard, there is no such simple key interface in the next battle. Is the key interface the interface between the users and handsets (man–machine interface), the interface between the handsets and application programs (operating systems), or the interface between the handsets and the Internet (browsers and language for representing contents)? And is the key handset a mobile phone, Personal digital assistant (PDA), or even a handheld game?

Further, is compatibility important between the different user interfaces, operating systems, and browsers that are used in mobile phones, PDAs, and desktop computers? Users would probably like to use similar user interfaces and most likely the same application programs

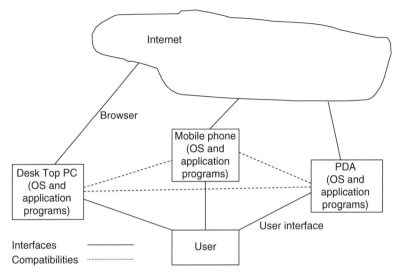

Figure 6.1   Key interfaces in mobile computing

and access the same content on the Internet that they can use and access on desktops. And the major suppliers of desktop computers, PDAs, mobile phones and even televisions and children's games are hoping and arguing that it is the interface between their products and the Internet that is the key interface and everyone else should have compatibility with their products.

Thus, it is not just competition between the standards for a specific interface but between the various interfaces themselves. And for each interface and type of handset, there are relevant committees and markets. Although analogies with war are often overused in describing business strategy, the differences between the methods of creating air interface and mobile computing/Internet standards can be easily described using the terminology of war. The competition to make your firm's, country's, or region's air interface technology has resembled large armies preparing for battle in a large open field. Firms and governments create open standard setting committees and announce their support for single standards. In the case of mobile computing/ Internet standards, the competition resembles jungle warfare where it is not clear where the actual battle will be fought and often who is your ally and who is your enemy. There are many committees and markets and it is not clear which committees and markets are the most important.

This section argues that there are three sets of battles simultaneously being fought concerning mobile computing and mobile Internet standards. First, there is a battle between different handsets (for example, mobile phones and PDAs) to determine which device will become the primary means of accessing the Internet. Here size is both an advantage and disadvantage for PDAs.[25] Second, there will be competition between standards for each specific interface. Third, as part of both the competition between different standards for a specific interface and the competition between different handsets, there will be a battle to see who can create the most compatibility between their handset (that is, mobile phone) and a different form of device (that is, PDAs or desktop computers). The latter is occurring because it is very possible that both PDAs and mobile phones will coexist for a long time.

Table 6.1 summarizes the key devices, firms, standards, committees, and markets for both browsers and operating systems in these battles to determine the mobile computing and Internet standards. Microsoft would of course like to transfer its control of desktops to PDAs and mobile phones. And the large installed base of its Windows software makes this a possibility. In PDAs, for a long time Japan was the leading user and thus some people saw Sharp's Zaurus as becoming the dominant force in mobile computing.[26] It was not until 1998 that there were more sales of PDAs in the US than in Japan in spite of the US's larger economy. Now both Palm Computing's[27] Palm Pilot (strong in the US) and Psion's PDA (strong in Europe) are sold in greater volume per year than the Zaurus and they are now perceived as the leaders in the field.[28]

In phones, most mobile phone manufacturers have supported WAP and EPOC since 1998 but real installed bases have not yet materialized. On the other hand, although there are only a small, albeit growing number of supporters for i-mode, they have a large number of users. Thus, the battle between WAP and i-mode in 2000 and 2001 can be characterized as a battle between a large forecasted installed base for WAP and a real installed base for i-mode that is growing very quickly. Similarly, the battle between phones and PDAs may also be characterized as a battle between a large and small installed base for phones and PDAs with questions concerning which device will be able to generate the larger installed base for mobile Internet users.

This great uncertainty over which interface or device will be the critical determinant of the mobile computing/Internet standards has caused firms to create a wide variety of committees/coalitions in order to generate support for their products and standards. This is similar to

217

Table 6.1 Competing standards for some of the interfaces/technologies shown in Figure 6.1

Device	Main supporter	Browser	Operating system	Committee (i.e., major supporters)	Market as of (1999)
Desktop computers	Microsoft	Internet Explorer	Windows	Major desktop and laptop manufacturers	#1 in world
PDAs	Palm	Palm Browsers	Palm OS	IBM, Sony, Handspring	#1 in US and world #2 in Japan and in Europe
	Microsoft Sharp Psion	Windows CE	Microsoft OS Sharp OS EPOC	Casio, HP None None	Low installed base #1 in Japan #1 in Europe
Phones	WAP Forum (WAP) Symbian (EPOC)	WAP (WML mark-up language)	EPOC	Most mobile phone, service, software and content providers	6 million 12/2000
	NTT DoCoMo	i-mode (c-HTML mark-up language)	Manufacturer Proprietary	Japanese firms	20 million 12/2000

the mobile phone air interface standards and many other standards where firms participate in a number of competing coalitions in order to prevent themselves from being left out of the winning standard. The first wave of important committees/coalitions that were created in the mobile computing/Internet area reflected inter-device competition while the second wave of these committees/coalitions reflected intra-device competition.

The first committees/coalitions: WAP, Symbian, and Bluetooth

The first important committees/coalitions that were created in the n obile Internet/computing area reflected the competition between different devices. Nokia, Motorola, Ericsson, and Psion created the WAP[29] (Wireless Application Protocol) Forum in June 1997, Symbian in mid-1998, and Bluetooth in June 1998 to fight both Microsoft's Windows CE and Palm Computing's operating systems and browsers. WAP is creating an open standard for mobile browsers, Symbian is creating an open operating system for mobile phones and PDAs, and Bluetooth is creating an open standard for wireless communication between handsets that are in close proximity. While a desire to promote the field of mobile computing/Internet was also a motivation for the creation of these organizations, it is clear that intra-device competition was not one of the motivations since any firm can join these organizations.

Although most handset manufacturers have joined these three organizations thus resulting in strong coalitions and the release of products compatible with these standards, by late 1999 tiny cracks began to appear in these alliances that reflected the change in competition in the mobile computing/Internet area from inter-device competition to intra-device competition. Once the mobile phone manufacturers had established credible alternatives to both Microsoft's Windows CE and Palm Computing's operating systems and browsers, they began to create coalitions in order to differentiate themselves from other mobile phone manufacturers. Many of these efforts to differentiate themselves were concerned with creating more compatibility between their phones and other devices (such as, PDAs and laptops) than the other phones had with these other devices.

The second wave of coalitions/committees: phone and PDA manufacturers

The second wave of coalitions began in late 1999 and reflected intra-device competition in that they were aimed at creating better compatibility between mobile phones and either PDAs or desktop computers. Nokia announced its plan to collaborate with Palm Computing to develop hybrids of smart phones and personal organizers (that is, PDAs) at Telecom 99 in October. Nokia licensed the Palm operating system, thus enabling it to implement the user interface (pen input), wire clipping technology and applications on the Symbian platform.[30] In December, Motorola announced it would also license the Palm operating system for use in Motorola products. Apparently Motorola was particularly interested in having the Palm Pilot's user interface sit on top of the EPOC operating system and thus Motorola still remained committed to Symbian. Both Nokia and Motorola also announced they would take equity positions in Palm Computing.[31]

Ericsson pursued a slightly different strategy choosing to work with Microsoft rather than Palm Computing. In early December 1999, Ericsson announced that it would use Microsoft's Mobile Exporer, a new version of Microsoft's Internet browser, in future phones. Since this browser runs on multiple operating systems including EPOC, it does not tie Ericsson to Microsoft. Analysts saw Microsoft's move as a reflection of its diminishing power in the mobile field in spite of the chance that it might convince Ericsson to put Windows CE in future phones.[32] Almost simultaneously, Ericsson announced that its new R380 phone, which is a combined mobile phone and handheld computer, will contain its own operating system albeit one that is based on the EPOC operating system.[33]

These announcements reflected differing perceptions about the key interfaces. Nokia, Motorola, and Ericsson said they remain committed to Symbian probably because they believe that the mobile phones will be used to connect to the Internet and run application programs. However, all three realized that other devices are also important. Nokia and Motorola were concerned that PDAs, in particular Palm Computing's PDA, may become a major entry point to the Internet and thus compatibility between mobile phones and PDAs is important. On the other hand, Ericsson apparently believed that the compatibility between desktops and phones is more important than the compatibility between PDAs and phones.

Further, from the beginning of 1999, the variety of these alliances began to expand dramatically. While the above discussion primarily focuses on the hardware and software shown in Figure 6.1, the providers of this hardware and software began to make alliances with service and content providers and the service and content providers began to make alliances with each other. The result is a bewildering array of alliances where most are said to merely involve the exchange of business cards. Some of these alliances have been established to create new products and services for mobile phone users while the vast majority have been most likely established to create a forecasted installed base for their own hardware, software, service or contents. The alliances that are being made between mobile phone manufacturers and both service and content providers reflect both intra-device competition and the desire to find the so-called killer applications and key interfaces.

However in spite of the extensive work on the committee side of standard setting, however, the market for WAP had still not materialized as of early 2001. This was in spite of the many optimistic predictions that had been made. Phones that include WAP browsers and EPOC operating systems had appeared by early 2000 and those with Bluetooth were expected to appear by mid-2001.

THE JAPANESE MOBILE INTERNET MARKET

The Japanese mobile Internet market surprised everyone and exploded in the year 2000. Japan had almost 30 million Internet subscribers by the end of 2000 and the market for mobile contents and services was almost 80 and 500 million US$ respectively in December 2000. NTT DoCoMo had more than 70% of these subscribers and an even larger percentage of the income from mobile Internet services. Japan expected to have about 50 million Internet subscribers by the end of 2001 and the market for mobile contents and mobile services (packet charges) was expected to exceed 2 billion US$ and 10 billion US$ respectively in Japan in 2001.

Contrast this with the rest of the world where the number of mobile Internet subscribers (that is, WAP subscribers) was less than four million as of mid-August 2000[34] and probably not more than eight million by the end of 2000.[35] Further, it is generally agreed that few WAP subscribers actually use the service, thus placing the market for WAP contents and services outside of Japan at almost zero in late 2000.[36] Part of the problem was technical as there were problems with the WAP mark-up language,[37] intellectual properly rights (IPRs),[38] and the lack of a packet communication systems (GPRS) and micropayment systems.

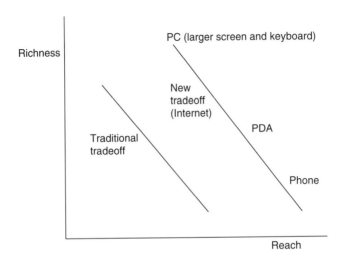

Figure 6.2   The new tradeoff between richness and reach

A more fundamental difference however, is the differences in perceptions about the mobile Internet. These differences in perception can
be explained using the concepts of reach and richness (see Figure 6.2).
"Richness" refers to the quality, depth, and bandwidth of information,
as defined by the user. "Reach" refers to the number of people who
participate in the sharing of that information. There is a strong tradeoff between richness and reach both in the "traditional" and "new"
economies. For example, general interest newspapers reach a large
number of people and thus enable a large number of people to share
in that experience. However, the information contained in newspapers is clearly not as "rich" as the information contained in special
purpose magazines or journals that do not have as large a "reach" as
the general purpose newspapers[39] (Evans and Wurster, 2000).

Many[40] people argue that the Internet enables firms to provide both
more reach and more richness, thus causing the tradeoff between reach
and richness to change and perhaps disappear (Evans and Wurster,
2000). This section[41] argues that the new tradeoff between reach and
richness involves the tradeoff between fixed line and mobile Internet
applications. As shown in Figure 6.3; mobile devices provide lower
richness but have higher reach than desktop computers. Mobile
phones have smaller screens and keyboards and thus cannot access
the level of rich information that can be accessed with a desktop

computer. The larger reach of mobile phones comes from their greater diffusion, greater mobility, and faster power-up as compared to desktop computers. There are more mobile phones being used than desktop computers in many countries in the world including Japan and it is expected that the number of mobile phone subscribers will exceed the number of installed desktop computers within a few years. Naturally, mobile phones are easier to carry than desktop computers and PDAs. Further, mobile phones can be used within seconds of turning them on versus several minutes for desktop computers.

Another implication of the tradeoff between reach and richness is that it is a function of age since in most countries young people place a greater importance on reach and a lower importance on richness than older people do. Younger people are more mobile than older people and due to their less experience place less value on rich information than older people do. People under 25 generally spend a much larger amount of their time away from home and the office (if they have one) and use public transportation (buses and trains) more than older people. Young people also place less emphasis on richness than older people do due to their less experience and thus lower specialization. This is also why young people are the major users of other portable devices such as portable music players and calculators.

Japan and the West have approached this market in different ways. As shown in Figure 6.3, while the West is trying to move the high

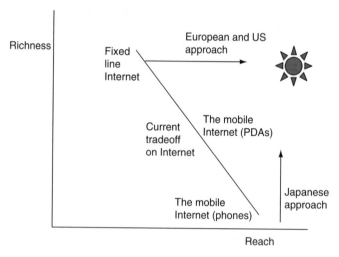

Figure 6.3   Japanese vs. US and European approaches to the mobile Internet

richness of the fixed line Internet onto the small screens of mobile phones,[42] the major applications in the Japanese mobile Internet are e-mail and simple entertainment with a significant fraction of the e-mail being part of entertainment and other simple content services. Within entertainment, the most popular contents are the downloading of ringing tones and cartoon characters, the playing of games, reading horoscopes, and finding information about videos and music. The major users are also young people. For example, more than 24%, 57% and 81% of users for the leading provider of video and music information (Tsutaya Online) are less than 20, 25 and 30 years old respectively.[43]

The fact that entertainment is the main content and young people are the main users of the Japanese mobile Internet suggests that Japan's low fixed line Internet usage has little to do with the success of Japan's mobile Internet. Few of the popular mobile Internet services are available on the Japanese or US fixed line Internet and even if they were, they would not be very popular as they are too simple to be of interest to Japanese fixed line Internet users. Although young people are the major users of the fixed line Internet in Japan, they are also the major users of the mobile Internet. The greater impact of the low fixed line Internet usage in Japan is that perceptions about the mobile Internet are not constrained by the fixed line Internet as they are in the US.[44]

In their focus on business users and popular fixed line contents, Western service and content providers are in danger of offering mobile Internet services that few people want. This is already creating a negative feedback loop where poor perceptions of the mobile Internet are leading to little investment in contents, phones, and appropriate services for the mobile Internet. Contrast this with Japan where the early success in e-mail and entertainment has caused phones with large color screens and embedded cameras, more interesting and useful contents,[45] and new services like Java to appear. Japan created this positive feedback loop by starting with the appropriate users and contents.

INTERFACE COMPETITION AS OF EARLY 2001

The success of the Japanese mobile Internet began to have a large impact on the competition between various interfaces by the middle of 2000 both in terms of market-and committee-based competition. Its effect on market-based competition was felt as several Western service providers announced they would start i-mode services. KPN announced in late September[46] that it would start such services followed by AT&T Wireless,[47] and Taiwan's KG Telecommunications in December;[48] all of these firms had previously received minority investments from NTT DoCoMo. And these numbers will increase as other service providers attempt to tap into NTT DoCoMo's understanding of the mobile Internet.

However, an equal or perhaps larger reaction to the success of the Japanese mobile Internet is being felt in the committee side of the competition between WAP and i-mode. The mark-up languages for WAP (WML) and i-mode (c-HTML) are converging through the participation of NTT DoCoMo and its key partners in WAP committees. It is expected that both mark-up languages will become compatible and be based on X-HTML. Since this WAP version, called WAP-NG, was expected to be available by mid-2001, it is likely that compatible phones will be available by the fall of 2001.[49] This will cause the battle between the i-mode and WAP mark-up languages largely to end. Then the West will have to deal with the more difficult and important issues of creating the appropriate contents and handsets for the mobile Internet along with introducing packet communication and micro-payment services.

The battle between PDAs and mobile phones will continue. Figure 6.3 suggests that desktop computers, mobile phones, and PDAs will coexist, with each device occupying a different place in the tradeoff between reach and richness. Many people will use these devices as complements where rich information will be handled on desktop computers and less rich information will be handled on PDAs and mobile phones. Content providers and other firms will provide services that make it easier to use these devices as complements.

However, there will also be competition between these devices. Mobile phones will always have a larger reach than desktop computers and even PDAs due to their lighter weight and lower costs. The challenge for the phone manufacturers is to increase the capability of phones to access rich information as shown in Figure 6.4. Manufacturers of mobile phones and even PDAs are attempting to do this by reducing costs, increasing display size, and improving input methods either through larger keyboards or new technologies like voice recognition. Further, as PDAs diffuse, they will begin to acquire more reach as shown in Figure 6.4. A critical issue in this diffusion is whether and when service providers will subsidize the price of PDAs with activation commissions as they do with phones.

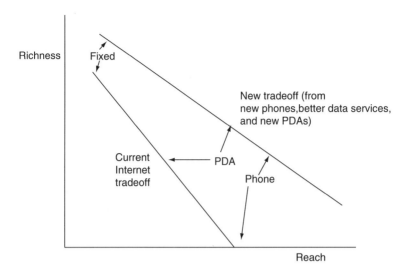

Figure 6.4   New phones, higher speed data services and new PDAs will continue to change the reach and richness tradeoff

The rest of Chapter 6 looks at how competition in third generation infrastructure and handsets may proceed. These discussions on third generation infrastructure and phones refer to the analyses carried out Chapters 4 and 5 respectively.

COMPETITION IN THIRD GENERATION INFRASTRUCTURE

This section uses the hybrid model of markets and committees to forecast competition in third generation infrastructure. Chapter 4 found that committee-based competition and its interaction with market-based competition played a stronger role in overall competition than just market-based competition by itself. Firms must participate in standard setting committees while they simultaneously develop technology in cooperation with a service provider due to the complexity of mobile communication standards and infrastructure. Since early orders for test and commercial systems are necessary to develop experience, it is critical to obtain orders from those service providers who provide the earliest orders and start the earliest services. Therefore, due to the high switching costs associated with mobile infrastructure, firms need to have provided these early service providers with infrastructure in the previous generation of technology. This form of committee-based competition will also probably determine the winners in third generation infrastructure. This is in spite of the claims by some infrastructure providers that since the technologies (that is, market-based competition) needed in third generation infrastructure will be very different than those needed in second generation infrastructure, market-based competition will be more important in the change from second to third than in the change from first to second generations. These people argue that the integration of data and voice and the integration of carrier and enterprise networks are becoming necessary capabilities. Just as in the past capabilities in both switches and base stations were critical to success, these people argue that capabilities in data and voice for both enterprise and carriers will be important.

Thus, this section provides an interesting test of the importance of committee-versus market-based competition. This section analyzes firms in terms of both their market-and committee-based capabilities followed by an analysis of the relative importance of committee-and market-based competition.

Market-based competition in third generation mobile infrastructure

This subsection compares mobile infrastructure providers in terms of those third generation capabilities that are usually associated with market-based competition. It is generally believed that the required technological capabilities for mobile infrastructure providers is expanding from both merely switches and base stations in second generation services to capabilities in data and voice for both enterprises (firms) and service providers in enhanced second generation and third generation mobile infrastructure. A 1999 report by the Yankee Group evaluated the leading firms in these areas in order to estimate which firm had the largest chance of success in third generation infrastructure.[50] It concluded that Nortel is the leader, Motorola/Cisco are in the middle, and Lucent, Ericsson and Nokia are at the bottom of these five firms in terms of capabilities in this order. Nortel's acquisition of Bay Networks and Motorola's alliance with Cisco (announced in February 1999) has made Nortel and Motorola considerably stronger. Cisco has 90% of the router access network market while Bay Networks is also strong in related areas. Motorola and Cisco are planning to invest up to $1 billion on the project between 2000 and

2004.[51] The acquisition as opposed to the alliance by Motorola makes Nortel appear stronger since alliances have a tendency to go sour as Motorola has experienced with both Nortel and Siemens. Presumably the better fit between Motorola and Cisco will reduce the chances of these problems.

The alliance with Alcatel may also help Motorola in the switch area. Although they only obtained four of the new 25 GSM orders in 1998, it is in the third generation area where the two alliances with Alcatel and Cisco are expected to help Motorola. Alcatel has decided not to develop third generation base stations (it still sells second generation GSM base stations) and thus there may be a better fit in third generation than in second generation mobile infrastructure.

Lucent has also improved its data communication capabilities with the acquisition of Ascend Communications. However, Ascend Communications is not perceived as being as strong as Cisco or Bay Networks, it is only strong in the carrier and not in the enterprise markets, and Lucent is apparently having trouble integrating Ascend Communications with Lucent.[52] Thus, the acquisition of Ascend Communications may not help Lucent as much as Nortel's acquisition of Bay Networks appears to be helping Nortel.

Ericsson and Nokia have largely focused on internal development as opposed to the acquisition of data communication capabilities. Neither firm has a core Internet Protocol (IP) switching product due to their focus on internal development. For example, Ericsson is trying to develop products using its existing switch platform. Further, both Nokia and Ericsson have declined offers from Cisco to work more closely with Cisco.[53]

A second way to evaluate the capabilities generally associated with market-based competition is in terms of success in cdmaOne. Both W-CDMA and cdma2000 are based on CDMA technology and thus the level of success in cdmaOne provides a measure of CDMA capabilities. Lucent is the leading supplier of cdmaOne infrastructure followed by Motorola and Nortel. Although Ericsson's purchase of Qualcomm's cdmaOne infrastructure unit will probably help Ericsson in the CDMA area, it is generally considered to be a distant fourth in terms of cdmaOne capabilities. Siemens and Nokia do not sell cdmaOne infrastructure.

The above discussion of those capabilities that are generally associated with market-based competition suggests that Nortel and Motorola will be the leading suppliers of mobile infrastructure with Lucent perhaps number three and Ericsson and Nokia numbers four and five respectively. Although Siemens and NEC were not evaluated in the Yankee Group report, they are generally considered to be weaker than the other firms and both firms have no or a negligible share of the cdmaOne market. Thus, by the market-based competition capabilities measure, these firms would be expected to obtain the sixth and seventh highest shares in the third generation infrastructure market.

Committee-based competition in third generation mobile infrastructure

This subsection compares mobile infrastructure providers in terms of those third generation capabilities that are usually associated with committee-based competition. Early orders are needed to develop experience and due to continuity in supplier–customer relationships, the early orders will most likely be received by those manufacturers who supplied the early service providers with second generation infrastructure.

As of early 2001, NTT DoCoMo was expected to be the first firm to start third generation services in May 2001 followed by a J-Phone affiliate[54] in the fall of 2001 and many GSM service providers in Europe in the fall of 2001 and early 2002. The Japanese Ministry of Posts and Telecommunications expects spending by the industry overall to reach 1430 billion yen ($14bn) in fiscal 1999 and spending on third generation infrastructure alone will come to 4340 billion yen between 2001 and 2010, with the bulk of spending concentrated in the first five years. NTT DoCoMo expects to spend about 800 billion yen on W-CDMA over the next few years and others, such as Japan Telecom, have similar spending plans of about 700 billion yen over a few years.[55]

NTT DoCoMo has awarded contracts for base stations to NEC, Matsushita, Fujitsu, Ericsson, and Lucent and contracts for switching equipment to NEC, Fujitsu, and Lucent.[56] Dollar values are not available but it is generally perceived that NEC and Ericsson are the leading suppliers of the equipment. The consortium of Japan Telecom, British Telecom, and Airtouch has chosen NEC, Ericsson, and Nokia as their infrastructure suppliers.

Some European countries such as Spain, Sweden, France, Germany, Britain, Italy, Finland, and the Netherlands are expected to start services in 2001 (Spain) and 2002 although most will be a little later.[57] This will provide the French manufacturers like Alcatel (with its partner Motorola) and Siemens with early orders. However, since Ericsson and Nokia are the leading suppliers of GSM infrastructure in Europe, they will probably be the main recipients of these early orders.

Japanese infrastructure providers may also benefit from NTT DoCoMo's investments in foreign service providers. As discussed above, during the year 2000, it made minority investments in KPN, AT&T Wireless, Taiwan KG Telecommunications, and Hutchison Telecom and it is also working with several Asian carriers. As of early 2000, DoCoMo was carrying out W-CDMA tests in collaboration with SK Telecom (Korea) and service providers in Singapore, Thailand, Malaysia, and China.[58] It is likely that NTT DoCoMo's suppliers in Japan will receive some orders from these Asian carriers.

Therefore, if committee-based competition has a greater impact than market-based competition in third generation infrastructure, Ericsson will probably be the leader in third generation mobile infrastructure as it was in second generation infrastructure. It is a major supplier of infrastructure to the two Japanese service providers who will start services in 2001 and it is a major supplier of GSM infrastructure to many of the European service providers who are expected to start services in late 2000 and early 2001. Further, as of mid-2000, it was supplying test equipment to many of these European service providers including Telecom Italia, Telia, Mannessmann, Deutsche Telekom, Telefónica and Vodafone.[59] Ericsson's weakness is cdma2000 since its recently-acquired Qualcomm division has a very small share of the cdmaOne market.

After Ericsson, it is more difficult to say which infrastructure vendor is better positioned in terms of relationships with service providers due to the recent alliances between NEC and Siemens, between Matsushita and Nortel, and between Fujitsu and Alcatel. These alliances enable these firms to utilize the Japanese infrastructure suppliers' access to early orders in Japan and the Western suppliers' access to customers outside of Japan.

NEC and Siemens in March 1999 announced their plan to cooperatively develop third generation base stations and switching equipment. They hoped to capture 20% of the global market for cellular phone systems equipment.[60] Subsequently, the two firms created a joint firm in Great Britain called Mobisphere to develop and design equipment in which Siemens will control 51% and Great Britain will control 49% of the new firm. The two firms believe they are combining technological and marketing capabilities. Siemens has strengths in one half of the European standard (the time division-based) and the GSM switching equipment while NEC has specialist expertise in the more mobility-oriented frequency division segment of the system. As for marketing, NEC believes that Siemens is strong in Europe while NEC has strengths in Asia.[61]

In theory, the combination of the two firms should succeed as long as they do not let pride interfere with an appropriate division of responsibilities. The alliance is really about combining NEC's relationship with DoCoMo and Siemens' relationships with service providers in more than 55 countries (as of mid-2000). They can use the initially large orders from DoCoMo (and perhaps Deutsche Telekom and Telecom Italia) to create the best base stations and switching equipment for the rest of the world. Thus, it would make sense if both firms were made responsible for marketing the infrastructure to their existing customers while the development work is divided between their existing capabilities of NEC in the frequency division segment and Siemens in the switching equipment and time division-based segment. This would make Siemens responsible for marketing the infrastructure outside of Japan to its existing customers except where DoCoMo has contacts. Further, it would make sense if this development work were effectively integrated with the development work in Japan. Whether these firms will be able to do this is still questionable, as these kinds of alliances did not work well in second generation infrastructure.

Matsushita and Nortel announced an alliance in October 1998 to develop third generation base stations and switching equipment. Matsushita was planning to develop the base stations while Nortel was planning to develop the switching equipment and base station controllers. This alliance is also about combining Matsushita's relationship with DoCoMo and Nortel's relationships with service providers in more than 34 countries (as of mid-2000). Although Matsushita has been a rather small supplier of base station-related equipment to DoCoMo in PDC, most people are predicting that its share with DoCoMo will rise in W-CDMA base stations.[62] The question is how well Matsushita and Nortel will cooperate on development and in marketing where Nortel should probably be made responsible for most of the marketing effort outside Japan. The fact that a joint company does not exist makes this alliance appear weaker than the NEC–Siemens alliance.

Nokia's order from Japan Telecom and Telecom Finland gives Nokia an opportunity to develop early capabilities in W-CDMA base stations.[63] Further, its strong relationships with GSM service providers could make Nokia one of the largest providers of W-CDMA base stations along the lines of the NEC–Siemens alliance and the Matsushita–Nortel alliance.

Alcatel and Fujitsu created a joint venture in May 2000 to develop equipment for third generation systems. Alcatel will own 66% and Fujitsu will own 34% of a venture that will employ 2000 engineers.

Alcatel will be responsible for selling systems in Europe and Fujitsu will be responsible for selling systems in Japan. They expect to obtain one-fifth of the market for third generation systems.[64] Although the existence of a joint company is a good sign, Fujitsu has never sold mobile communications infrastructure outside of Japan, it is weaker than NEC and Matsushita, and Alcatel is somewhat weaker than both Nortel and Siemens.

Lucent has been a small supplier of infrastructure to DoCoMo and is expected to supply some W-CDMA infrastructure to DoCoMo. The small volume of this order and Lucent's small installed base outside the US, particularly in GSM, means that Lucent may have a hard time generating early orders for W-CDMA infrastructure. Lucent's bigger opportunity is in cdma2000, particularly in the US where Lucent has by far the largest share of the cdmaOne market.

Motorola and Alcatel have sold infrastructure to the second and seventh largest number of countries. Their challenge is to obtain early orders for third generation equipment. They will not be suppliers of W-CDMA infrastructure to DoCoMo or the Japan Telecom-led consortium. They will probably get some early orders from the European, in particular the French, service providers. Their real opportunity is in cdma2000 where Motorola has the second largest share worldwide. Although most of these service providers will be slow to introduce third generation services, they are expected to improve incrementally their data rates and two of Motorola's largest customers, DDI Cellular and IDO, are expected to continue being the first service providers to install this new equipment. Thus, it is likely that Motorola will be able to challenge Lucent for position as the leading supplier of cdma2000 infrastructure.

The relative importance of market- and committee-based competition

The relative importance of market- and committee-based competition in third generation infrastructure will probably depend on three factors; the percentage of new versus existing service-providers, the degree of technological change in the move from second to third generation services, and global carriers. First, the larger the percentage of licenses that are offered to existing service-providers, the greater the importance of relationships. Chapter 4 found that market-based competition played a stronger role with new than existing service-providers. For example, orders from new service-providers helped Nokia and to some extent Nortel expand their shares of the GSM market. Thus, a large number of new service-providers could also offer infrastructure suppliers the opportunity to be more successful in third generation than in second generation infrastructure.

There is a general agreement, however, that existing service-providers or consortiums of existing service-providers will probably receive the majority of third generation service licenses. For example, the US does not plan to offer licenses for third generation services, Japan will offer three licenses but they are going to existing service-providers, and it appears as if consortiums of existing service-providers will receive most of the licenses in the European countries.

This will also probably be true in other countries due to the large amount of existing competition in the mobile sector. A report by the Yankee Group found that worldwide, the average number of service-providers per market is 2.2, though these numbers vary depending on the region. The Japanese and North American markets have an average of 6.5 and 4.5 competitors in the major markets respectively, while only in Latin America and Africa do more than half of wireless subscribers have a choice of just one or two providers. Thirty percent of the world's addressable wireless population have at least four providers available and only 7% live in true monopoly markets.[65]

Second, the more incremental the changes the service-providers make in moving from second to third generation services, the greater the continuity in customer–supplier relationships. Japanese service-providers like NTT DoCoMo and the consortium of Japan Telecom, BT, and Airtouch are making a big jump from second generation PDC to third generation W-CDMA services. The reason is that these service-providers have not defined an evolutionary path from low data to high data rates in PDC and they are employing a new network interface that will be to some extent compatible with the evolution of the GSM network interface.

However, outside Japan, most service-providers have already defined evolutionary paths from second to third generation services in order to reduce the cost and risk of introducing third generation services. Many GSM service-providers have been in the process of introducing GPRS (General Packet Radio System) services between 1999 and 2001.[66] Interestingly, by summer 1999, European GSM service providers had given 20 of their 21 contracts for GPRS to their previous GSM infrastructure supplier. The only exception was Deutsche Telekom, who gave its GPRS contract to Ericsson. Including this contract, Ericsson received six of the contracts versus seven for Nokia, four for Alcatel, three each for Motorola and Nortel, and one each for Siemens and Lucent.[67] In terms of dollars, Ericsson claimed that it had over 50% of the global market for GPRS systems as of December 1999 followed by Nokia and Alcatel.[68]

DAMPS and cdmaOne service-providers also appear as if they are following a similar pattern of evolutionary evolution toward third generation services. As mentioned earlier, the DAMPS industry group or UWCC (Universal Wireless Communications Consortium) has elected to move in the same direction as GSM and adopt many of the GSM enhancements such as GPRS and EDGE. Ericsson has been a major proponent of these developments since this will make it easier for Ericsson to move its DAMPS customers to improved second generation and eventually to third generation services.[69] Similarly, cdmaOne service-providers are incrementally improving their data rates with Japan's DDI Cellular leading the way. It was the first cdmaOne service-provider in the world to introduce 64 kilobit per second services in the fall of 1999 and it plans to introduce 144kbps capability before it introduces third generation services in the fall of 2002.

The degree at which carriers move from second to third generation services may depend on the timing of their third generation services. An early start of third generation services would suggest a large technological jump from second to third generation services while a slow start would suggest an incremental move from second to third generation technologies. NTT DoCoMo and a second consortium plan to start services in 2001 and some European service-providers (primarily in Germany, France, and Italy) are talking about starting services in 2002. After that, most European service providers are taking a cautious approach and US service-providers are largely satisfied with second generation technology. This suggests an incremental move towards third generation services.

The third factor determining the importance of relationships versus capabilities is the degree to which global carriers emerge. Many people argue that 15–20 carriers may dominate the world market within a few years. This argument is strengthened by the recent acquisitions of Airtouch (US) and Mannessmann (Germany) by Vodafone, which now has the largest number of subscribers in the world followed by NTT DoCoMo. Other carriers like Deutsche Telekom, France Télécom, British Telecom, and AT&T have also been busily investing in foreign service-providers and are considering the types of large acquisitions that Vodafone has done.

The emergence of these global carriers will cause changes in vendor–service-provider relationships and may reduce the importance of these relationships. It is expected that these global carriers will negotiate global contracts in order to reduce the cost of infrastructure and improve the compatibility of their different systems. The high global roaming charges are one factor that is driving these global acquisitions and in order to improve the efficiency of global roaming greater compatibility in these systems will be necessary.

These types of global contracts will probably change the nature of the vendor–service-provider relationships. They may move towards the pattern found in the US. As discussed in Chapter 4, the fragmented US market led to the service-providers acquiring markets that had been supplied by multiple vendors. This caused the service-providers to develop capabilities of working with multiple vendors. In other words, they reduced their switching costs. If this happens, we can probably expect the global carriers to work with two vendors in order to promote competition while at the same time retaining some compatibility. This may reduce the importance of relationships and increase the importance of capabilities.

The remaining question is when these global carriers will emerge. Many of the vendor decisions for the enhanced second generation technologies had been decided by mid-2000 and the vendor decisions for the third generation services had been decided by early 2001. Thus, the emergence of global carriers may not have an effect on competition in the mobile infrastructure market until the fourth generation, which by the way is under development by NTT DoCoMo.

In summarizing the three factors that will probably impact on the relative importance of market-versus committee-based competition in the third generation, it appears that committee-based competition and its interaction with market-based competition will play a stronger role than just market-based competition. Global carriers will not emerge before many of the orders are placed, there will be an incremental move towards third generation services, and most third generation service providers will have offered second generation services.

COMPETITION IN THIRD GENERATION HANDSETS

This section uses the hybrid model of committees and markets to forecast competition in third generation handsets. Chapter 5 argues that while participation in the relevant standard setting committees is necessary to succeed, market-based competition has largely deter-mined the winners in the open standards. Further, product line/platform strategies have been the determinants of success in this market-based competition. The product line/platform strategies used by Nokia, Motorola, and Ericsson in the GSM handset market, in particular their subsidization of entry-level models, act as an entry barrier to other firms. This has made it difficult for Japanese firms to use their incremental improvement strategy in the GSM market. And Nokia's superior product line/platform strategy has enabled it to obtain the highest share and profitability in this market. Further, Nokia's effective use of global platforms has enabled it to extend its domination of the GSM phone market to the DAMPS and to some extent cdmaOne market.

Market-based competition will probably play a more important role than committee-based competition (particularly outside of Japan) in third generation handsets since the W-CDMA standard-setting process is completely open. It also appears as if product line/platform strategies will play a role in this market-based competition. One question is whether the Japanese manufacturers can use the early start of services in Japan to develop an advantage in this market-based competition.

Advantages for Japanese manufacturers in third generation handsets

The early start of services in Japan in 2001 will probably provide Japanese manufacturers with an advantage over Western firms. Up until now, Western firms have not done well in the Japanese market and this is expected to continue, partly due to the emphasis on committee-based competition in the Japanese market. DoCoMo may continue providing its preferred domestic suppliers with preferential information and the poor performance by the foreign manufacturers in weight competition will probably provide DoCoMo with little incentive to change its procurement methods.

The question is whether the Japanese phone suppliers can transfer their domination of the Japanese market to the European market. Although the Japanese manufacturers will have about a 6–12-month lead over their European rivals in terms of service start dates, it is not clear that the Japanese or any market will generate a large number of third generation phone shipments. According to interviews with manufacturers, most of them expect fewer than 150,000 dual-mode PDC and third generation phones to be sold in the first year of NTT DoCoMo's service.

As this book was going to press, it appeared that the success of Japan's mobile Internet would provide more foreign opportunities for

Japanese firms than the adoption of W-CDMA by Europe. Japanese firms have acquired more experience than Western firms in the mobile Internet and it appears that they will be able to use this experience to increase their shares of the foreign handset market.

Interestingly, Japanese firms might have increased their share of the GSM market in 2000 if DoCoMo had adopted the WAP browser and WML as opposed to i-mode and c-HTML. As discussed earlier, Japan's MPT had demanded that DoCoMo either adopt or create a global third generation standard. This encouraged them to work with Ericsson and Nokia and to agree to the adoption of the evolution of the GSM network interface. However, it now appears that the mobile Internet is now more important than 3G services. Thus, while DoCoMo adopted a more global policy towards a third generation air and network interface, its adoption of a unique albeit rather open browser standard may have temporarily placed the Japanese manufacturers at a disadvantage. I say "temporarily," since the convergence of the mark-up language will make the choice of c-HTML by DoCoMo less important.

To be fair though, it is not clear that it is only DoCoMo who has wanted to use a unique as opposed to a global standard in micro-browsers. Since DoCoMo decided to adopt the evolution of the GSM network interface in its third generation standard, some Japanese manufacturers have grumbled that this has made it even easier for foreign firms to enter the Japanese mobile infrastructure market.[70] Thus, Japanese manufacturers probably also have mixed feelings about the adoption of a global micro-browser language like WAP. They realize that they have done well with a protected Japanese market and DoCoMo's suppliers have done even better with their own little playing field within the Japanese market.

Dual-mode phones and thus very little change in market shares?

It is quite possible that there will be very little change in market shares due to the initial use of dual-mode phones and the continued existence of the structural differences between the Japanese and other markets. As shown in Figure 6.5, the service providers currently plan to expand their coverage very slowly. Thus, dual-mode phones will dominate the market for many years: the Japanese service providers will initially introduce dual-mode PDC and W-CDMA phones while GSM service-providers will initially introduce dual-mode GSM and W-CDMA phones. Naturally, cdmaOne and DAMPS service-providers will also

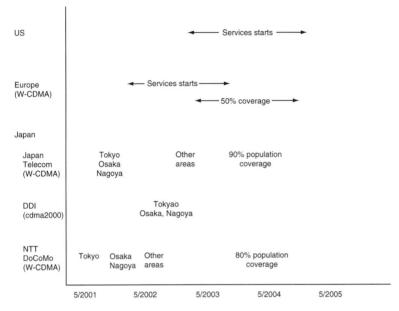

Figure 6.5   3G service schedules and thus the need for dual-mode phones

introduce other forms of dual-mode phones. It is likely that single-mode phones will not appear before the year 2004 in any country and thus the same phone will not be able to be used effectively in both Japan and Europe until at least the year 2005.

In other words, it is quite possible that the start of third generation services will have little effect on the current mobile phone shares. Different phones will be sold in Europe and Japan until at least 2005 and possibly long after that due to these dual-mode phones. Further, the structural differences between the two markets that are discussed at the end of Chapter 5 may continue in the third generation markets. Thus, Nokia may continue to dominate the European market through its effective product line/platform management strategy while Matsushita may continue to dominate the Japanese market through its ability to create the lightest phones.

A global development capability

The ability to succeed in both the Japanese and other markets will most likely require an effective global development capability. Firms that can develop dual-mode phones for both the Japanese and GSM markets using a single global platform will be able to introduce a much wider variety of phones for the same development resources than other firms. This will be particularly important and difficult due to the introduction of new functions such as game-playing, music-playing, video-viewing, personal navigation, and business capabilities in these phones. Further, the similarities in the W-CDMA and cdma2000 standards will also require a global development capability. Firms that can develop phones for the W-CDMA and cdma2000 standards from a single platform will be able to use development resources more effectively than other firms will.

Nokia and to some extent Ericsson have created this organizational capability and Motorola is moving strongly in this direction. Motorola has made substantial changes in its platform management strategy since it recognized the need for these changes in 1998. These changes have already led to increased market share in the US digital phone market and it is expected that its share of the GSM market will also increase due to a better use of platform products. Further, it is expected to introduce phones for both the GSM and DAMPS standards that are based on a single platform beginning in 2001.

The other firms will probably take much longer to develop global platforms. Although Matsushita, NEC, and Mitsubishi have all participated in the GSM market for many years, they still manage their Japanese, European, and US development centers independently. Matsushita may be the fastest to create such a capability since it claims that it will begin integrating its global development centers once it begins introducing W-CDMA phones. Toshiba's alliance with Siemens[71] may help them create this capability while Alcatel and the other Japanese manufacturers will need a global alliance to succeed.

Thus, it appears as if competition in third generation handsets will be determined by whether the Western or Japanese firms can most quickly overcome their weaknesses. Nokia has strengths in global platform management while the Japanese firms have an advantage in terms of the early starts by their service-providers. Will Nokia or perhaps Ericsson or Motorola be able finally to succeed in the Japanese market or will Matsushita, NEC, or Mitsubishi be able to create a global platform capability?[72]

Notes

1. Banding together: the future of IS-136, Jo Wheeler *Mobile Communications International* 2/99, pp. 79
2. For example, it is generally believed that its infrastructure and handset businesses were losing money when they were sold to Ericsson in March 1999 and Kyocera in February 2000 respectively.
3. NTT DoCoMo and Ericsson have argued that W-CDMA doesn't completely rely on Qualcomm-patented technology and they had the necessary patents to bypass Qualcomm technology. Although no one, including the antagonists actually knows who was right, the fact that DoCoMo cited 1500 Qualcomm patents in its submission to the ITU suggests that Qualcomm held the majority of patents – both critical and otherwise. Thus, it was generally recognized that Ericsson's claim concerning patents that could be used to bypass Qualcomm patents was a negotiating ploy, albeit a necessary negotiating ploy, 17/11/1998, *Wall Street Journal* Interactive Edition, Asian Technology.
4. Qualcomm and the CDMA Development Group argued that they would not allow their patents to be used in W-CDMA unless the third generation standard contained backward compatibility with cdmaOne. A critical aspect of this compatibility is the chip rate used in the standard. W-CDMA must use a chip rate that is a multiple of the cdmaOne rate if W-CDMA is to be backward compatible with cdmaOne systems. Thus, the CDMA Development Group requested a chip rate of 3.686, which is three times the chip rate (1.2288) used in cdmaOne. Meanwhile, the W-CDMA supporters have wanted to use a much higher rate since this increases network capacity. They have continuously argued that reducing its proposal from 4.096 to 3.686 mcps would be counterproductive for non-cdmaOne operators.
5. This difference is partly due to more stringent rules concerning patents and Qualcomm's desire to defend its cdmaOne business. The International Telecommunications Union (ITU) has been responsible for choosing a third generation mobile communications standard that is known as IMT-2000 (International Mobile Telecommunications 2000). It received 15 different proposals by its deadline of June 1999 of which the two main proposals were UTRA (ETSI's compromise between W-CDMA and TD-CDMA) and cdma2000.

   The ITU has taken a very strong stance towards intellectual property rights. For example, it is generally argued that the holder of any known patent or any pending patent application related to any proposal made to the ITU in the process of international standards-setting must submit a written statement, either waiving those rights or committing to negotiate licences on a non-discriminatory basis and on reasonable terms and conditions. Failure to provide this statement ultimately excludes the proposal from the international standards-setting process. Ericsson was willing to conform to these rules while Qualcomm was not since it depended on patent royalties for its existence. Thus, Qualcomm probably believed that it could make higher profits defending its cdmaOne business than in licensing its technology for third generation systems. Without compatibility between W-CDMA and cdmaOne, there is clearly less reason for service providers to adopt cdmaOne or even expand their cdmaOne business.

6. 17/11/1998, *Wall Street Journal* Interactive Edition, Asian Technology.

7. The ITU began threatening to throw out the W-CMDA and cdma2000 proposals in November 1998 if the long-standing dispute surrounding the IPRs of the various CDMA proposals was not resolved. Eleven major European and Asian cellular operators made similar pleas and argued that any IPR issues should be discussed separately from the ITU's standard setting activities and that IPR licenses should be granted on fair, reasonable and non-discriminatory terms and conditions (*Total Telecom*, Operators Side with ITU over 3G Dispute, Vanessa Clark, 18/12/1998).

8. Although the ITU expected to finalize specifications for IMT-2000 at its March 1999 meeting the long-running IPR dispute between Qualcomm and Ericsson caused it to settle for a compromise of three next generation air interfaces. The three systems were cdma2000, wideband-CDMA and TDMA, which was supported by groups like the Universal Wireless Communications Consortium. It then placed the responsibility for making this family of standards work back in the hands of the manufacturers. The only people that were happy with the outcome were the TDMA supporters since their standard was the only one without IPR problems and few observers expected their TDMA proposal stood much chance of being first past the post in the race to back the standard chosen for IMT-2000 (*Bloomberg*, ITU Gives Up on Single 3G Standard, Vanessa Clark, 22/3/1999).

9. For example, at a 1995 conference, a Qualcomm representative cited a Cellnet report that stated there were many problems with GSM technology. A Cellnet attendee had to point out that the Qualcomm representative was citing a 1991 report; GSM technology had evolved considerably in four years. In a more flagrant example, without presenting any evidence, Qualcomm argued that cdmaOne had fewer harmful health effects than GSM. This type of alarmist statements scared the European service providers who were trying to avoid the health effects issue.

10. Ericsson's proposal did reduce the component costs of W-CDMA and cdmaOne dual-mode phones, which would make it easier for cdmaOne operators to move from cdmaOne to W-CDMA. However, Ericsson's claim that its proposal would make W-CDMA compatible with cdma2000 was not entirely true since the proposed chip rate was not a multiple of the cdmaOne chip rate.

11. *Mobile Communications International*, 7/98, p. 21, UMTS licensing raises eyebrows.

12. For example, many US officials argued that the choice of a single standard, in particular linking licensing with a particular technical standard is a trade barrier. *Mobile Communications International*, 7/98, p. 21, UMTS licensing raises eyebrows.

13. *Wall Street Journal*, 2/6/2000 Qualcomm Has High Hopes for Deal With Chinese Mobile-Phone Operator, Matt Forney.

14. China Unicom spent more than a year considering the implementation of cdmaOne before announcing in May 2000 that it would not install cdmaOne and would stick with GSM. Many analysts believed the delay was a Chinese negotiating tactic during talks with the United States on China's entry to the World Trade Organization. The talks led to a China–US market-opening agreement in November 1999, and in May 2000 the U.S. House of Representatives endorsed the deal by passing a bill that gives China permanent normal trade status (PNTR). 30/5/2000, Qualcomm's Hope for China Unicom CDMA Appear Dead, Tony Munroe. A more complete discussion of these issues can be found in UCI Graduate School of Management case study on Qualcomm, Joel West (Qualcomm's CDMA (B): China Market Entry, 31/1/2001).
15. Ericsson documents.
16. For example, while Qualcomm was encouraging developers to move to its three-channel multicarrier model called 3XRTT, European developers were expected to move towards a direct-sequence spreading method for data services. Rally by 3G camps excludes W-CDMA interface, Loring Wirbel, *EE Times*, 3/3/2000.
17. Susie Helms, "You say you want a revolution," *Mobile Communications International*, July/August, p. 46.
18. See p. 239 n.l.
19. Total Telecom, Ericsson Wins $200 Million Contract In Venezuela, Paul de Bendern, *Reuters*, 13/12/1999.
20. Rally by 3G camps excludes W-CDMA interface, Loring Wirbel, *EE Times*, 3/3/2000.
21. Dundee's Securities Corporation Report, "Global Industry Wireless Report: Part 2," by Mark Sam *et al.* 20/12/2000.
22. *NY Times*, Technology, 8/7/2000, Three South Korean Phone Firms Reject Qualcomm's Standard, Carolyn Koo, Nytimes.Com/Thestreet.-Com. Technology News, *Sun*, 23/7/2000, Korea Picks Nokia, DoCoMo Mobile System Over Qualcomm (Update5), Ian King
23. For example, this is argued in a report by the Dundee's Securities Corporation called "Global Industry Wireless Report: Part 2," by Mark Sam *et al.*, 20/12/2000.
24. "Only fakirs need apply," *Economist*, 3/2/2001, pp. 67–8.
25. There is a wide perception that mobile phones are too small to effectively send and receive e-mail and files, access the Internet, and use application programs, particularly in the US. As discussed in the next section, this perspective is very country-dependent in that in Japan and to some extent Europe size is considered a liability.
26. Sales of Sharp's Zaurus began to grow in the mid-1980s due to its popular pen-input system. While Japanese, particularly older Japanese, are more comfortable with writing than typing in characters since they never became used to a keyboard, Americans and Europeans have been using typewriters and computers for a long time. This caused the Japanese PDA market to be much larger than the US or the European PDA market until recently.
27. Palm Computing was a subsidiary of 3Com until it went public in March 2000.

28. Windows CE has generally not been considered a viable candidate for the PDA operating system due to its high power consumption and lack of support from PDA manufacturers. For example, both Philips and Sharp quit Windows CE in favor of EPOC. Total Telecom, Psion & 3Com Make Software Compatible – Rival Microsoft, Bundeep S. Rangar *Bloomberg News*, 13/10/1999.

29. The WAP Forum was created in June 1997 by Ericsson, Motorola, Nokia, and Unwired Planet. It is not a standards body; it submits its specifications for adoption by appropriate standards bodies. It is independent of the air interface standard and thus can be used with cdmaOne, GSM, DAMPS, cdma2000 and W-CDMA. It is also independent of the handset and thus can be used with any multiple displays, devices, input methods, transports, and applications.

30. *Mobile Communications International*, November 1999, p. 6, "Nokia breaks ranks," Guy Daniels and Mike Hibberd.

31. *Yahoo News*, 15/12/1999, Motorola to Use Palm Pilot Operating System, Emily Kaiser.

32. Microsoft and Ericsson to Create Wireless Venture Software Giant Gets New Edge in Industry Lawrence M. Fisher 9/12/1999, *Wall Street Journal* Technology, Microsoft Enters Cell-Phone Market Through Alliance With Ericsson, Ericsson Says It Remains Committed To Symbian Venture With Nokia, Others.

33. AllNet Devices, Ericsson: No Plans To Work With Palm, 16/12/1999 *Reuters*.

34. See *South China Morning Post Publication* (2000), Anonymous, "China and Japan seen as key drivers for new-generation Internet access Source," 19/9/2000.

35. Another estimate claimed that there were less than 4 million WAP subscribers outside Japan with 3 million of these in Korea by November 2000. http://www.eurotechnology.com/imode/faq-wap.html

36. See K. Chan (2000).

37. Presently, Web-based pages are written in HTML while WAP is based on WML and thus content must be rewritten for WAP-based handsets to access the Internet. The World Wide Web Consortium recommended in January that Web-based pages be written in XHTML or XML in order to make it easier for small handsets such as mobile phones to access the Internet. *Yahoo News*, 27/1/2000, Standards group recommends XHTML 1.0, Jennifer Mack. And since WML is a subset of XML, conversion between XML and WML is expected to be much easier than between HTML and WML. The problem is that content providers are only just beginning to write their pages in XML.

38. GeoWorks claims that it holds the essential intellectual property rights (IPRs) for WAP and there are disagreements about the level of patent charges. (*Total Telecom*, GeoWorks Claims Could Finish Off WAP 26/1/2000). Geoworks initially said that it would seek 10% royalties from vendors of WAP-based hardware, software and content. Although it has now rescinded this demand and agreed that it will follow Forum policies regarding intellectual property rights, the exact licensing terms

are still unclear (*Allnetdevices*, Geoworks Says It Will Play By The Rules On WAP Patent Claim 8/2/2000).

39. Many of these special purpose magazines have not only been traditionally difficult to obtain; it has often been difficult to even identify them due to their limited circulation. Traditionally, only specialists are familiar with these special purpose magazines and journals and the identifying and contacting of the relevant specialists has been difficult. Thus, traditionally there has been a strong tradeoff between richness and reach.

40. US and European firms have made a large number of announcements concerning their plans in the mobile Internet. Most of these announcements suggest that they are focusing on contents that are currently successful in the fixed-line Internet. Chan, K., "Mobile internet hits bumps but next year looks better – despite flaws WAP is set," *Dow Jones Newswire*, 25/9/2000. Dodge, J, "The wireless Web is going nowhere fast," e*WEEK Dow Jones Newswires*; 25/9/2000. Tiernan, R., "Moving at WAP speed," *Dow Jones Newswires*, 12/10/2000.

41. More details can be found in Jeffrey Funk, "The Mobile Internet Market: Lessons from Japan's i-mode System," presented at the E-Business Transformation: Sector Developments and Policy Implications, Washington, DC, 25–26/9/2000.

42. See n.40

43. Source: Tsutaya Online.

44. See Christensen (1997) for a discussion of how existing customers often cause firms to misunderstand new technologies.

45. Popular contents now include train and other navigators, restaurant search and discount coupon services, and ski information services.

46. DoCoMo, KPN to Create European i-mode Portal Latest News, *allNet-Devices*, 29/9/2000 Japan's NTT DoCoMo has signed an agreement with Dutch wireless operator KPN Mobile to develop wireless services based on its i-mode specification for the European market.

47. Support for i-mode Grows, *allNetDevices*, 12/12/2000 Two vendors have announced software products that support both i-mode and the competing Wireless Application Protocol (WAP), confirming that i-mode is gaining momentum outside its base in Japan. At least one European wireless operator is creating an i-mode portal. In addition, AT&T Wireless will license i-mode technology in the wake of a major investment by NTT DoCoMo, which developed and controls i-mode.

48. *Yahoo News*, 11/12/2000, DoCoMo Allies With Taiwan's Telco (Associated Press): Japan's NTT DoCoMo Inc. forged an alliance with Taiwan's KG Telecommunications Monday to bring the Japanese mobile giant's multimedia services to Taiwan and eventually to mainland China.

49. Global equity research report (11/2/2000) from Warburg.

50. Yankee Group, Positioning for an IP Mobility World – Part 2: *Infrastructure Vendor Strategies*, Report Vol. 3, No. 8, March 1999.

51. New York Times, 4/12/1999, Technology, Cisco Seeks Deals With Nokia and Ericsson, Reuters, Stockholm

52. *Yahoo News*, 24/2/200, What's Ailing Lucent?

53. See n.51.
54. A consortium consisting of Japan Telecom, British Telecom, and Airtouch. Tsushin shinchouryuu (3) jisedai keitai, takamaru kitai – sekai shijou shiya ni. The high expectations for next generation mobile phones – globalization of the mobile market, *Nikkei Industrial*, 11/10/1999.
55. Financial Times (FT.com), 12/14/99, Japan: Mobile phone market rings true Mobile telecoms is bucking the economic trend, thanks largely to start of third generation services, Michiyo Nakamoto.
56. These suppliers have been mentioned in several *Nikkei* articles.
57. Europe's Telecom Firms Launch Bid For Share of New Wireless Licenses, Gautam Naik, *Wall Street Journal* 7/3/2000. Nikkei Electronics, 15/1/2000, "keitai, sekai seiha, mobile phones, global domination," pp. 121–145.
58. Seikoku unyu, I-mo-do wo katsuyou, raigetsu kara yusou joukyou tsutaeru. Seikoku unyu will begin transmitting transportation conditions using i-mode next month, *Nikkei*, 28/1/2000, p. 7.
59. *Total Telecom*, Ericsson To Pilot UMTS System, 5/1/2000, Total Telecom, TIM Says Europe's First UMTS Call Made, Reuters 24/11/1999.
60. NEC doitsu shi-mensu, jisedai idotai tsuushin de hokatsu teikei – oo ni gappei setsuritsu. NEC and Germany's Siemens are pursuing a comprehensive tie-up in next generation mobile phones – will establish a joint company in Europe, *Nikkei Industrial*, 25/3/1999, p. 7. NEC Teams with Siemens to Develop Mobile Phone Technology. Peter Poole-Wilson, *Bloomberg News*, 24/3/1999,
61. NEC to doitsu Shi-mensu, Ei de gappei Kaisha Setsuritsu – Jisedai Keitai Infura Kaihatsu. NEC and Germany's Siemens have established a joint company in England to do next generation infrastructure development, *Nikkei*, 13/11/1999, p. 9; Siemens and NEC Team for 3G Development *Total Telecom*, Jeremy Scott-Joynt, 12/11/1999.
62. Matsushita Tsuukou, Jisedai Keitai Denwa de Teikei – Bei No-teru Nettwa-kusu toto. Matsushita Communications has tied-up with America's Northern Telecom in next generation mobile phones, Nikkei Industrial, 21/10/1998, p. 5.
63. Jisedai Keitai Denwa chuukaku Setsubi, Nokia kara mo Choutatsu, Nihon Terekomu – Hacchusaki 3sha Kettei. Japan Telecom has decided to purchase next generation mobile infrastructure from 3 firms including Nokia, *Nikkei*, 17/2/2000, p. 11.
64. *Bloomberg.com.*, Technology News, 9/5/2000, Alcatel Allies With Fujitsu in Mobile Phone Equipment (Update2), Daniel Tilles.
65. Wireless Operators Multiply Around The World – Report, Steven Bonisteel, *Newsbytes*, Boston, Massachusetts, U.S.A., 30/11/1999. *http://www.newsbytes.com.*
66. Total Telecom, French Telcoms Operators To Seek 3G Licences, Gillian Handyside, Reuters, 19/11/99.
67. Susie Helms, "You say you want a revolution," *Mobile Communications International*, July/August 1999, p. 46.
68. *Yahoo News*, 15/12/1999, Ericsson Says It Has 50 Pct of GPRS Market.
69. See page 239 n.l.

70. "Gekika suru sekai hyoujun senso, nihon kigyo ni hitsuyo na gaikor-yoku – asia to renkei, obei ni taiko wo: the escalation of the global standard battle, needed diplomatic strength – alliances with Asia and opposition to US and Europe," *Nikkei*, 11/8/1999, p. 7.
71. Jisedai keitai, Toushiba Doitsu Shi-mensu Teikei – Kaihatsu kara Han-bai made, sekai de Kyoudou Kaihatsu. Toshiba and Germany's Siemens are cooperating on next generation mobile phones from development to sales in the global market, *Nikkei*, 11/3/2000, p. 1.
72. A dark horse in this competition is Kyocera. Kyocera has the fourth largest share in the Japanese market and the largest share of the non-DoCoMo suppliers. Kyocera has always been an innovator in the Japanese market both technologically and organizationally. It is the world leader in ceramic packages and it created DDI (Japan's second largest long-distance provider), DDI Cellular (Japan's second largest mobile phone service provider following its merger with IDO), and DDI Pocket (Japan's largest PHS service provider). In mobile phones, it has often introduced the first phone features and it is now manufacturing some of the smallest phones in the Japanese PDC and cdmaOne markets. Its purchase of Qualcomm's cdmaOne phone business now provides it with an opportunity to compete with Nokia and Motorola in the US and Korean markets and perhaps the rest of the world. Further, Kyocera has always been an organizationally innovative firm. Unlike Japan's electronic giants, Kyocera has consistently created the necessary organizational capabilities without being trapped in long planning cycles and letting tradition and consensus be an organizational obstacle. Kyocera may be the Japanese firm that is able to create a global platform capability and thus take advantage of its capability in making small and light phones.

7 A Proposed Model of Technological Change

This chapter proposes a new model of technological change that incorporates the hybrid model and other ideas from this book. The model of technological change is intended to be exploratory and is not expected to explain all industries. It is offered as an alternative explanation of technological change in industries where standards play a key role. Hopefully, future research by the author and others will modify and extend the framework.

Figure 7.1 summarizes the new model of technological change, which is somewhat similar to the one previously discussed in Chapter 2. These similarities include the circular nature of technological change where technological discontinuities cause competition to return to the competition between alternative standards, designs, or systems.

The major differences in the proposed as opposed to the traditional model of technological change are as follows:

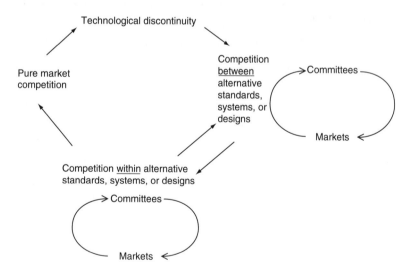

Figure 7.1   A new model of technological change for network industries

1. Global standards are created through the interaction between committees and markets, both of course at the global level.
2. There is also competition within standards and this competition starts long before a global standard is selected. This is why "the emergence of a standard or a dominant design" has been replaced by "competition within standards."
3. At some point, most products will enter a phase in which pure market competition including incremental change drives the market.
4. There is simultaneous competition between and within standards as shown by the bi-directional arrows connecting these two factors in Figure 7.1.

GLOBAL STANDARDS AND THE COMPETITION BETWEEN ALTERNATIVE SYSTEMS, DESIGNS, OR INTERFACE STANDARDS

Results from the mobile communications industry

Large countries (such as the US) or regions (such as Europe) that created a single open standard in an international committee-based standard-setting process and promoted competition between manufacturers and other key suppliers were able to create an early installed base and thus a global mobile communication standard. For example, when Scandinavia, the US, and Europe announced their plans to adopt a single open standard, the forecasted installed bases for these systems rose dramatically. These forecasts for installed base continued to rise as the countries or regions received participation from domestic and foreign firms in the standard-setting processes, awarded licenses to multiple service-providers, started services that were based on the single standards, and experienced the synergistic effect from falling prices and an increasing number of subscribers.

Many of the failures further illuminated the key aspects of this process. For example, although the US service-providers initially used an open standard-setting process to select an open digital standard, DAMPS, the lack of new licenses left the installation of DAMPS to the incumbents who were more interested in making money from the old technology. And when new licenses were finally made available, the support for a single standard had disappeared and the US government refused to intervene. Japan's failures with PHS demonstrate the importance of a standard-setting committee that is open to both domestic and foreign firms.

Several examples also illuminate the difficulties of catching up to a standard with a large installed base. The new standard must be clearly technologically superior or it does not have a chance of displacing the established standard, as the French and Germans learned in the analog era. However, even when the challenger is clearly superior, as subsequent events now show with cdmaOne, it is very difficult to catch up unless the challenger is able to create a much superior committee-and market-based approach, as the supporters of cdmaOne did not.

Learning played a key role in the creation of second and third generation standards. Most of Europe and Japan moved from a relatively closed approach in analog standard-setting to a committee-based approach that is open to both domestic and foreign participants in second and third generation digital standard-setting. The US on the other hand has moved in a different direction due to both changes in overall US regulatory policy and the fact that the initial method used to create the AMPS standard was merely a semi-committee-based approach in which support for a full committee-based approach was not generated.

Firms played a much different role in the setting of standards than is ordinarily found in the literature on standards. In many ways individual firms had very little influence on the setting of mobile communication standards due to the large number of participants on individual standard-setting committees and the openness of them. And when they did influence the setting of standards, as in the case of Ericsson and Nokia in the setting of third generation standards, it occurred in a very unusual way. Ericsson and Nokia were able to utilize Europe's international committee-based standard-setting process, including Europe's decision to adopt a single standard, as a negotiating tool with Docomo.

Applicability of the results to other industries

One question is the applicability of these results to other industries. There certainly are a growing number of formal and informal standard-setting committees not just for mobile phones and telecommunications, but for products such as computers, broadcasting, and consumer electronics that require large investments to implement the new standards. For example, standards are created by such organizations as the Institute of Electric and Electronic Engineers, the National

Institute of Standards and Technology, and the Association for Computing Machinery.[1] As for informal standard-setting activities, 55 firms created the digital video camera standard, more than 100 firms created the 8-millimeter video standard, and two competing DVD standards were created by more than 50 firms each.[2]

Also like the mobile phone industry, in spite of the large number of formal and informal standard-setting committees, in most of these cases it is the market that chooses a winner. And in the choice of the winners, openness is important and thus there is a linkage between the committees and the competition between manufacturers (that is, market). Thus, it is believed that the hybrid model of committees and markets is very applicable to a broad number of industries.

The second commonality is, probably, learning. The growth in the number of these formal and informal standard-setting committees mainly reflects learning. Many firms have recognized that they need to build large and open coalitions to get standards accepted where these large and open coalitions utilize committee and market mechanisms. Why some firms and countries are able to learn faster than others is of course an interesting question for further research.[3]

But beyond these two commonalities it becomes more difficult to generalize. How much openness is needed to create a global standard? When is the choice of a single standard by a country or region useful? When should governments become involved to help create a single standard?

Previous research has found that the degree of required openness is a function of a firm's strength. A firm's strength in network markets can be measured in terms of its existing market position (existing installed base), technical capabilities (ability to innovate, manufacturing abilities, strength in complementary products), and control of intellectual property such as patents and copyrights.[4] Previous research has also found that the tradeoff between performance and compatibility depends on the degree to which one must be sacrificed for the other and the number of new users (Shapiro and Varian, 1999).

This book argues that investment size and interface ambiguity are also important variables.

Investment size

It is hypothesized that the higher the investment required by the new standard, the higher the openness that will be required, the larger the alliances and committees will be, and the greater the importance of compatibility. As the required investments increase, the technology adopters become more risk averse and place more importance on openness, individual firms became less able to control changes to the standard, and the alliances become larger. This is seen in the growing number of formal standard-setting activities and informal alliances for not just mobile phones and telecommunications, but for products such as computers, broadcasting, and consumer electronics that require large investments to implement the new standards.

Further, as these investments become very high as in the case of mobile phones, telecommunications, computers, and broadcasting, governments tend to become involved with these activities and have in some cases played a critical role in creating global standards. Their involvement in these standard-setting activities is partly due to the historical role played by governments in some of these industries. Governments have controlled frequencies, supplied licenses, and set prices indirectly through determining the level of competition in not just mobile phones but also other telecommunication industries like satellites and broadcasting.

However, the fact that governments have also played a critical role in creating *global standards* suggests there is another reason for their involvement in these standard-setting activities. In the mobile communications industry, it was found that governments were the only organizations capable of ensuring competition between hardware and service-producers and ensuring the choice of a single open standard. The choice of a single standard can be looked upon as the creation of a very large alliance/committee and the government as an important entity that has facilitated the creation of this large alliance/committee. AMPS, GSM, and W-CDMA were all supported by large alliances that were to some extent brought together by in some cases one (AMPS) and, in others, multiple governments.

It is argued that governments can and probably should play a similar role in other industries that require large investments to implement a new standard. For example, Appendix 4 presents other examples of industries that require large investments to implement new standards. These include intelligent highway vehicle systems and broadcasting.

Interface ambiguity

It is also hypothesized that the type and number of alliances/committees will be shaped by the degree of definition in the interface. In most of the examples mentioned in Chapter 7 so far for mobile phones, broadcasting, and many types of consumer electronic products, the interface is fairly well-defined so the competition focuses just on this interface. Further, as argued above, the importance of the openness of the interface and its compatibility with previous systems becomes more important as the required investments increase.

However, it is hypothesized that as uncertainty increases in what constitutes the key interface, the variety of alliances/committees will increase. As discussed in Chapter 6, there are a number of interfaces involved with mobile Internet/computing and thus in addition to competition between various standards for each interface there is also competition *between* the various interfaces. In the mobile computing and mobile Internet markets, these interfaces include the interface between the users and various types of handsets (man–machine interface), the interface between the handsets and application programs (operating systems), or the interface between the handsets and the Internet (browsers and language for representing contents). The various types of handsets include mobile phones, PDAs, and handheld games.

Compatibility probably also plays an important role in this competition between different interfaces. But unlike the air interface for mobile phones, it is not clear which compatibilities are important in the competition between the different interfaces. Is it important to have compatibility between different user interfaces, different operating systems, or the different browsers that are used in mobile phones, PDAs, and desktop computers?

The lack of a well-defined single interface in the competition to create mobile computing and mobile Internet standards has caused firms to create a wide variety of alliances/committees. As discussed in Chapter 6, the first wave of important coalitions that were created in the mobile computing/Internet area reflected inter-device competition. Nokia, Motorola, Ericsson, and Psion created the WAP Forum in June 1997, Symbian in mid-1998, and Bluetooth in June 1998 to fight both Microsoft's Windows CE and Palm Computing's proprietary operating systems and browsers.

However, once the mobile phone manufacturers had established credible alternatives to both Microsoft's Windows CE and Palm Computing's proprietary operating systems and browsers, they began to create coalitions in order to differentiate themselves from other mobile phone manufacturers. Thus, the second wave of coalitions began in late 1999 and reflected intra-device competition in that they were aimed at creating better compatibility between mobile phones and either PDAs or desktop computers. Further, from the end of 2000, the variety of these alliances began to expand dramatically as mobile phone manufacturers begin to make alliances with service and content providers; these alliances also reflect intra-device competition and the desire to find the so-called killer applications and key interfaces.

Examples of this phenomenon are not limited to mobile computing and the mobile Internet. Actually, the battle to create mobile computing and mobile Internet standards is part of a larger battle to create Internet standards and Internet businesses. The list of these standards' battles is endless for a variety of reasons. But one reason is because different firms are trying to make their product (desktop, game, or appliance) the main platform for connecting to the Internet.

The competition between different interfaces will probably be affected by the industry structure. Research on standards in the semiconductor industry concluded that incumbents succeeded by building central positions in a cooperative network, which included start-ups. The entry of start-ups was a function of network centrality, as a measure of technological dominance in the standard. Medium levels of centrality lead to the highest amount of entry (Kogut *et al.*, 1995). Thus, in the competition between different interfaces, the number of start-ups will probably be determined by the industry structure, in particular the degree of network centrality in the industry.

COMPETITION *WITHIN* A SPECIFIC STANDARD, DESIGN, OR SYSTEM

The proposed model of technological change also includes competition *within* alternative standards, systems, and designs. And this competition is much more complex than the traditional literature portrays it. In particular, competition within a specific standard starts before a global standard is established and in fact before the specific standard is itself established. This early competition occurs in the committee side of the competition where participation in the standard-setting activities is a prerequisite to success in the market-based competition. For example, Nortel, Lucent, and Japanese handset manufacturers did not initially succeed in GSM because they did not participate in the relevant standard-setting activities.

Committee-based competition and the case of CoPS: mobile infrastructure

This book found that committee-based competition played a much stronger role in infrastructure than in phones due to the complexity of infrastructure. Infrastructure suppliers participated in standard-setting committees while they simultaneously developed technology in cooperation with a service provider due to the complexity of mobile communication standards and infrastructure. Early orders for test and commercial systems are necessary to develop experience as is shown by the similarities between the shares of the early orders and the eventual breakdown of shares.

Although market-based competition played a stronger role in obtaining orders from *new* service-providers while committee-based competition played a stronger role in obtaining orders from existing service-providers, committee-based competition played a stronger role than market competition in the mobile infrastructure market since existing service-providers tended to place the earliest orders for a new generation of infrastructure. This committee-based competition primarily manifested itself in high switching costs and strong continuity in the relationships between infrastructure and service-providers. This continuity appeared to be independent of the maturity of the technology as the strong continuity in GSM and non-US orders for digital infrastructure demonstrated.

Within a single generation of technology, the most successful firms used committee-based capabilities to develop market-based capabilities. For example, in GSM, firms like Ericsson and Nokia developed these market strengths while Lucent, Nortel, Matra, and Philips failed. These latter firms were forced to acquire these capabilities through mergers or acquisitions of which only the Nortel–Matra merger can be considered successful. Other firms, like Motorola, initially succeeded but later failed as committee-based competition began to cross product lines, thus requiring firms to offer both base station and switching equipment or have a strong alliance with a single firm.

Interestingly, the US exhibited a slightly different pattern from the rest of the world. Although even in the US, committee-based competition and its interaction with market-based competition played a stronger role than just market-based competition played, it was less dramatic in the US than elsewhere. In spite of the smaller technological discontinuity and greater compatibility between first and second generation systems in the US than elsewhere, the US market exhibited less continuity than elsewhere in vendor–customer relationships within the analog market, between the analog and digital markets, and in the activities of US service-providers when they invested in foreign service-providers. This suggests that the relative importance of committee-versus market-based competition (in the form of switching costs and continuity in relationships) is more a function of market fragmentation than the level of technological change.

It appears that some aspects of the mobile infrastructure case may be generalizable across other complex products and systems (CoPs). As discussed in Chapter 2, CoPS such as broadcasting equipment, computer systems, and telecommunications equipment tend to be complex, have low volumes, and strong continuities in customer–supplier relationships. Potential research questions for future research on CoPS include the following:

1. What are the degree of switching costs and continuity of orders?
2. Are the switching costs and continuity of orders more a function of market fragmentation, degree of technological change, or other factors?
3. How do firms use committee-based strengths to develop market-based strengths?
4. Does the committee-based competition cross product lines?

Further, although standards do not always play a major role in CoPS, there are often technological discontinuities where dominant designs play a similar role to standards. This brings up the question of how dominant designs and standards are different: a question that is still unresolved. In general, standards deal with interfaces while dominant designs deal with product structure.[5] Due to the growing importance of committees in modern society, future research should look at whether, and if so, how, both committees and markets influence the emergence of dominant designs in recent technologies. Here, it is probably formalized relationships as opposed to formal standard-setting committees that influence the dominant designs.

This discussion suggests that the above four questions can also be applied to CoPS even if standards do not play an important role in the specific product. Questions 1 and 2 can be considered solely in terms of technological discontinuities. Questions 3 and 4 can be framed in terms of technological discontinuities, dominant designs, and how the dominant designs emerge and effect competition.

Market-based competition and the case of mass-produced products: phones

The proposed model shown in Figure 7.1 argues that competition will change from a combination of committee- and market-based competition to just market-based competition at some point after the standard has been established. This characterization is of course quite different from the existing models of technological change, which focus on the emergence of a dominant design or standard and its effect on costs, the relative frequency of product versus process innovation, the nature of the production system, and incremental versus radical innovations. Clearly these variables do not represent the key changes in competition for a CoPS-like mobile infrastructure where volumes never rise significantly and process innovation remains relatively unimportant.[6] And here it is argued that the proposed model also better describes technological change in a mass-produced product like mobile phones than the existing models do.

It is expected that competition will change from committee-based to market-based competition faster in mass-produced products than in CoPS both for reasons of complexity and volumes. As discussed in Chapter 5, although some phone manufacturers failed to create and others did create a temporary advantage in a specific standard through committee-based competition, in the end it was market-based competition that determined the winners. Assuming the standard is relatively open, market-based competition probably plays a more important role than committee-based competition in most mass-produced products. This is certainly the dominant conclusion of most research on this topic (Shapiro and Varian, 1999) and in these industries.[7] Future research should consider whether firms were able to establish any form of committee-based advantage in open standards for mass-produced products like still and video cameras, DVDs, and other consumer electronic products.

Clearly there are a number of ways in which market competition occurs and this chapter will not attempt to discuss them. Nevertheless, it is believed the use of the term "market competition" is a more robust term than "incremental improvement" since it encompasses a much broader set of firm actions than just incremental improvement. In this discussion, however, I will only focus on product line and platform management since this played the key role in market-based competition in the mobile phone market. Other research has found that this plays a key role in industries like automobiles (Cusumono and Nobeoka, 1998) and other products (Dertouzos and Lester, 1990).

The evolution of the appropriate form of product line and platform management is also a new concept. The existing literature does not recognize the effect of industry structure on the appropriate form of product line and platform management not the evolution of this appropriate form. The evolution of the successful strategies over time in the mobile phone industry suggests that volumes, costs, and the diversity of user needs impact on the appropriate product line and platform management strategy.

Future research should attempt to look at the appropriate method of product line and platform management differ by product type and evolve over time in a single product. Where standards play a critical role, the research can look at this in terms of a broader question of how competition evolves from committee-to market-based competition and how this market-based competition evolves in other mass-produced products where standards play a critical role. Industry structure, regulation, and other country-specific variables will probably play a critical role. As with the mobile phone example, it is possible that competition in PDAs, video cameras, digital TVs, and other consumer electronic products will evolve in a manner similar to how competition has evolved in the mobile phone market.

INTERACTION BETWEEN COMPETITION "BETWEEN" AND "WITHIN" ALTERNATIVE STANDARDS

A fourth key difference between the traditional and proposed models of technological change is the interaction between "the competition between" and "the competition within" standards. While the traditional model of technological change describes the emergence of a standard as a critical event that changes the competition in the industry, the new model allows there to be simultaneous competition "between" and "within" standards. Research on the mobile communications industry suggests two reasons why this simultaneous competition between and within standards might exist.

The first reason for the simultaneous competition between and within standards is the coexistence of different standards. For example, in the mobile communications industry, even after AMPS emerged in the mid-1980s, NMT continued to be used by the early adopters and adopted by new countries. Even after GSM began to diffuse in the early 1990s, both AMPS and NMT were still being used by the early adopters and adopted by new countries. Further, new second generation standards such as DAMPS and cdmaOne were also introduced even as the success of GSM had become apparent.

The coexistence of these standards is partly due to different needs including different frequency bands that each country allocated to mobile communications. It was also because service-providers did not want to stop providing services while users were still quite happy with them and they had large fixed costs invested in them. This caused manufacturers to find ways to upgrade existing systems with new technologies. Thus, we see a number of standards coexisting and a variety of paths being built to connect the existing and new standards.

Other industries like the television and radio broadcasting industries have also seen the coexistence of different national standards over many years. It is probably not an accident that these industries have very high fixed costs and thus a change in standards by firms would be very expensive.

The second reason for the simultaneous competition between and within standards is the desire by firms to cover all of their bets. As stated above, competition within a specific standard starts before a global standard is established and in fact before the specific standard is itself established. This is particularly true in committee-based competition where firms must participate in the relevant standard-setting committees and, in the case of CoPS, develop the technology in co-operation with key customers. Thus, firms do not know which standard will win until long after the competition *within* the standard has been decided. Further, when industries require firms to open their technology and proposed standards and these standards are created in open standard-setting committees, it becomes very difficult for a single firm to dominate a specific standard.

This is why the most successful firms in the mobile communications industry have supported multiple standards. For example, the leading suppliers of GSM infrastructure and handsets did not push GSM at the expense of the analog standards. Ericsson, Motorola, and Nokia maintained their shares in the NMT, TACS, and AMPS markets as they competed in GSM infrastructure and phones. Further, to some extent these firms have also become major suppliers of products for other non-GSM digital standards such as the US DAMPS and cdmaOne standards and the Japanese (PDC) digital standard.

This is clearly very different from the two-firm model of standard-setting where firms support only one standard. In some ways, the support of multiple standards by the most successful mobile communication firms reminds us of the way firms will offer a complete product line of say automobiles and trucks. While Porsche may try to convince users to buy sports cars since that is its main product, General Motors does not care whether people buy sports cars, sports utility vehicles, or station wagons, as long as they buy a GM vehicle. To some extent, Ericsson also does not care whether service-providers purchase infrastructure that is based on the GSM, DAMPS, or PDC standards.

In the mobile communications industry, however, support for multiple standards has actually helped firms succeed in the subsequent generation of technology. Ericsson and Motorola were able to develop greater committee-based strengths in GSM than other firms partly because they had supported TACS and supplied several European service-providers with TACS infrastructure. This increased the number of their early orders in GSM. In W-CDMA, it appears that Ericsson's support of PDC enabled it to develop relationships with NTT Docomo and J-Phone and that these second generation orders are leading to early and probably critical W-CDMA orders.

In phones, Nokia's support of multiple analog and digital standards helped it create a global development capability and thus has made it less dependent on determining the winning standard. Nokia's support of multiple analog standards such as AMPS, TACS, and NMT caused it to create global analog platforms. It extended and expanded this strategy in digital phones such that it can develop more than twice the number of models as its competitors for the same development efforts. This enables Nokia to create global economies of scale in development, manufacturing, and purchasing. More importantly, this global development capability has enabled Nokia to change the competition from competition within a single standard, including its relevant committees and markets, to competition at the global level.

Future research should look at other standards to see if there was simultaneous competition "between" and "within" standards. For example, in products such as cable television (set-top boxes), digital television, and PDAs there are many different regional standards and it is still unclear which standard will become the global standard. It is quite possible that there is simultaneous competition between and within standards in these industries. Research on industries like these will further illuminate the issues discussed in this book.

Notes

1. Shapiro and Varian, 1999, p. 237.
2. Yamada (1900).
3. See Kash and Rycoft (2000) for a discussion of how networks learn.
4. Shapiro and Varian, 1999.
5. For example, see Clark (1985).
6. Hobday *et al.* (2000) make a similar argument.
7. Dertouzos and Lester (1990) *Made in America: Regaining the Productive Edge.*

Appendix 1 Interviews

Table A.1 shows the number of interviews carried out with the relevant firms between 1996 and 1999. The interviews are classified according to the person's expertise either as a phone, infrastructure or standard representative. However, in many cases, the issue of standards was discussed with many of the phone and infrastructure representatives since it was often difficult to separate the issue of standards and the product itself. The location of the representative is also noted although of course the constant transfers of people between Europe, Japan, and the US often made this unimportant. In particular, many of the Ericsson, Nokia, and Motorola people who were interviewed in Japan had

Table A.1   Number of interviews each year

Region	Firm	Product type	1996	1997	1998	1999
US	Lucent	Infrastructure		1	3, (1)	1, (1)
	Motorola	Infrastructure	1		(1)	1, (1), **2**
		Phones	1	1	1	1, **1**
		Standards	1	1	1, (1)	
	Nortel	Infrastructure			1, (1)	(1)
European	Alcatel	Infrastructure			(1)	(1)
		Phones			(1)	(1)
	Ericsson	Infrastructure	1	1		(1)
		Phones	1	3	2, (1)	(1)
		Standards		2	1	
	Nokia	Infrastructure				2
		Phones		3	2, (3)	1, (1)
		Standards			2	1
	Philips	Phones			2, (2)	
	Siemens	Infrastructure			(1)	(1)
		Phones			(1)	
	Bosch	Phones			(1)	
Japanese	Fujitsu	Infrastructure		1		
		Phones		1	3	
	Kyocera	Phones	1	3	2	1
	Matsushita	Phones	1	1	2	2
	Mitsubishi	Phones	1		1	1
	NEC	Infrastructure			1	1
		Phones	3	4	2	2
	Toshiba	Phones			2	
	Other	Phones	3	7	6	
	Other	Service providers	3	1		2
Total			17	30	34, (15)	16, (9), **3**

Note: Interviews carried out in Japan are in plain text, in Europe in (parentheses), and in the US in **bold**.

260

Ericsson, Nokia, and Motorola people who were interviewed in Japan had extensive experience in either the US or Europe or both.

The Japanese interviews were carried out regularly in trips to Tokyo while the interviews in Europe were carried out in three separate occasions: May 1998, March 1999, and September 1999. One additional interview was conducted with Motorola in June 2000. The US interviews were carried out in June 1999.

Appendix 2   Analysis of the First 20 GSM Orders

Of Ericsson's eleven base station orders, eight were the result of continuity in the customer–supplier relations, several of these eight orders were helped by alliances, and one additional order was through an alliance with Matra who had previously supplied France Télécom. Although the alliance with Matra was short-lived, it helped Ericsson to obtain early orders from France Télécom, Spain's Telefónica, Italy's SIP, and Vodafone.[1] Ericsson's orders from Italy's Telecom Italia Mobile and Vodafone were helped by its previous supply of analog equipment to these service-providers and alliances with Italian (Italtel[2]) and British firms. Ericsson created a joint venture with Orbitel, which itself was a joint venture between Racal Telecom (Vodafone's parent company) and Plessey, to supply infrastructure for the European market in 1987.[3] Ericsson was to supply switches and Ericsson and Orbitel together planned to supply base stations. This alliance with and eventual acquisition of Orbitel was important since although Vodafone is not a national carrier, it had received a lot of pressure to support UK manufacturing in the selection of both digital and analog infrastructure. Further, Racal Telecom, the major investor in Vodafone, had long harbored dreams of becoming a major supplier of mobile infrastructure.[4]

Motorola's early success in GSM was largely a result of the global customer relationships that it created with such service-providers as Millicom and the joint venture that it created with Siemens. Of Motorola's seven base station orders from the first twenty carriers, three were from previous TACS customers, two were from Millicom's investment in Netcom in Norway and Comvik in Sweden, and two were from a joint venture with Siemens who had previously supplied DeT Mobile's predecessor Deutsche Telekom and TMN in Portugal. In the UK, Cellnet, who was a previous TACS customer, was only able to award the contract to Motorola after it agreed to manufacture the equipment in the UK since, like Vodafone, Cellnet was also being pressured to support British industry.[5]

Siemens, PKI, Alcatel, and Matra received all of their orders either through continuity or preferences for national suppliers. Although Siemens had wanted to work solely with Motorola, it was encouraged to use PKI base stations (as it did in analog systems) by Deutsche Telekom. Siemens supplied the switches and PKI initially supplied the base stations to Deutsche Telekom, TMN, PTT Austria, SFR, and Mannessmann. The orders from Deutsche Telekom and TMN in Portugal were due to continuity while the orders from the Austrian PTT and SFR were obtained through preferences for national suppliers since Siemens had subsidiaries in Austria and France. Alcatel also received an order from Deutsche Telekom through preferences for national suppliers since it had acquired the German firm Standard Elektrik Lorenz. Alcatel's two other orders and Matra's one order were through continuities in customer–supplier relations with France Télécom and SFR. Subsequently, Siemens achieved some orders from Italy's SIP through its acquisition of the Italian firm Italtel in 1993.

Nokia was the sole exception in that of its six orders, only two orders (Telecom Finland and SFR) were from continuity in customer–supplier relations. Nokia's joint venture with Alcatel helped it obtain orders for an NMT and subsequently for early GSM orders from SFR (now called Cegetel) and the Dutch PTT.[6] As this NMT system was being developed by Nokia and Alcatel in 1989, a digital agreement was concluded which also briefly included AEG Telefunken.[7] Although this consortium did not last very long (the only subsequent order was the Dutch PTT), Nokia was able to acquire NMT and GSM orders from SFR in addition to both firms benefiting from technology exchanges.

Notes

1. Ericsson and Matra planned to sell systems that used Matra's small base-station controller to small communities. The relationship was terminated in 1992 largely since Ericsson had other products that it wanted to sell (Meurling and Jeans, 1994; *Le Monde*, 30/9/1988), La France et l'Allemagne choisissent leurs fournisseurs pour le radiotelephone des annees 90, p. 36.)
2. Meurling and Jeans, 1994.
3. *Financial Times*, 25/6/1987, p. 48, "Talks on cellular joint venture."
4. When Plessey was taken over by Siemens and GEC in 1988, Racal Telecom purchased Plessey's share of Oribitel (*Financial Times*, 4/7/1988 7a, "Orders for European car phone network expected"). Eventually, Ericsson purchased half of Orbitel from Racal Telecom (*Financial Times*, 18/1/1991, p. 17, "Racal Telecom sells half of Orbitel") although Racal Telecom was primarily interested in selling half of Orbitel to a service provider who would buy Orbitel equipment. Racal Telecom was even willing to invest in a service provider in order to obtain an order. However, apparently no carrier would give Racal Telecom a deal as good as Ericsson provided (*Financial Times*, 8/11/1989, p. 31, "Racal approached over Orbitel stake," Hugo Dixon).
5. *Financial Times*: 2/8/1988 -7a, "Cellnet mobile phone order goes to Motorola."
6. Nokia's joint NMT order with Alcatel from SFR in 1987 was partly a result of a failed agreement between Alcatel and Motorola. Motorola lost interest when it became clear that France would not license the 900MHz band, which is more appropriate for TACS (*Le Monde*, 20/4/1987, L'accord sur le radiotelephone, p. 28.)
7. *Handelsblatt*, 14/1/1988, Mobilfunk/Weitere europaische Gruppierung – Konsortium mit AEG, Alcatel und Nokia, p. 9.

Appendix 3 Example of Standard Setting in Other Industries That Require High Investments

This appendix applies the hybrid model of standard-setting to two industries where government involvement in standard setting should and will emerge since many technologies in these industries require very large investments by users and even more so by firms. In both of these two examples, intelligent highway vehicle systems and broadcasting, governments choose the mix of committee and market mechanisms.

INTELLIGENT HIGHWAY VEHICLE SYSTEMS

Intelligent highway vehicle systems are expected to provide traffic and other forms of information, automatic toll collection services, accident avoidance services, and eventually remote vehicle control of which the latter will clearly require huge investments in various forms of equipment. The equipment will probably be located in the cars, on the highways themselves, and in distributed base stations.

The government could manage these services in a manner similar to how they manage air traffic control systems or they could award licences to private firms for specific stretches of highway. In either case, the technology and standards for these systems must be created and implemented using both committee and market mechanisms. The large investments needed to create and implement these technologies suggest that an open standard setting committee and the selection of a single standard are necessary to create such services. Without such an open standard-setting committee and the adoption of a single standard, it is unlikely that such technologies would be developed privately.

This is not just because governments own most of the highways and are responsible for safety standards, it is also due to the large investments needed to implement the system. Firms will be unwilling to develop the technologies unless they believe that the technologies will be implemented. And the creation of a single standard in an open standard-setting process, the aggressive awarding of licences or the creation of plans for the government to operate the systems, and competition among manufacturers will partly demonstrate that the technologies will be implemented. This happened in Europe when a single digital standard was created and licences were awarded for GSM services. The country that moves the fastest with creating and implementing the appropriate technologies and standards has the best chance of creating a global standard. This global standard will benefit the consumers and manufacturers from the country or region that creates the standard. By early 2000, although there was a joint program between the National Highway Traffic Safety Administration, the Federal Highway Administration, and the Federal Transit Administration in the US and similar programs in Japan and Europe, Japan probably has some advantages in this area due to their greater needs for such a system including extensive traffic problems. It expects to have implemented a nationwide automatic toll collection system by the end of 2001 and to have automatic control of vehicles on some highways by 2010.

THE BROADCASTING INDUSTRY

The broadcasting industry is similar in many ways to the mobile communications industry. Governments have affected the mix and role of committee or market mechanisms at the national level through their allocation of frequency spectrum and licences. And since large investments are required in many new key technologies governments should probably promote the adoption of a single standard and competition between service-providers and manufacturers, something they have not consistently done.

For example, the lack of a single open standard and competition between hardware and software producers were and continue to be the problems to varying degrees in AM stereo, digital radio, and digital high-definition television (HDTV) in the US. In the first two cases it was partly the lack of a single national standard that discouraged the incumbents from investing in the new technology in the US, which is why you have not heard of AM stereo[1] or digital radio. In all three cases, it was partly due to the lack of licences for new radio and television broadcasters (that is, lack of competition). For example, it is generally believed that the US television broadcasters only participated in the HDTV standard-setting activities to acquire spectrum for free. This is spectrum that the US Congress had planned to auction until the broadcasters promised in the late 1980s (and many times after that) to start services based on HDTV.[2]

A short summary of the history of the television industry, including color television, HDTV, and digital television will make these points clearer. The US government used an open standard-setting committee that was managed by the Federal Communications Commission (FCC) to announce a color TV standard in 1950. However, the market rebelled against the standard since there was already a large installed base for black-and-white televisions (and these investments were seen by users as fairly large at that time[3]) and users wanted compatibility between the black-and-white and color TVs. Thus, the FCC was forced to change in 1953 from the CBS to the RCA-supported standard, since the latter was compatible with black-and-white television sets. Nevertheless, color television did not become popular until RCA purchased from ABC and began showing *Walt Disney's Wonderful World of Color* in 1960.

This example clearly shows the hybrid model at work where committees selected the standards but the market ended up choosing the winning standard. Further, the choice of a single standard was necessary to reduce uncertainty albeit several other developments such as that of the appropriate contents were necessary before color television became a reality. The only mistake may have been the lack of a standing committee that continually updated the standard as was done for GSM in Europe. This may have enabled the US to incorporate elements of the supposedly superior European system.[4]

High-definition television (HDTV) is supposed to provide higher-resolution televisions and programming than regular color television. Although programming for HDTV has apparently existed for some time due to the way in which movies and programs have been filmed, an HDTV standard requires new hardware and the use of a limited frequency spectrum. The lack of diffusion of HDTVs is for reasons that are very similar to the lack of diffusion of DAMPS in the US in the early 1990s. An open standard-setting process was established albeit in this case by the US Federal Communications Commission; both US and foreign manufacturers were allowed to participate in the creation of the standard.

However, also similar to DAMPS, new licences were not awarded and thus the implementation of HDTV was left to the incumbents who did not want to use the allotted frequency spectrum for HDTV. They believed that this spectrum could be more profitably used to provide additional conventional programming and thus made little effort to have HDTV programming created and begin HDTV services. The mobile communications industry study suggests that HDTV would have had a much higher chance of success if the FCC had also offered HDTV television licences to new and not just existing broadcasters. It is generally believed that the US television broadcasters only participated in the HDTV standard-setting activities to acquire spectrum for free. This is spectrum that the US Congress had planned to auction until the broadcasters promised in the late 1980s (and many times after that) to start services based on HDTV.[5]

Digital television

Digital television offered the possibility of crystal-clear, high-resolution pictures and first-quality digital sound – as well as the possibility of interactivity and other advanced digital services that have yet to be devised. Like the HDTV example, mistakes on the market side of the hybrid model (that is, the lack of new licences) have slowed the diffusion of services. In addition, mistakes have also been made on the committee side where all of the important parties were not included in the beginning.

Partly due to the time it has taken to create and implement the digital television standard (like US digital mobile services), new firms have also become involved with the standard's battle. This includes new hardware manufacturers (computer manufacturers) and service-providers (cable operators) along with Hollywood since digital television makes intellectual property protection even more important. The computer manufacturers saw digital television as their opportunity to enter the television market where their computers could be used as television receivers. However, they wanted a standard that was compatible with the Videographics Array (VGA) video standard that dominated the computer world. These disagreements were somewhat solved by the creation of a standard that did not specify the display format, such as scanning formats, aspect rations, and lines of resolution. The FCC approved this standard in December 1996 and conventional analog broadcasting was to be ended after about ten years.[6]

However, since more than two-thirds of the nation's television viewers subscribe to cable, digital sets must be cable-compatible if the transition to digital television is ever to succeed. But the cable operators are like the television broadcasters: they want to offer more channels as opposed to higher-quality programming and without the threat of new service-providers they will probably not introduce higher-quality programming. Just as with the initial US digital mobile standard and HDTV, the threat of new entrants is a necessary incentive for firms to introduce new technologies.

Further, a major problem for digital television is how to provide copy protection. Hollywood will not release digital copies of current movies for use on cable unless they are protected against the making of multiple copies. Hollywood believes this is a bigger problem with digital than analog television since analog copies degrade over time.[7] Under pressure from the FCC in the fall of 1998, the television manufacturers and cable operators claimed they had solved the connection problem with an agreement in November 1998. But when no televisions appeared in the stores in 1999 due to a lack of a copy-protection plan to address Hollywood's concerns and disagreements over the connection standard, the FCC again put pressure on them to come up with an agreement. A new digital connector standard was announced in February 2000 but Hollywood is still dissatisfied with the copy protection plan.[8]

The unsuccessful attempts to implement HDTV and digital television between 1985 and 1999 highlight the challenges in implementing a standard that has very large investments. On the market side of the hybrid model, existing broadcasters and cable-television operators have shown very little interest in HDTV or digital television largely since there has not been a threat of new licences. The committee side has also been difficult to manage since the emergence of digital television further complicated the matters; computer manufacturers were now interested in making the standard compatible with their technology while Hollywood became more concerned about intellectual property protection. The US government is the only entity that could have offered new licences and it is probably the only entity that can get the competing firms to create an effective standard. Nevertheless, most observers believe that the FCC has consistently mishandled both HDTV and digital TV with Commissioner Reed Hundt (from 1993 to 1998) receiving a great deal of criticism. Further, the US Senate was unwilling to auction the HDTV/digital television licences for fear of angering the US television broadcasters.[9]

European digital television

It appears as if Europe has utilized the committee and market mechanisms in digital television better than the US, just as they did in digital mobile phones.

Europe appears to have created its digital standard for digital television in a manner that is very similar to how they created GSM. While in the US, manufacturers were the primary participants in the creation of the HDTV and digital standards, a broader group including broadcasters and regulatory bodies formed a European Launching Group in 1991. This group drafted and the participants signed a Memorandum of Understanding in 1993 establishing the rules by which the standard would be established and implemented.[10]

A key realization was that satellite and cable would most likely deliver the first broadcast digital television services. These alternatives presented fewer technical problems and a simpler regulatory climate meant that they could develop more rapidly than terrestrial systems. Further, these alternatives had much greater competition than in terrestrial broadcasting and thus enabled Europe to avoid the major problem faced in the US of broadcasters not wanting to move to digital. Finally, the European regulatory bodies are requiring a complete switchover from analog to digital terrestrial broadcasting by 2010 with many countries setting more rigorous timetables.

While it is still too early to tell whether Europe's digital television standard will become a global standard, it is probably safe to say that Europe now has a larger chance than the US does of creating such a global standard in digital television. Variants of this standard exist for satellite, cable and terrestrial (regular television) broadcasting. By the end of 1998, there were more than 100 cable, satellite, and terrestrial broadcasters of digital television in Europe and more than five million subscribers to digital television in Europe. It appears that most of the world (Japan may be the only exception) will adopt one form of Europe's digital television standard that is called digital video broadcasting.[11] And similar to how GSM has become widely used in the US, several US broadcasters want to use the digital transmission standard that is now used in Europe. In late 1999 more than 1600 television stations expressed support for the Sinclair Broadcast Group's campaign to revise the US digital standard. These stations claim that receivers cannot easily pick up a watchable television signal in anything short of ideal circumstances with the current US standard.[12]

Notes

1. Shapiro and Varian, *Information Rules*, pp. 263–4.
2. Joel Brinkley, *Defining Vision*, 1997.
3. A 21-inch black-and-white television cost $300 in 1954 or almost $2000 in 1998 dollars. Brinkley, *Defining Vision*, p. 421, and Shapiro and Varan, *Information Rules*.
4. See Shapiro and Varian (1999) and Fisher and Fisher (1997) for a more detailed discussion of color television.
5. Brinkley, *Defining Vision*. 1997
6. *New York Times*, 11/10/1999, "Stations Challenge Digital-TV Standard," by Joel Brinkley.
7. *New York Times*, 28/2/2000, Accord on Digital TV Technology Still Lacks Hollywood's Input, Joel Brinkley.
8. See n. 7.
9. See n. 2.

10. Digital video broadcasting home page (*http://www.dvb.org/dvb_framer. htm*)

11. Digital video broadcasting home page (*http://www.dvb.org/dvb_ framer. htm*). Analysis: Broadcasting review of 1999, 14/12/1999, BBC Worldwide Monitoring, Source: Monitoring research 1999/BBC Worldwide Monitoring/(c) BBC, Text of editorial analysis by Peter Feuilherade of BBC Monitoring's publication *World Media*.

12. *New York Times*, 1/11/1999. More Stations Back Revised DTV Standard. By Joel Brinkley.

Appendix 4 Large Investments and Interface Ambiguities: The Internet

This appendix applies the hybrid model of standard-setting to the standards that have been and still are created for the Internet. Not only does the hybrid model apply to standard-setting for the Internet, many of these standards were initially created in a surprisingly similar way to how standards were developed for mobile phones and broadcasting. Most Internet-related standards, particularly the initial standards, are completely open, they were developed in government-sponsored committees (institutions and/or research projects), and in some cases they were implemented as a single standard by a government agency. The key differences between standard-setting for the Internet and mobile phones involve the use of smaller committees for the Internet standards and, since the mid-1990s, complete decentralization of the Internet standard-setting including almost no role by governments. I argue that the initial similarities in standard-setting are due to similarities in investment levels and interface definition while the recent differences are due to lower investments (for a specific standard) and most importantly the rapid expansion in the number and complexity of critical interfaces.

The US Defense Department began sponsoring the creation of a decentralized nationwide communications network in the 1960s. This included the development and implementation of IMP (Interface Message Processors) in 1969 and TCP/IP (Transmission Control Protocol/Internet Protocol) in 1974. The IMP standard enabled communication between different mainframe computers and was the basis for the first network (ARPAnet) and much later for the routers developed by Cisco Systems. TCP/IP enabled communication between different research networks such as ARPAnet, SatNet, and BITNET. These networks eventually became the NSFNet, which was opened to commercial operation in 1992 and was the basis for the Internet.[1]

Further, the TCP/IP standards are an important part of the Internet in other ways. The most widely used version of UNIX called the Berkeley UNIX, which is still the basis for most Internet servers, utilized the TCP/IP standards. The Ethernet standard, which enabled communication between distributed PCs, was made compatible with the TCP/IP standards when it was created in the early 1980s.[2]

The World Wide Web was created at the European Particle Physics Laboratory (CERN) in 1992 by Tim Berners-Lee in order to improve communication between physics researchers in various countries. The World Wide Web included URL (the Universal Resource Locator), HTTP (HyperText Transfer Protocol), and HTML (HyperText Mark-up Language).[3] The first Internet

270

browser, Mosaic, Netscape browsers, and all subsequent Internet browsers are based on URL, HTTP, and HTML.

With its openness, low price, and the fact that it made Internet access possible for the average person, Mosaic (and its successor the Internet Explorer from Microsoft) changed the Internet overnight. Internet businesses were started and the proprietary systems like CompuServe, Prodigy, and America Online (AOL was the only one who made the change to the World Wide Web) went out of business. It is probably safe to say that there would not be an Internet if we still relied on those proprietary systems. There is a number of reasons for this of which the largest is that firms were not willing to invest in creating contents for the Internet until a single open standard existed. The creation of the World Wide Web and a browser capable of accessing the information on the World Wide Web was the catalyst for change. And these technologies are open technologies because they were created in government-sponsored institutions or projects.

Of course these technologies were not created by large coalitions of firms or even researchers. But I argue that this is only because few people understood the importance of the Internet when these technologies were created. Very few people cared about what kind of technology or standard the Department of Defense, Berkeley, or Xerox PARC chose for making communications possible between different researchers in the 1960s, 1970s, and 1980s.

Standard-setting has changed a great deal since the start of the Internet primarily since the number of critical interfaces has grown dramatically. For example, in 1995 and 1996, the battle between the Mosaic and Explorer browsers directly involved just one interface (desktop computers and the Internet) but indirectly involved many interfaces. One account claims that the key interfaces in this browser battle included those between operating systems, application programs like Word, Excel, and Front Page, and Web servers. Microsoft's control of many of these interfaces is a major reason for its victory.[4]

Simultaneously with this battle, the growing interest in the Internet has caused the number of critical interfaces to explode. For example, the Open Systems Interconnect model defines seven layers in a network and updates to each layer are made continuously. There are many types of data that people want to transmit such as text, tables, figures, pictures, music, and video. There are issues of security and encryption, digital signatures and certificates, and how to develop home pages, Internet businesses, and applications that take into account all of the above standards. Thus, standard-setting has become very decentralized and the complexity of loose coalitions and alliances has increased dramatically. Most standards are created in a large variety of industry standard-setting activities where loose coalitions are the norm.

Notes

1.   Segaller, pp. 82, 110–12, 224–5, and 294.
2.   Segaller, pp. 232–3 and 276.
3.   Segaller, pp. 288.
4.   Ferguson, 1999.

Bibliography

Abernathy, W. and Clark, K. (1985), "Innovation: Mapping the Winds of Creative Destruction," *Research Policy*, 14, 3–22.

Abernathy, W. and J. Utterback (1978), "Patterns of Innovation in Technology," *Technology Review*, 80 (July), 40–47.

Adams, S. and O. Butler (1999), *Manufacturing the Future: A History of Western Electric*, Oxford University Press.

Afuah, A. (1997), *Innovation Management: Strategies, Implementation, and Profits*, Oxford University Press.

Anderson, P. and M. Tushman (1990), "Technological Discontinuities and Dominant Designs: A Cyclical Model of Technological Change," *Administrative Science Quarterly*, 35(4), 604–633.

Arthur, B. (1989), "Competing Technologies, Increasing Returns, and Lock-in by Historical Events," *Economic Journal*, 99(394), 116–131.

Asaba, Shigeru (1995), *Kyoso to Kyoryoku no Senryaku: Gyokai Hyojun wo Meguru Kigyo Kodo (A Strategy of Competition and Cooperation: Firm Actions in the Search for an Industry Standard)*, Tokyo.

Bartlett, C. and S. Ghoshal (1998). *Managing Across Borders: The Transnational Solution*, 2nd edn., Boston. Harvard Business School Press.

Berg, S., (1989), "Technical Standards as Public Goods: Demand Incentives for Cooperative Behavior," *Public Finance Quarterly*, 17(1), 29–54.

Besen, S. and J. Farrell (1994), "Choosing How to Compete: Strategies and Tactics in Standardization," *Journal of Economic Perspectives*, 8(2), 117–131.

Brinkley, J. (1997). *Defining Vision: How Broadcasters Lured the Government into Inciting a Revolution in Television*, New York: Harcourt Brace.

Christensen, C. (1997), *The Innovators' Dilemma: When New Technologies Cause Great Firms to Fail*, Boston: Harvard Business School Press.

Christensen, C. and R. Rosenbloom (1995), "Explaining the Attackers' Advantage: Technological Paradigms, Organizational Dynamics, and the Value Network," *Research Policy*, 24, 233–257.

Conner, K. R. and R. P. Rumelt (1991), "Software Piracy: An Analysis of Protection Strategies," *Management Science*, 37 (2).

Crane, R. (1979), *The Politics of International Standards: France and the Color TV War*, Norwood, NJ: Ablex Publishing.

Cusumano, M. and K. Nobeoka (1998), *Thinking Beyond Lean: How Multi-Project Management Is Transforming Product Development at Toyota and Other Companies*, New York: Free Press.

David, P. (1986). "Narrow Windows, Blind Giants and Angry Orphans: The Dynamics of Systems Rivalries and Dilemmas of Technology Policy," in P. David, *Innovation Diffusion*, 3, New York: Oxford University Press.

David, P. and S. Greenstein (1990), "The Economics of Compatibility Standards: An Introduction to Recent Research," *Economics of Innovation and New Technology*, 1 (1/2), 3–41.

David, P. A. and W. E. Steinmueller (1994). "Economics of Compatibility Standards and Competition in Telecommunication Networks," *Research Policy*, 217–241.

Dertouzos, M. and R. Lester (ed.) (1990), *Made in America: Regaining the Productive Edge*, Cambridge, MA, MIT Press.

Dobbin, M. (1998), "Pricing IPR," *Mobile Communications International*, (December, 1998/January 1999), 23.

Farr, J. (1993), "The Portable Jungle," *Cellular Business*, (June), 24–58.

Farrell, J. and G. Saloner (1985). "Standardization, Compatibility and Innovation," *Rand Journal of Economics*, 16(1), 70–83.

Farrell, J. and G. Saloner (1986). "Installed Base and Compatibility: Innovation, Product Preannouncements and Predation," *American Economic Review*, 76, 940–955.

Farrell, J. and G. Saloner (1988), "Coordination Through Committees and Markets," *Rand Journal of Economics*, 19(2), 235–52.

Farrell, J. and G. Saloner (1992), "Converters, Compatibility, and the Control of the Interface," *Journal of Industrial Economics*, 40(1), 9–35.

Farrell, J. and C. Shapiro, (1988) "Dynamic Competition with Switching Costs," *Rand Journal of Economics* 19 (1) 123–37.

Fransman, M. (1995), *Japan's Computer and Communications Industry: the Evolution of Industrial Giants and Global Competitiveness*, Oxford University Press.

Funk, J. (1998), "Competition between Regional Standards and the Success and Failure of Firms in the Global Mobile Communication Market," *Telecommunications Policy*, 22 (4/5), 419–441.

Funk, J. (2000), "The Mobile Internet Market: Lessons from Japan's i-mode System," paper presented at the E-Business Transformation: Sector Developments and Policy Implications, Washington, DC (September 25–26).

Funk, J. and D. Methe (2001), "Market- and Committee-based Mechanisms in the Creation and Diffusion of Global Industry Standards: The Case of Mobile Communication," *Research Policy*, 30, 589–610.

Garrard, G. (1998), *Cellular Communications: Global Market Development*, Boston and London: Artech House.

Grindley, P. (1995), Standards Strategy and Policy: Cases and Stories, Oxford Univeristy Press.

Hayashi, K. (1992), "From Network Externalities to Interconnection: The Changing Nature of Networks and Economy," in C. Antonelli, (ed.), *The Economics of Information Networks*, Amsterdam: Elsevier Science Publishers BV.

Hobday, M., (1998), "Product Complexity, Innovation and Industrial Organization," *Research Policy*, 26, 689–710.

Hobday, M., H. Rush, and J. Tidd (eds.) (2000), Special Issue on Innovation in Complex Products and Systems, *Research Policy*, 29, 793–804.

Hulten, S. and B. Molleryd (1995), "Mobile Telecommunications in Sweden," in Schenk, K.-E., J. Muller and T. Schnoring (eds.), *Mobile Telecommunications: Emerging European Markets*, Boston and London: Artech House.

Johnson, C. (1982), *MITI and the Japanese Miracle*, Stanford University Press.

Juran, M. (1992), *Juran on Quality Design*, New York: Free Press.

Kash, D. E. and R. Rycoft. (2000), "Patterns of Innovating Complex Technologies: A Framework For Adaptive Network Strategies, *Research Policy*, 29, 819–833.

Katz, M. and Shapiro, C. (1985), "Network Externalities, Competition, and Compatibility," *American Economic Review*, 75(3).

Khazam, J. and D. Mowery (1994), "The Commercialization of RISC: Strategies for the Creation of Dominant Designs," *Research Policy*, 23.

Klemperer, P. (1995), "Competition when Consumers have Switching Costs: An Overview with Applications to Industrial Organization, Macroeconomics, and International Trade," *Review of Economic Studies*, 62, 515–539.

Klemperer, P. and A. Padilla (1995), "Do Firms' Product Lines Include Too Many Varieties?," *Oxford University Working Paper*.

Kogut, B., G. Walker and D. Kim (1994), "Cooperation and Entry Induction as an Extension of Technological Rivalry, *Research Policy*, 77–95.

Meurling, J. and R. Jeans (1994). *The Mobile Phone Book: The Invention of the Mobile Telephone Industry*, London: Communications Week International.

Meyer, M. and A. Lehnerd (1997), *The Power of Product Platforms*, New York: Free Press, 12.

Mobile Communications International (1999), Telecom 99 Supplement: the A–Z of Wireless Technologies, 65 (October), 65–107

Paetsche, M. (1993), *The Evolution of Mobile Communications in the US and Europe: Regulation, Technology, and Markets*, Boston and London: Artech House.

Pelkman, J. and R. Bueters (1986), *Standardization and Competitiveness: Private and Public Strategies in the EC Colour TV Industry*, Maastricht, European Institute of Public Administration (November).

Prestowitz, C. V. (1988). *Trading Places: How We Allowed Japan to Take the Lead*, New York: Basic Books.

Shapiro, C. and H. Varian (1999), *Information Rules*, Boston: Harvard Business School Press.

Shosteck, H. (1997), *The Retail Market of Cellular Telephones*, London: Wheaton.

Teece, D. (1986), "Profiting from Technological Innovation: Implications for Integration, Collaboration, Licensing, and Public Policy," *Research Policy*, 15, 285–305.

Tushman, M. and P. Anderson (1986), "Technological Discontinuities and Organizational Environment," *Administrative Science Quarterly*, 31, 439–456.

Utterback, J. M. (1994), *Mastering the Dynamics of Innovation: How Companies Can Seize Opportunities in the Face of Technological Change*, Boston: Harvard Business School Press.

Wakabayashi, H, (1994), "Japan's Revolution in Wireless," *Nomura Research Institute Quarterly* (Autumn).

Williamson, O. E. (1975). *Markets and Hierarchies: Analysis and Anti-Trust Implications*, New York: Free Press.

Woodward, J. (1958), *Management and Technology*, London: HMSO.

Yamada, Hideo (1997), *Defacto Standard: Strategic Standard Setting for Controlling the Market (Defakuto Sutanda-to: Shijo wo seiha suru kikaku senryaku)*, Tokyo: Nihon Economic Publishing.

Yoshihara, H. (1999), "Global Operations Managed by Japanese and in Japanese, Kobe University, *Research Institute for Economics and Business Administration Working Paper* (December).

Index

Index abbreviations:
f = figure; n = endnote or footnote; and t = table.

3Com, 242(n28)
360 Communications (1996–), 102t, 125, 139(n18), 143(n58)

ABC, 268
advertising, 166, 190, 204(n83)
AEG Telefunken, 61, 67, 89(n30), 90(n43)
Aerial Communications, 143(n61)
Africa, 46, 76, 104, 107, 208, 232
Air Call (private mobile radio service), 88(n20)
air interface, 70, 140(n24), 177, 185, 208, 214, 215, 218, 240(n8), 242(n29)
Airtouch (USA), 101t, 122–6, 141–2(n42), 143(n51–2), 228, 232, 233, 244(n54)
Airadaigm, 143(n61)
Airtel (Spain), 113t, 140(n26), 142(n42)
Alcatel, xiii, 8, 8t, 10t, 11t, 49t, 51f, 59, 60–1, 67, 82, 89(n26–7), 90(n43), 96, 104–13, 116–17, 119, 120t, 122t, 127, 134, 135–6, 139(n19), 140(n24), 140(n26), 141(n41), 158, 160, 181, 227–33, 238
    global customer base (1981–98), 105f
    market share (GSM base stations), 108t, 162f
Alcatel-Fujitsu joint venture, 230–1
Alltel, 102t, 143(n58)
amakudari ('descent from heaven'), 144(n64)
America Matsushita Communications Industries, 198(n9)
America Matsushita Electronic Parts, 198(n9)

American Cellular Communications, 103
American Radio Telephone Service, 57
Ameritech, 97t, 101t, 103t, 103, 123, 125, 142(n45), 174
AMPS (Advanced Mobile Phone System), 9, 10–12t, 13–18, 39–44, 46, 47t, 49t, 51–3, 55–62, 68, 72, 76, 81, 84–6, 89(n23), 90(n38), 94, 95t, 99, 100, 104–8, 124–5, 128, 139(n19), 140(n23), 142(n49), 143(n63), 145, 146, 161, 176
    first generation global standard, 56–8, 88(n17)
    Japanese firms, 149–51, 155–7
    Motorola's strategy, 151–4
    non-European countries, 68, 91(n59)
    rising share of Nokia in AMPS and TACS, 154–5
    US analog market (AMPS), 148–70
analog
    cellular, 91(n65)
    equipment, 103, 105, 106, 119, 127, 139(n19), 143(n60)
    handsets, 68
    infrastructure, 9, 263
    market, 96–9, 107, 128, 133, 167, 171, 174, 192
    services, 68, 69, 106, 110, 125, 141
    signals, 38
    standards, 31, 43t, 51, 58–63, 70
    suppliers, 111–12t, 120t, 144(n65)
    systems, 65, 71, 85
    technology, 6, 10–12t, 16, 17, 20(n11–12), 39t, 41t, 47t, 49t, 52f, 53f, 61, 63, 73, 126–7, 134
    vendor, 101–2t

Antel (Uruguay), 143(n63)
APC, 143(n61)
APC/Sprint, 143(n61)
ARIB (Association for Radio Industry Businesses, Japan), 51f, 70, 185
ARM, 63
ARPAnet, 273
Ascend Communications, 227
Ascom (Switzerland), 160, 200(n25)
Asia, 27, 40, 46, 50t, 55, 76, 77, 82, 104, 107, 137, 160, 176, 208
Astel, 50t, 194
Astronet, 138(n6)
AT&T, 57, 67, 92(n72), 97, 118, 123, 125, 126, 138(n4–5), 139(n13), 145, 149, 171, 174, 201(n41), 213, 233
AT&T Wireless, 100, 102t, 179, 224, 229
Atlanta (Georgia), 198(n10), 198(n10)
Audiovox, 197(n3)
Australia, 45t
Australia Telstra, 92(n71)
Austria, 43t-45t, 46, 62, 106, 111t, 113t, 140(n25), 213
automobiles, 22, 30, 34
AXE (Ericsson), 64

Baby Bells, 57, 96, 97, 98t, 100, 103, 107, 124, 138(n5), 149
Bahrain, 43t, 45t, 120t
bandwagon effect, 4, 23, 36, 37, 85
bankruptcy, 91(n63)
barriers to entry, 147f, 156, 160–1, 181, 235
base stations, 38–9, 38f, 56, 76, 87(n3), 87(n6), 88(n17), 89(n23), 94, 96, 99, 108–19, 127, 133, 134, 139(n21), 142(n49), 144(n64), 144(n65), 185, 194, 203(n74), 226, 227, 229, 230
  market share, 108t, 118t
  providers, 131
baseband, 163–4, 166, 177, 178, 180
batteries, 179, 183–4, 186, 205(n85)
  lithium ion, 187–9, 204(n77–9)

Bay Networks, 226, 227
Belgacom, 111t, 113t, 142(n42)
Belgium, 43t, 45t, 54, 59, 60, 90(n51), 111t, 113t, 141(n35)
Bell Atlantic, 97t, 101t, 103t, 123, 125, 126, 142(n45), 143(n51), 173, 174
Bell Canada, 96, 98
Bell South, 97, 97t, 100–3, 101t, 103t, 122t, 123, 124, 126, 127, 138(n6), 142(n43), 143(n60), 171
Bell South Mobility, 143(n61)
Bluetooth (1998–), 218, 220
Bosch, xiii, 82, 89(n29–30), 90(n43)
Bouygues Télécom, 113t, 117, 119
brand image, 34, 160, 165–6, 167, 173, 190, 194, 196
Brazil, 44t, 45t, 104, 140(n23), 141(n36), 213
British Telecommunications, 59, 88(n20), 228, 232, 233, 244(n54)
broadcasting, 23, 26, 28, 33
Brunei, 43t, 45t

c-HTML, 224, 236
C-Netz system (Siemens), 39t, 43t, 47t, 49t, 51f, 52f, 53f, 58–62, 64, 90(n38,40), 111t, 112t, 116
Cable & Wireless, 88(n20), 121, 122t, 124, 142(n49)
Canada, 43t, 45t, 57–8, 96, 98, 126, 128, 143(n61), 198(n10)
car phones, 150, 198(n10)
Caribbean, 46, 106, 142(n49)
Casio, 194, 217t
CDMA (Code Division Multiple Access), 12t, 42, 101–2t, 126, 227, 240(n7)
  IS95 CDMA, 10t, 42, 74, 135
CDMA Development Group, 51f, 239(n4)
cdmaOne (Qualcomm) 9, 11–12t, 16, 20(n8), 39t, 40, 41, 41t, 42, 42f, 45t, 48t, 50–3, 75–6, 79–86, 95t, 125–32, 135–6, 143(n53,60), 145, 146, 161, 169, 171, 189, 201(n45,47), 206, 209, 210, 213,

cdmaOne (*contd*)
  227, 228, 233, 235, 236, 239(n4),
  240(n9–10), 241(n14), 242(n29)
  handsets, 75
  narrow-band, 81
  previously known as IS95 CDMA,
    74
  subscribers, 210
cdmaOne market, 172–4
cdmaOne phones, 177
cdma2000, 53f, 132, 209, 211, 229,
  231, 237f, 238, 239–40(n5),
  240(n7,8,10), 242(n29)
  "wide-band version of cdmaOne",
    81, 208
  see also W-CDMA
CDs (compact discs), 26, 28, 149
Cellcom (Israel), 143(n59,63)
Cellnet, 62, 104, 112t, 114t, 137,
  240(n9)
cellular
  phones, 18, 78, 92(n69), 149, 197(n1)
  services, 71, 72, 100
  systems, 76, 87(n3), 106
  technology, 12t, 39t, 41t
Cellular Communications, 100, 101t,
  138(n8), 139(n15)
Cellular Radio, 88(n20)
Cellular Subscriber Group
  (Motorola), 174
Centel, 102t, 103t, 103, 138(n7),
  139(n18)
Centennial Cellular, 125
Central America, 46, 106, 198(n10)
Century Cellunet, 143(n58)
CEPT (European Postal and
  Telecommunications
  Conference), 63–6, 70, 74
Charisma Communications, 139(n12)
Chevènement, Jean-Pierre, 89(n26)
Chicago, 57, 198(n10)
China, 43t, 45t, 80, 104, 119–20,
  141(n36), 143(n62), 206, 210,
  229, 241(n14)
China Telecom, 92(n72)
China Unicom, 241(n14)
chips, 152f, 163n, 167, 172, 173, 178,
  209, 211, 212, 239(n4)
Christensen, C, 243(n44)

Cingular, 213
Cisco Systems, 226–7
CIT Alcatel, 60
CMS St Cloud, 143(n58–59)
commissions, 153, 183, 189, 196, 197,
  203(n68), 204(n81), 224
committee- and market-based
  competition in the mobile
  infrastructure market, 14–16,
  93–144
committee-based competition,
  96–9, 109–10, 119–24, 127–9,
  131–6
competing in subsequent
  generation of technology, 136–8
consolidation by US service-
  providers, 99–104
early years of mobile infrastructure
  analog market, 96–9
GSM infrastructure market, 108–24
infrastructure competition in
  Japan's PDC market, 130–4
infrastructure competition in US
  digital standards, 124–30
international AMPS and TACS
  infrastructure markets, 104–8
market-based competition, 99–104,
  104–8, 110–15, 134–5
relative importance of committee-
  versus market-based
  competition, 134–5
summary and discussion,
  134–8
committees/standard-setting
  committees, 1, 2t, 9, 18, 28–9, 31,
    94, 145
  committee- and market-based
    competition in mobile
    infrastructure, 14–16
  committee- and market-based
    competition in mobile phones,
    16–17
  defined, 3
  hybrid model, 2–7, 18, 19
  global, 6
  national and regional, 6, 13
Communications Industries, 101t
competition, 1–7, 13, 36–8, 52–4, 57,
  58, 77, 79, 84

competition (*contd*)
  committee- and market-based,
    14–17, 29, 93–144
  committee-based, 14
  intra-device, 218, 220
  lacking (in Japan), 150
  market-based, 14, 16, 206–45
  mobile infrastructure, 14–16
  mobile Internet, 19, 213–20
  mobile phones, 16–17
  multiple standards, 3
  theoretical issues, 21–35
  third generation, 206–45
  two-firm, 1, 4, 17, 29, 86
competition: theoretical issues within
    and between standards, 21–35
  committee-based competition
    within standards, 29–31
  customer-supplier relationships,
    29–31
  interface ambiguity as moderating
    variable on standard-setting,
    28–9
  investment size as a moderating
    variable, 25–8
  models of technological change,
    22–3
  network-related products, 29–31
  role of global development, 31–3
  role of product line/platform
    management, 33–5
  standards: committees, 25
  standards: market competition,
    23–4
  switching costs, 29–31
competitive advantage, 61, 72, 146
components, 152f, 191, 193, 205 (n85)
  TCXO, 205(n86–87)
computers, 23, 26, 34, 249, 251
  desktop, 29, 214, 215f, 216, 217t,
    219, 221–2, 224
  personal, 7, 28, 75, 156, 221f
computing standards, 213–20
Comvik (Sweden), 88(n11),
    88–9(n20), 106, 113t, 116
Conestoga Wireless, 143(n61)
Connex (Romania), 142(n42)
consumer electronics, 17, 22, 26, 28,
    34, 156, 161, 175

consumers, 3, 6, 27, 30, 58, 69
Contel, 97t, 103, 139(n17)
Contel Cellular, 102t, 138(n8)
cooperative development work,
    29–30
CoPS (complex products and
    systems), 5, 6, 14, 19–20(n5), 93,
    104, 121
Corpac (car phone system), 59
Costa Rica, 44t, 143(n63)
costs, 33–4, 35(n12), 76, 87(n3),
    143(n64), 146, 147f, 156, 162,
    163t, 173, 174, 179, 196, 224
  development, 18, 148, 164,
    200(n30), 205(n87)
Croatia, 44t, 45t, 111t
CT-2, 48t
CTIA (US Cellular
    Telecommunications Industry
    Association), 49t, 51f, 71–2, 73,
    74, 126, 142(n50), 143(n53), 171
customer/supplier continuities, 99,
    110
customer/supplier relationships,
    29–30, 32, 103–4, 110, 124, 232
Cyprus, 43t, 45t, 111t
Czech Republic, 45t, 111t, 113t
Czechoslovakia, 44t

DAMPS (Digitalized Advanced
    Mobile Phone System), 9–12, 16,
    20(n7–8), 39t, 42, 47t, 49t, 51–3,
    72, 73–6, 86, 91(n61), 95t,
    101–2t, 125–30, 135, 142(n50),
    143(n63), 146, 148, 169,
    174, 177–8, 201(n45), 213, 233,
    235–6, 238, 242(n29)
  "digitalized version of AMPS", 41
  improved version (IS136), 171
  initial version called IS54, 170
  market, 202(n60)
  "often called TDMA in the USA",
    41
  standard-setting process, 137
  standards, 133
  US market, 170–2
Dancall, 160
data networking, 169
data transmission, 79, 211–12

David, P., 25, 277
DDI, 106, 130t, 132, 137, 194, 237f,
   245(n72)
DDI Cellular, 71, 131, 132, 145, 184,
   231, 233
   merger with IDO, 246
DDI Cellular Group, 69, 130, 132, 184,
   189, 190, 194, 203(n72), 204(n83)
DDI Pocket, 50t, 194, 246
dealers, 149, 197(n2)
decentralization, 180
DECT, 77
Denmark, 43t, 45t, 54, 55, 68,
   90(n51), 111t, 113t, 141(n41),
   180
Denso, 194
deregulation, 67–8, 85
derivative products, 196
designs, 22, 177t, 179, 180
   competition *within* specific, 253–7
Deutsche Telekom, xiii, 49t, 90(n40),
   96, 109, 116, 117, 140(n30), 230,
   232, 233
Deutsche Telekom Mobil (DeT
   Mobile), 109, 111t, 113t, 116,
   118, 121, 122t, 123, 124, 229
DGT (*Direction Générale des
   Télécommunications*, France), 59
Digifone, 113t
digital
   cellular, 91(n65)
   equipment, 139(n19)
   infrastructure, 9, 10t
   market share, 11t
   markets, 148
   mobile technology, 3
   orders, 20(n12)
   phone market (global), 17, 147f
   phones, 17, 74
   services, 110
   signals, 38
   switch (DX 200 system), 115,
      140(n27)
   systems, 19, 65, 73, 101–2t, 132–4,
      144(n65)
   technology, 12t, 13–14, 16, 31,
      39–40, 39t, 41t, 47–50t, 52f, 53f,
      61, 62, 73, 95t, 127
   vendors, 101–2t

Digital Phone Group, 184, 203(n70),
   204(n73)
   "also called J-Phone", 190
   "subsequently changed its service
      name to J-Phone", 203(n73)
digital standards, 6, 41, 43t, 51, 71
   actual committee-based
      competition: actual continuity in
      orders, 127–9
   differences in expected and actual
      committee-based competition,
      129–30
   expected committee-based
      competition (USA), 125–7
   expected continuity in customer
      relationships and effect on
      development decisions, 125–7
   infrastructure competition (USA),
      124–30
Digital Tsuka, 130t, 132–3, 203(n70)
digital video discs (DVD), 19(n1), 24,
   26, 27t
DRAM (dynamic random access
   memory), 183
DSC Communications, 127, 135
DSPC, 172, 205(n85–6)
dumping, 149–50, 156, 198(n7),
   199(n22)

E-Plus (Germany), 113t, 141(n38)
early orders, 109–10, 228
Eastern Europe, 46, 55, 107,
   142(n44)
economies of scale, 7, 17, 24, 34, 151,
   155, 156, 179, 197
EDGE (enhanced data rates for GSM
   evolution), 212–13, 233
Eesti Mobiltelefon, 141(n40)
EF Johnson (US firm), 57, 88(n11,16)
Egypt, 45t, 62, 120t
Eircell, 111t, 113t
employment, 63, 88(n20)
EMT, 111t, 113t
engineers, 174, 175, 182, 185
EPOC, 216, 217t, 219, 220, 242(n29)
EraGSM (Poland), 142(n42)
Ericsson, xiii, 7–11, 14–17, 20(n7),
   50t, 51, 59–60, 63–5, 77, 79,
   82–3, 84–7, 87(n6), 89(n30),

Ericsson (*contd*)
91(n61–2), 92(n71), 94, 96,
98–105, 107–16, 119–23, 125–37,
132–4, 138(n8–9), 139(n13–14,
19, 21), 140(n24,28), 141(n38,
40–1), 141–2(n42), 142(n44,49),
143(n61), 145–8, 154, 156–75,
178–81, 191–2, 201(n41),
202(n60), 206–12, 218, 219,
226, 227, 228–9, 232–3, 235,
236, 238, 239(n2–3, 5),
240(n8,10), 242(n29)
alliance with NTT DoCoMo and
Nokia, 80–2
battle with Qualcomm (third
generation standards), 208–11
derivative products, 168
evolution of GSM 900 MHz
phone line (1994–8), 159f
global customer base (1981–98),
105f
GSM 900 platform management
strategies, 163t
market share, 99t, 108t, 129t, 162f,
170t
problems with (GSM)
implementation, 166, 168–9,
201(n35)
success, 7–9, 14–16, 157–69
tiger teams, 119
Ericsson Toshiba KK (1992–),
133
Esat Digifone, 141(n39)
Esselte, 154, 199(n17)
Estonia, 44t, 45t, 111t, 113t
ESWD switches (Siemens), 64
ETRI (Electronics and
Telecommunications Research
Institute, Republic of Korea),
92(n73)
ETSI (European
Telecommunications Standards
Institute, 1988–), 51f, 63, 65–7,
68, 70, 79, 82, 83, 86–7,
90–1(n53), 206, 208, 211,
239(n5)
Europe, xiii, 3, 6, 7, 12t, 13, 14,
26–7, 31, 36, 39, 41t, 46,
49t, 50t, 51, 52f, 55, 58–63,
76–7, 82–5, 94, 95t, 104,
109, 110, 176, 207–9, 236,
237, 237f
domination of (third-generation)
standard-setting process,
18–19
European Commission, 63, 65
European Community, 63, 155
European Council of Ministers, 65
European Launching Group (1991),
271
European Technology Standards
Institute (ETSI), 25
Europolitan (Sweden), 141(n38)
Eurotel, 111–13t

fast-moving vehicles, 76–7
FCC (Federal Communications
Commission, USA), 51f, 57, 72,
73, 96, 171
FDMA (frequency division multiple
access), 73, 91(n62), 126, 132,
133, 142(n50), 143(n53)
Finland, 7, 43t, 45t, 54, 68, 90(n51),
111t, 113t, 115, 140(n26–7), 155,
180, 228
firms, 1, 4–7, 13–18, 19(n1), 23–30, 36,
37, 54, 61, 79, 134, 136, 237–8
acquisitions, 154
alliances/coalitions, 13, 19, 25, 26,
28–9, 82, 86, 87, 110, 115, 116,
207
cellular, 92(n68)
communication, 180–1
content providers, 26
criteria for success, 18
Japanese, 8, 9, 16, 22, 146, 148–50,
154–8, 178–81, 202(n58–9)
Korean, 9
mergers, 98
mergers and acquisitions, 32, 100,
101–2t, 103–4, 123, 124, 156
multinational, 32
service providers, 26, 32
US, 9, 19, 138
France, 39t, 39, 43t, 45t, 46, 47t, 52f,
58–61, 63–5, 68, 85, 89(n26),
90(n51), 92(n71), 111t, 113t, 114,
228, 233

France Télécom, 59, 61, 96, 113t, 117, 121, 122t, 123, 124, 140(n25–6), 141(n31,41), 233
frequency bands, 38, 46, 54, 55, 59, 60, 61, 63–4, 66, 71, 74, 79–80, 87(n1), 89(n26,n29), 91(n63), 91(n65), 92(n73), 114, 118–19, 144(n66), 163, 164, 166, 172, 176, 177t, 177, 178, 200(n30), 202(n59)
  1800, 118–19, 123, 141(n41)
  900, 119
Frontier (Lucent/Bell Atlantic joint venture), 125
Fujitsu, xiii, 10t, 35(n7), 49t, 50t, 54, 56, 91(n61), 92(n71), 107, 130t, 132, 133, 144(n65), 149, 150, 154, 184, 185, 186, 187, 187f, 188f, 188, 189, 191, 192, 193, 194, 198(n10), 204(n77,79), 205(n85), 228, 229
  market share (cellular phones, 1994–8), 190f
Funk, J., 25

Galvin, Christopher, 174
games/entertainment, 28, 29, 34, 223, 238
Garrard, G., 138(n3)
GEC (UK), 62, 63
GEC Plessey (UK), 138(n6)
GEC-Marconi (UK), 59
General Communications Industries, 100, 101t, 138(n8), 139(n14)
General Electric (USA), 98, 98t
Geostar, 172
GeoWorks, 243(n38)
Germany, 39t, 39, 43t, 45t, 46, 52f, 58, 60–1, 63–5, 68, 85, 89(n26), 92(n71), 96, 111t, 113t, 114, 160, 180, 213, 228, 233
  East Germany, 140–1(n30)
  West Germany, 47t, 59, 60, 90(n51)
global
  carriers, 233–4
  customer base, 105f, 106, 140(n23)
  customer relationships, 136–7
  development, 18, 21, 31–3, 34–5
  platforms, 147f, 155, 175, 202(n60)

Global Wireless Industry Alliance Forum (Motorola), 136
globalization, 156, 157
GlobTel, 113t
governments, 2, 27–8, 37–8, 52, 61–3, 69, 71, 75, 80, 83, 85, 120, 131, 134, 139(n21), 156–7, 192, 206, 210, 215
GPRS (General Packet Radio System), 211–13, 220, 232–3
Graphic Scanning, 101t, 103, 138(n8)
Greece, 45t, 113t, 141(n41)
Groupe Spécial Mobile (1982–), 64, 66
GSM (Global System Mobile) 9–12, 14–18, 20(n7–8), 39–42, 45t, 46, 48t, 49t, 51–3, 73, 75, 79, 80, 82–6, 94, 95t, 101t, 104, 105, 125, 129, 133–7, 140(n25), 141(n36,n40), 145–8, 157–69, 176, 177, 185, 200(n24), 207–9, 241(n14), 242(n29)
  base station market, 108–9
  committee-based competition in early orders, 109–10
  committee-based competition outside Europe, 119–24
  creation, 63–8
  differences in product line/product management and rise of Nokia, 162–9
  digital technology, 170
  enhancements, 211–13, 233
  firms struggle to strengthen their committee- and market-based capabilities, 115–19
  global digital standard, 9
  handsets, 68, 162f, 235
  infrastructure market, 108–24
  Japan, 71–2
  market, 128, 156, 173, 175, 180, 181–2, 184, 200(n25), 236, 238
  market-based competition, 110–15
  models, 182
  network interface, 81, 83, 86, 236
  non-European countries, 68, 91(n59)
  orders from second and third service-providers, 110–15

GSM (*contd*)
  platform management as barrier to
    entry, 160–1
  second generation global standard,
    63–8, 90–1(n53)   standards, 70,
    79, 133
  strategic differences, 163–6
  subscribers, 210
  suppliers, 111–12t, 120t
  switching market, 108–9
  technology, 213, 240(n9)
  US market, 170–2
GSM 900, 159f, 163t, 176, 177, 178,
    180, 192, 202(n58–60)
GSM 1900, 127, 129–30, 136, 171–2,
    174, 177, 180, 202(n59)
GTE, 97t, 98t, 100, 102t, 103t,
    103, 125, 138(n7), 139(n17),
    143(n60)
Guatemala, 44t, 143(n62)
Gulf War (1991), 120, 121

Hagenuk (Denmark), 160, 200(n25)
Hambros Bank, 88(n20)
Handelsblatt, 20(n11)
handsets, 9, 20(n8), 28–9, 38, 38f, 53f,
    54, 62, 67, 69, 70, 75, 83, 86,
    87(n5), 89(n23), 90(n37),
    90(n53), 92(n71), 180, 183, 184,
    186, 189, 193, 194, 201(n41),
    203(n69,74), 204(n81), 214, 215,
    216, 218, 224, 239(n2), 242(n29),
    242(n37)
  charges, 57
  Japanese manufacturers, 235–6
  third generation, 18, 234–8
Handspring, 217t
hardware, 24, 219–20, 242(n38)
health effects, 240(n9)
Helsinki, 88(n9)
Hillsborough (Oregon, USA),
    198(n10)
Hitachi, xiii, 54, 150
Hong Kong, 43t, 45t, 48t, 56, 57,
    92(n72), 118, 140(n23)
Hong Kong Telecom, 142(n49)
Hughes, 50t, 51f
Hundt, Reed, 270
Hungary, 44t, 45t, 111t

Hutchison Telecom, 229
hybrid model (markets and
    committees), 2–7, 18, 27, 36,
    51, 53, 82, 84, 206, 212, 214, 234
  competition between firms in a
    single standard, 4–6
  competition in a single standard at
    a global level, 6–7
  global standards creation, 3–4
  markets and committees, 2–7, 18,
    19, 19(n1)
Hyundai, 92(n73)

i-mode, xiii, 216, 217t, 224, 236
IBM, 67, 217t
Iceland, 45t, 55, 88(n13), 111t
IDO, 69, 71, 130t, 131–2, 145, 184,
    189, 231
IMT-2000 (International Mobile
    Telecommunications 2000), 212,
    239(n5), 240(n8)
India, 45t, 118
Indonesia, 44t, 45t, 92(n72–3), 104,
    139(n19)
infrastructure, 18, 26, 36, 38–9,
    53f, 67, 71, 75, 80, 81, 83, 86,
    92(n72), 100, 101–2t, 105f, 115,
    185, 207, 239(n2)
  committee-based competition,
    228–31, 231–4
  digital, 135
  market share (USA 1997), 129t
  market-based competition, 226–8,
    231–4
  third generation, 18, 225–34
infrastructure markets: AMPS and
    TACS, 104–8
installed base, 24, 27, 37, 38, 46, 51,
    52, 65, 68, 70, 75, 81, 84, 85,
    87(n5), 210, 213, 216, 220, 231
Intel, 75, 115
intellectual property rights (IPRs),
    209, 220, 239(n5), 240(n7–8),
    242(n38)
  copyrights, 250
  patents, 56, 66, 67, 71, 75, 83,
    140(n24), 145, 157, 200(n24),
    206, 208–9, 210, 239(n3–5),
    242(n38)

intelligent vehicle systems, 26, 27t, 35(n3)
interfaces, 206, 207, 214–18, 223–5
  ambiguity, 28–9
Internet, xiii, 7, 18–19, 23, 29, 33, 78, 169, 194, 213–14, 219, 222f, 223, 225f, 241(n25), 242(n39–40, 42)
  browsers, 215–20
  e-mail, 214, 223
  home pages, 18, 20(n13)
Intranet, 206, 214
investment, 3–4, 13, 39, 87(n2), 95, 121, 123–4, 127, 131, 132–3, 136, 138(n3), 139(n19), 141(n37), 141–2(n42–5), 142(n49), 143(n61), 145, 160, 214, 226–7, 228
  size as a moderating variable on standard-setting, 25–8, 35(n3)
IP (Internet Protocol), 211–12, 227
Ireland, 43t, 45t, 46, 62, 90(n51), 111t, 113t, 141(n39), 199(n22)
Iridium (satellite system), 87(n2)
ISDN interface, 81
Israel, 45t, 106
Italtel (Telecom Italic Mobile), 49t, 61, 64, 82, 96, 110, 113t, 139(n21)
Italy, 39t, 39, 43t, 44t, 45t, 46, 47t, 49t, 52f, 54, 58, 59, 60, 61, 62, 64, 90(n51), 92(n71–2), 96, 112t, 113t, 141(n41), 213, 228, 233
ITT (later acquired by Alcatel), 104
ITU (International Telecommunications Union), 51f, 79–80, 82, 209, 211, 239(n3,5), 240(n7–8)
Iusacell, 139(n19)

J-Phone, 130t, 132–3, 144(n66), 203(n70), 228
  "brand name", 203(n70)
Japan, 6, 7, 12t, 18, 19, 20(n10), 27, 31, 32, 39t, 39, 41, 41t, 43t, 45t, 47t, 48t, 49t, 50t, 51, 52f, 52, 53, 54, 55–6, 60, 68, 69–72, 75, 83, 85, 94, 96, 106–7, 179,

183–94, 203(n76), 208, 216, 232, 235, 237, 237f, 241(n26)
  cellular phones (market share, 1994–8), 190f
  committee- versus market-based competition in analog market, 184
  committee-based competition and foreign manufacturers, 191–2
  committee-based competition helps Motorola and Ericsson in digital systems, 132–4
  Docomo's four phone suppliers develop lighter phones, 186–8
  infrastructure competition in PDC market, 130–4
  internal procurement policies, 156, 199(n20)
  lack of success in mobile phone industry, 8
  market-based competition becomes stronger, 190–1
  market-based competition in Japan's PHS phone market, 193–4
  mobile Internet "booming", xiii
  mobile Internet market, 220–3
  Motorola enters the market through committee-based competition, 131–2
  NTT DoCoMo refines its committee-based strategy, 185–6
  "protected, overregulated economy", 157, 199(n23)
  results of DoCoMo's committee-based strategy, 189–90
  "richness" and "reach", 221–2, 243(n39)
Japan: MITI (Ministry of International Trade and Industry), 77
Japan: Ministry of Posts and Telecommunications (MPT), 56, 70, 76, 77, 78, 80, 86, 91(n61), 131, 185, 193, 204(n81), 228, 236
Japan: Ministry of Transportation, 56
Japan Denpa Industries, 205(n85)

Japan Telecom, 92(n72), 130t, 133, 194, 203(n70), 228, 230, 231, 232, 237f, 244(n54)
Japanese firms, 207, 217t, 235–6
JIT (just in time), 155
JRC, 150, 199(n22)

"Kansai", 130t, 132, 184, 189
"Kansai (Osaka)", 69
Kansai Cellular (subsidiary of Kyocera), 189
KDDI, xiii, 131–2, 184
  formed by merger of DDI Cellular and IDO, 145
Kenwood, 187, 194
KG Telecommunications (Taiwan), 224, 229
Klemperer, P., 138(n2)
Kokusai Electric, 199(n22)
Korea, South, 12t, 41t, 41, 43t, 45t, 48t, 57, 75, 80, 83–4, 85, 92(n73), 126, 128, 146, 155, 172, 213, 242(n35)
Korea Mobile Phone, 92(n71)
KPN, 224, 229
Kuwait, 44t, 45t, 89(n27), 120, 120t
Kyocera, xiii, 131, 174, 184, 187f, 187, 188f, 189, 239(n2)
  "dark horse", 245(n75)
  market share (cellular phones, 1994–8), 190f
Kyushu, 184, 189

LA Cellular, 126
language, 156, 181
laptop computers, 207, 218
Latvia, 44t, 45t, 112t, 113t, 141(n40)
LCT (French telecommunications company), 64
Lebanon, 44t, 45t, 141(n39)
Libancel, 141(n39)
liberalization, 184, 203(n73)
Libertel, 113t, 140(n26)
licences, 4, 13, 14, 27, 36, 38, 52, 57, 58, 59, 66, 67–8, 72, 73, 74, 82, 98, 100, 121, 131, 171, 207, 213, 232
licensing fees, 56, 67, 145, 157, 172, 186, 211

lifestyle, 54, 88(n9)
Lin Broadcasting, 100
LMT, 112t, 113t
LSI Logic, 172
Lucent, xiii, 8, 8t, 10t, 50t, 63, 81, 82, 91(n62), 92(n71), 96–110, 117–21, 124, 125, 126, 128, 134, 138(n4,7–9), 139(n13–14, 16–17), 141(n31,33), 142(n50), 143(n52), 161, 175, 205(n85), 226, 227, 228, 231, 233
  (then ATT&T) acquires PKI (1995), 118
  global customer base (1981–98), 105f
  market share, 99t, 108t, 129t
  Original equipment manufacturing wing (OEM) agreement with PKI, 118
Lucky Goldstar, 92(n73)
Luxembourg, 43t, 45t, 116

McCaw Cellular, 100, 102t, 103t, 123, 126, 127, 137, 139(n13), 142(n45)
MacLaren, Peter, 209
McTighe, Mike, 161
magazines, 18, 20(n13), 221, 243(n39)
Magnetic (Swedish company), 87(n6)
Malaysia, 43t, 45t, 92(n71), 118, 229
Mannesmann, 113t, 116, 141(n42), 229, 233
manufacturers, 3, 4, 13, 26, 36–7, 49–50t, 52–4, 56–8, 61–2, 66–7, 69–70, 72, 75, 77, 82–3, 208–9
manufacturing, 22, 31, 34, 139(n21)
market and committee mechanisms in setting global standards, 36–92
  adoption overseas, 68
  another proprietary standard, 69–71
  awarding of new licences, 67–8
  characteristics of global standards, 46–53
  committee side, 65–7, 69–71, 74–6
  creation of ETSI, 65–7
  creation of GSM (second generation global standard), 63–8

DAMPS (failure on market side), 73–4
downside of government involvement in standard-setting, 61–3
emergence of DoCoMo-Ericsson-Nokia alliance, 80–2
evolution of 'global' standards, 39t, 40–6
failed efforts to create a pan-European analog standard, 58–63
first generation global standard: America's AMPS, 56–8
first regional standard: Scandinavia's NMT system, 53–6
French and German collaboration, 60–1
Great Britain adopts TACS, 59–60
Japan and GSM, 71–2
Japan introduces competition, 69
Japan tries a little harder, but fails again with PHS, 76–8
Japanese create another proprietary standard, 69–72
Japanese and European collaboration in third generation systems, 78–84
lack of national digital standard in USA, 72–6
late responses by manufacturers, 82–4
market side, 67–8, 69, 73–4
no process to select a single digital standard: a failure on committee side, 74–6
overview of mobile communications systems and standards, 38–53
summary, 84–7
technological change in mobile communication industry, 39–40
marketing, 5, 22, 31, 229, 230
markets, 1, 2t, 2–7, 9, 18, 29, 128
committee- and market-based competition in mobile infrastructure, 14–16

committee- and market-based competition in mobile phones, 16–17
transition from business to personal, 17, 148, 195–6
Matra, 10t, 49t, 51f, 59–61, 82, 89(n29–30), 90(n39), 96, 106, 107, 109–11, 113t, 116–19, 134, 135, 140(n24)
Matra Communications, 141(n31)
joint venture with Nortel, 117, 141(n31)
MATS-E system (Philips), 49t, 51f, 58, 59–62, 89(n23,27)
Matsushita, xiii, 8t, 91(n61), 92(n71), 150, 180, 184–92, 194, 198 (n9–10), 199(n22), 200(n24), 203(n69), 204(n77–8), 205 (n84–5), 228–9, 238
internal procurement, 179
market share (cellular phones, 1994–8), 190f
Matsushita-Nortel alliance, 230
Maxcell Telecom Plus, 139(n12)
Maxon, 92(n73)
MCI, 139(n12)
message service, 190
Methe, D., 25
Metro Mobile, 101t, 103t, 103, 125, 138(n8)
Metro One, 143(n60)
Metromedia, 102t, 103, 138(n8)
Metroplex Telephones, 197(n5)
Mexandeau, Louis, 89(n26)
Mexico, 43t, 45t, 104, 139(n19), 198(n10)
Microcell, 143(n61)
microprocessors, 115
Microsoft, 30, 75, 216, 217t, 219
Mobile Explorer, 219
Windows CE, 217t, 218, 219, 242(n28)
Windows software, 30, 216
Microtac models, 154
Middle East, 46, 55, 120t, 120–1, 140(n23)
Millicent, 122t
Millicom, 105–6, 110, 121, 137, 263
Millicom Services, 57, 88(n20)

Mitsubishi, xiii, 8t, 11t, 87(n6), 91(n61), 92(n71), 130t, 133, 138(n6), 149, 150, 154, 157, 181–3, 184–8, 190–2, 194, 198–9 (n9–10), 199(n22), 200(n24), 203(n69), 238
  market share (cellular phones, 1994–8), 190f
Mobilais Telephone (Latvia), 141(n40)
Mobile Choice, 20(n13), 158–9f
Mobile Communications, 20(n12)
mobile communications, 2t, 2–3, 7–9, 19(n4), 27t, 28–32, 36, 54, 55, 88(n26)
  equipment, 96
  infrastructure, 5–9, 13–16, 20(n7), 21, 29–30, 31, 80, 93–4, 95, 95t, 98, 99–100, 138(n1), 146
  infrastructure market, 10t, 104, 135
  market (USA), 127
  outline, 38f
  overview of systems and standards, 38–53
  providers, 5–6
  services, 46, 56, 63, 78, 87(n2), 96
  standards, 46
  systems, 18, 26, 30, 37, 38, 58
mobile computing, 28, 138, 252
mobile Internet, 19, 28, 138, 206, 213–20, 222f, 224, 235–6, 242–3(n37), 243(n40,42,45)
  competition between different interfaces, 214–18
  first committees/coalitions: WAP, Symbian, Bluetooth, 218
  Japanese market, 220–3
  second wave of coalitions/ committees: phone and PDA manufacturers, 218–20
mobile phone market: committee and *particularly* market competition, 16–17, 145–205
  cdmaOne market, 172–4
  committee-based competition, 184, 185–6, 189–90, 191–2
  DAMPS and GSM markets in the US, 170–2
  Ericsson, 168–9

Japanese firms, 149–51, 155–7
Japanese market, 183–94
mobile phone market-based competition, 190–1, 193–4
Motorola, 151–4, 166–8, 174–6
Nokia, 154–5, 162–9, 169–83
NTT Docomo refines its committee-based strategy, 185–6
success of Nokia, Motorola and Ericsson in GSM, 157–69
summary and discussion, 194–7
US analog market (AMPS), 148–57
US digital phone market and Nokia's global platforms, 169–83
mobile phones, 5–6, 7, 13, 18, 20(n10), 21, 28, 33, 34, 63, 146, 149, 150, 154, 187f, 188f, 193–5, 213–17
  battery time, 183–4, 186
  cellular, 156–7, 180, 182, 190, 203(n76)
  design, 163–4, 165–6, 170, 187–8, 190–1, 200(n30), 203(n73), 205(n84–5)
  digital, 176f, 177t, 181, 187f, 191, 201(n45), 238
  dual-mode, 166–7, 170, 208, 235, 236–8
  fast-moving industry, xiii
  folding, 188, 204(n78)
  infrastructure market, 93–144
  market share, 11t
  penetration rates, 7–8
  size, 168, 174, 183, 186, 192, 194, 203(n75), 221, 241(n25)
  standards, 32
  systems, 131
  third generation, 174
  voice quality, 39, 40, 74, 79, 190, 204(n83)
  weight, 158–9f, 162, 164, 167, 168, 181, 183–4, 186, 187f, 187–8, 188f, 189–94, 196, 203(n75), 204(n78–9)
  worldwide market share (1997–9), 8t
Mobilkom, 111t, 113t
Mobisphere, 229

Mobistar, 113t, 140(n26), 141(n41)
Mobitel (Slovenia), 112t
Mobtel (Serbia), 112t
models: 3XRTT, 241(n15)
modems, 28
monopolies, 27, 31, 37, 66, 232
Morocco, 43t, 45t, 120t
Motorola, xiii, 8–11, 14, 16–17,
    20(n7–8), 50t, 54, 57, 60, 63, 67,
    71, 75, 81, 82, 85, 86, 87(n2),
    89(n23), 91(n61–2), 92(n71),
    97–122, 125, 127–37, 131–2,
    132–4, 138(n6–8), 139 (n14,
    16–17,19,21), 140(n22, 24–6),
    141(n39), 142(n43), 143
    (n52–3,60), 146–50, 155, 156,
    171–3, 178–81, 184, 191, 192,
    197(n2), 199(n22), 200(n24),
    202(n58–9), 203(n72), 208, 218,
    219, 226–8, 231, 232, 235, 238,
    242(n29)
  evolution of GSM 900 MHz
    phone line (1994–8), 159f
  global customer base (1981–98),
    105f
  GSM 900 platform management
    strategies, 163t
  market share, 99t, 108t, 129t, 162f,
    170t
  problems with GSM
    implementation, 166–8
  slow move to digital, 174–6
  Startac series, 164, 167, 172
  strategy, 151–4
  subsidiaries, 89(n30)
  success in GSM, 157–69
multi-media services, 79
Murata, 205(n88)

Nagoya, 69, 237f
NAMPS, 74
national champions, 3, 61
National Semiconductor,
    205(n85)
NEC, xiii, 8t, 10–11t, 35(n7), 49t, 50t,
    54, 56, 91(n61), 92(n71), 96, 102t,
    104, 106, 107, 109, 120, 120t,
    122t, 130t, 132–4, 139(n14),
    140(n23), 142(n49), 144(n64),

144(n65), 149, 150, 154, 184–92,
    194, 198(n9–10), 199(n22),
    203(n69), 204(n77), 205(n85),
    228, 229–30, 238
  folding phone, 204(n78)
  market share (cellular phones,
    1994–8), 190f
NEC-Siemens alliance, 229–30
Netcom (Norway), 106, 113t, 263
Netherlands, 43t, 45t, 54, 59, 90(n51),
    112t, 113t, 228
network industries, 1, 22–3, 32, 33,
    34
network interface, 81, 214, 232
network managements systems, 38
networks, 24
New Zealand, 43t, 45t, 92(n71)
Newscable, 117
Nextel, 213
Nilsson, Sven-Christer, 168–9
Nippon Ericsson (technical office,
    1985–), 133
Nippon Ericsson KK (1991–), 133
Nissan, 130t
NMT (Nordic Mobile Telephone)
    standard, 9, 10–12t, 16, 20(n8),
    39–44, 46, 47t, 49t, 51–9, 61–2,
    84, 85, 86, 87(n6), 88(n13),
    90(n38), 98–9, 104–5, 107, 111t,
    112t, 120, 139(n19), 140(n22),
    141(n40), 142(n44), 145, 146,
    151, 154, 155, 176
  first regional standard, 53–6
Nokia, xiii, 7–11, 14, 20(n7–8), 51, 63,
    65, 67, 77, 79, 83, 85–7, 92(n71),
    96, 98, 99, 106, 109, 111–16, 118,
    119, 123, 127, 134, 139(n19),
    140(n24,26,27), 141(n40),
    143(n61), 145–9, 151f, 154–67,
    170–84, 187f, 188f, 191, 192,
    200(n26), 201(n41,47), 202(n58),
    207–9, 218–19, 226–8, 230–3,
    235–8, 240(n9), 242(n29)
  alliance with NTT DoCoMo and
    Ericsson, 80–2
  derivative products, 164, 165,
    201(n31)
  evolution of GSM 900 MHz
    phone line (1994–8), 158f

Nokia (*contd*)
    evolution of TDMA-based digital
      phone lines, 176f
    failure in Japanese market, 197
    global customer base (1981–98),
      105f
    global platforms, 175–6, 176–9
    GSM 900 platform management
      strategies, 163t
    market share (GSM base stations),
      108t
    market share (GSM handsets,
      1993–9), 162f
    market share (GSM switching), 108t
    market share (US infrastructure,
      1997), 129t
    multiple standards, 155
    rising share in AMPS and TACS,
      154–5
    share of US digital phone market
      (1995–8), 170t
    strategy "difficult to replicate",
      179–83
    success, 7–9, 16–17, 157–66
    "tiger teams", 114
Nokia Mobira, 154
Nortel (Northern Telecom), xiii, 8, 8t,
    10t, 10 n, 50t, 81, 91(n62), 96–9,
    101–7, 109, 113t, 117, 118, 119,
    126, 127, 128, 134, 135, 138
    (n5–8), 139(n15), 141(n31,32,39),
    143(n52,61–3), 226–7, 209, 229,
    231, 232
    acquisition of Matra, 118
    global customer base (1981–98),
      105f
    joint venture with Matra, 117,
      141(n31)
    market share, 99t
    market share (US infrastructure,
      1997), 129t
Nortel-Matra, 82, 113t, 117–18, 122t,
    134
    market share (GSM base stations),
      108t
    market share (GSM
      switching), 108t
North America, 8, 12t, 41t, 76–7,
    91(n65), 91(n71), 143(n62), 232

Norway, 43t, 45t, 54, 90(n51), 112t,
    113t, 140(n25)
NPI Wireless, 143(n61)
NSFNet, 273
NTT, 39t, 43t, 49t, 51–3f, 55f, 56, 58,
    71, 85, 87(n3), 91(n61),
    92(n68,n70), 96, 107, 130t,
    133, 142(n49), 150, 184,
    203(n72)
    "still partly-owned by Japanese
      government", 77, 78
    wireline system, 76
NTT Docomo (1992–), xiii, 14,
    18, 20(n10), 35(n7), 50–2,
    69–72, 78–9, 80, 83, 84, 86–7,
    91(n61), 92(n70–1), 130–3, 137,
    143–4(n64), 144(n65–6), 145,
    146, 183–94, 203(n75),
    204(n77,80–1,83), 205(n86), 206,
    217t, 220, 224, 228–37, 239(n3)
    spun-off from NTT (1992), 69–70
NTT Docomo-Ericsson-Nokia
    alliance, 80–2
NTT Personal, 50t, 193, 194
NTT Procurement Agreement, 133
NTT systems (Japan), 55–6, 59,
    140(n23), 150
Nynex, 97t, 101t, 103t, 103, 123, 125,
    142(n45), 143(n51)

OEM (Original Equipment
    Manufacturing), 118, 161,
    200(n25)
Oki Electric, 145, 146, 149, 150, 184,
    198(n9), 199(n10)
Omnipoint (USA), 141(n32),
    143(n61)
Omnitel, 113t
One-2-One, 114t, 140(n26)
openness, 5, 7, 13, 16, 24, 26, 36,
    37–8, 46, 47–48t, 49–50t, 51,
    52, 58, 61, 66, 67, 70, 72, 73, 79,
    80, 83, 146, 207, 235
    see also standard-setting
operating systems, 28–9, 214, 217t,
    219
Optimus (Portugal), 140(n28),
    141(n35)
Orange, 114t, 141(n35), 143(n61)

Orbitel, 168
Osaka, 237f
Oslo, 88(n9)

Pacific Telephone, 97t
Pacific Telesis, 101t
PACS, 50t, 51f
PacTel, 100, 101t, 103t, 125, 139
    (n14–15), 143(n51)
Padilla, A., 138(n2), 279
Palm Computing, 216, 217t, 218, 219,
    242(n27)
Panafon, 113t, 141(n41)
Panasonic, 8, 149, 154
PCS (Personal Communications
    Services), 73, 79, 83, 91(n63),
    92(n73), 125, 171
PDA (personal digital assistant), 207,
    214–17, 218–20, 221–2, 224,
    225f, 241–2(n27), 242(n28)
PDC (Japanese digital standard),
    10–12t, 10 n, 16, 20(n7), 39t,
    41–2, 48t, 50–3, 69–72, 80, 86,
    106, 130–3, 145, 146, 148, 177,
    185–7, 189, 191–4, 204(n83), 208,
    230, 232, 235, 236
PDC market, 205(n87)
penetration rates, 7–8, 47–48t, 58, 62,
    69, 78, 80
Philippines, 44t, 45t, 92(n70)
Philips, xiii, 11t, 49t, 51f, 59, 60,
    89(n23,n27), 90(n43), 140(n30),
    154, 158, 160, 242(n28)
    Fizz, 161
    Genie, 161, 164
    market share (GSM handsets,
        1993–9), 162f
    Spark, 161
PHS (Personal Handyphone System,
    Japan), 12t, 39–41, 48t, 50–3,
    69, 76–8, 84–6, 87(n3),
    92(n68–69), 156, 194, 205(n87),
    193–4
PKI (Philips Kommunikations
    Industrie AG), 10t, 10 n, 49t,
    60, 96, 106–9, 111–13t, 116–18,
    134, 140–1(n30), 141(n31,33)
    market share (GSM base stations),
        108t

platform management, 16, 17, 18,
    33–5, 146, 148, 157–60, 162–9,
    170, 200–1(n32), 208, 234–5
Plessey, 59, 62, 63, 263, 264(n4)
Plexys (USA), 142(n49)
Plus GSM (Poland), 142(n42)
PNTR (permanent normal trade)
    status, 241(n14)
population, 40, 54, 55, 57, 58, 77, 80,
    87(n3), 91(n65), 98, 99t, 170,
    237f
Portugal, 43t, 45t, 62, 68,
    90(n38,n51), 112t, 113t, 116,
    140(n25), 141(n41)
Powertel, 143(n61)
prepaid cards, 169
prices, 17, 23, 33, 34, 36, 37, 38, 59,
    67, 87(n5), 91(n61), 118, 138(n1),
    148, 150, 151–4, 157, 164, 165,
    167–8, 172, 173, 175, 179, 183,
    198(n7), 203(n69)
PrimeCo, 101t, 125, 143(n51,60)
product lines, 16, 18, 33–5, 146,
    147f, 157–60, 162–9, 170, 207–8,
    234–5
products: mass-produced, 5, 6,
    20(n5)
profits, 23, 35(n12), 78, 88(n13), 169,
    173, 174, 183, 209
Psion, 216, 217t, 218
PTTs (national wireline service
    providers), 51f, 59, 66, 96, 109,
    111t, 112t, 113t, 120t, 139(n19)
    Austria, 106
    France, 64
    Luxembourg, 116
    South Africa, 141(n38)
    Switzerland, 112t

Qatar, 45t, 62, 89(n27), 120t
QPE (Qualcomm Personal
    Electronics), 172
Qualcomm, 11t, 50t, 50 n, 51f, 74, 75,
    81, 83, 92(n73), 145, 146, 169,
    172, 173, 174, 206, 227, 229,
    239(n2–5), 240(n8–9), 241(n15)
    acquired by Ericsson, 229
    battle with Ericsson (third
        generation standards), 208–11

Qualcomm (*contd*)
  share of US digital phone market
    (1995–8), 170t

Racal Electronics (and Racal
    Telekom), 59, 88(n20), 139(n21),
    168
radio, 24, 26, 27t, 35(n3)
Radiocom, 111t
Radiocom 2000, 62
Radiolinja, 113t
Radiomobil (Czech operator), 113t,
    115
RAM Broadcasting, 97t, 100, 101t,
    138(n8), 139(n14)
Rarpac (private network system), 59
RC-2000 system (Matra), 39t, 47t,
    49t, 51f, 52f, 53f, 58, 59, 61, 62,
    90(n39)
RCA, 268
RCCs (radio common carriers), 96–7,
    98, 98t, 100, 138(n9)
regions/large countries, 13, 27, 36, 84
regulation/regulators, 86, 104, 194
research and development, 66,
    91(n61)
retail, 151, 183, 199(n12), 204(n81)
Retrovision (Spain), 141(n35)
risk, 3, 13, 27, 28, 37
Rogers AT&T, 213
Rogers Cantel, 98, 126
royalties, 92(n73), 208–9
RSAs (Rural Statistical Areas),
    58, 96
RTMS, 39t, 47t, 49t, 51f, 53f, 62
Russia, 44t, 45t, 104, 141(n36)

Samsung, 8t, 92(n73), 146, 170t, 172
Sanyo, xiii, 8, 187f, 188f, 194,
    203(n73)
Saudi Arabia, 43t, 45t, 54, 120t, 121
Scandinavia, 7, 9, 12t, 39t, 39, 41t,
    47t, 49t, 52f, 53–6, 58, 61, 62, 64,
    65, 68, 69, 84, 85, 88(n9,n17), 96,
    122t, 123, 124, 194
  see also NMT
Secre (Jeumon-Schneider group),
    89(n30)
Securicor, 59, 88(n20)

segments, 161, 195, 196
semiconductors, 166
service charges, 54–5, 57, 58, 78,
    88(n10–13)
service-providers, 3, 4, 13, 20(n10),
    26, 27t, 29–30, 33, 36–7, 40,
    49–50t, 52–6, 58, 61, 62, 66–7,
    70, 72, 75, 77, 79, 81–6, 87(n2),
    93–5, 98, 105, 106, 110–14,
    121–5, 127, 132–3, 138(n3,9),
    140(n22), 146, 153, 183–4, 186,
    189, 192, 203(n68,75), 204(n81),
    207, 208, 213, 231–3
  analog, 125
  cooperative development work,
    14–15
  digital, 128–9
  Japan, 130t
  Japanese, 28, 35(n4)
  USA, 97t, 98t, 99–104
SFR (later called Cegetel), 111t, 113t,
    140(n25)
shares, 150, 168, 169, 211
Sharp, 92(n71), 193, 194, 203(n73),
    216, 217t, 242(n28)
  Zaurus, 216, 241(n26)
Shintom, 150
Siemens, xiii, 8, 8t, 10–11t, 49t, 51f,
    60–1, 64, 82, 88(n9), 89(n26–7),
    96, 104–17, 119, 120t, 121, 122t,
    127, 134, 135–6, 139(n19),
    140(n24), 141(n31,38,39), 158,
    160, 161, 173, 181, 200(n26),
    227–30, 233
  global customer base (1981–98),
    105f
  market share (GSM base stations),
    108t
  market share (GSM handsets,
    1993–9), 162f
  market share (GSM switching),
    108t
Sinclair Broadcast Group, 271
Singapore, 43–45t, 56, 81, 229
Singapore Telecom, 92(n71),
    140(n23)
SK Telecom (Korea), 229
Slimlite, 164, 167
Slovakia, 45t, 112t, 113t

Slovenia, 44t, 112t
SM, 39t
SNET (Southern New England
 Telephone), 97t, 102t, 103t,
 138(n7), 139(n13)
*Société Anonyme de
 Télécommunications* (SAT), 61,
 89(n30), 90(n43)
software, 24, 26, 29, 30, 162,
 163–4, 165–6, 170, 175,
 177t, 178, 200(n30), 219–20,
 242(n38)
Sonera (Finnish carrier), 143(n61)
Sonofon (Denmark), 113t, 141(n38)
Sony, xiii, 8, 11t, 75, 82, 145, 146, 161,
 169, 172–4, 184, 187, 187f, 188f,
 200(n26), 203(n73), 217t
 market share (cellular phones,
 1994–8), 190f
 share of US digital phone market
 (1995–8), 170t
South Africa, 45t, 62, 90(n38)
South America, 46, 76, 104, 106, 107,
 142(n43), 177, 198(n10), 232
Southwestern Bell, 97t, 102t, 103t,
 103, 123, 125, 142(n45),
 143(n60), 171
Southwestern Bell Mobile Systems,
 197(n5)
Soviet Union, 46, 55
Spain, 43t, 44t, 45t, 46, 54, 59, 62,
 90(n51), 112t, 113t, 116,
 140(n25), 228
sponsors, 49–50t, 50 n, 51, 51f, 52f,
 59
Sprint, 102t, 126, 139(n18)
Sprint PCS, 143(n52)
Sri Lanka, 43t, 44t, 45t
Standard Elektrik Lorenz (SEL)
 (German subsidiary of ITT), 61,
 89(n29–30), 90(n43)
standard-setting, 51f-52f, 56, 72–3,
 78–9, 86–7, 220, 206–7
 committee-based, 51f
 domestic, 51f
 hybrid model, 36, 51, 53, 84
 international, 51f
 Internet, 273–5
 "jungle warfare", 215–16

mobile Internet, 206
 process, 46, 50 n, 51, 61, 70, 72, 77,
 109–10, 146, 157, 194, 235
 third generation, 81, 206
 see also openness
standards
 8mm video, 19(n1)
 analog, 57, 61–2, 63, 65, 72, 75, 85,
 86, 90(n53), 94
 closed, 249
 competition, 21–35
 de facto (chosen by markets), 1, 23,
 24, 40, 70
 de jure (created by committees), 1,
 19(n1), 23
 digital, 57, 63, 64, 69, 72, 74, 76, 85,
 90(n53), 91(n61), 94, 125
 domestic, 9
 global, 9, 12t, 13, 18, 26–7, 32,
 36–92, 146, 184, 208
 introduction, 1–20
 literature, 1, 4, 17
 market competition, 23–4, 35(n2)
 miscellaneous, 177t, 178, 180,
 242(n29)
 multiple, 36, 17, 155
 non-global, 47–48t, 58
 non-GSM digital, 86
 open, 84, 218, 234
 open digital, 84
 proprietary, 69–72, 107
 second generation, 51, 53
 success, 9–14
 theoretical issues, 21–35
 third generation, 18, 51, 53, 76, 83,
 94, 137, 208–13, 239(n5)
 two-firm model, 86
Startac, 174–5
STET, 61, 90(n37)
Storno, 154, 199(n17)
subscribers, 7, 40–1, 47–48t, 54, 55,
 55f, 56, 57–8, 60, 61–2, 68,
 69, 74, 78, 83, 84, 107, 121,
 140(n23), 151, 170, 183, 189,
 190, 194, 204(n81), 210, 220,
 222, 232, 233
 cancellation rates 189, 204(n80–1)
 digital, 205(n84)
 non-business, 151

supplier/customer relationships, 228
suppliers, 77, 113–14t, 122t, 184, 185–6, 186, 188, 190–1, 203(n73), 204(n76), 205(n85)
Sweden, 43t, 45t, 54, 68, 88(n10–11), 90(n51), 92(n71), 112t, 113–14t, 116, 140(n25), 228
Swedish Telecom Radio Laboratory, 54
switches/switching equipment, 38, 54, 64, 78, 87(n17), 94, 96, 99, 110–16, 117, 118, 119, 127, 131, 140(n25), 144(n65), 226, 227, 229, 230
  market share (Europe, 1997), 118t
switching costs, 6, 18, 21, 29–32, 93, 94, 118, 124, 134–5, 136, 207, 225, 234
switching stations, 38, 38f, 76, 87(n3)
Switzerland, 43t, 45t, 60, 112t, 200(n25), 213
Symbian (1998–), 217t, 218, 219

TACS, 9–13, 39t, 41–4, 46, 47t, 55, 55f, 62, 71, 85, 86, 90(n38), 104–8, 111–12t, 117, 120, 130t, 131–2, 137, 140(n23), 142(n49), 151, 154–5, 176, 184, 192, 199(n22), 203(n72)
  adopted by United Kingdom, 59–60
  derivative from AMPS, 9, 57, 104
  non-European countries, 68, 91(n59)
Taiwan, 43t, 45t, 118, 141(n32), 198(n9)
Talkline, 154, 199(n17)
Tandy, 149, 197(n5)
  Radio Shack stores, 149, 155
tapes, 28
TD-CDMA, 50t, 51f, 239(n5)
  "hybrid of TDMA and CDMA", 82
TDMA (time division multiple access), 10 n, 41–2, 64, 65, 72, 73, 91(n62), 126, 132, 133, 142(n50), 143(n53), 176f, 177, 240(n8)
  "third generation (wide-band) version of DAMPS", 208, 212–13
technological change

models, 22–3
  proposed new model, 22, 247–60
technological discontinuities, 21–3, 30–1, 35(n1), 95t, 96, 135, 137
technology
  data transmission capabilities, 39, 40
  first generation, 39, 39t, 41t, 47t, 52, 96
  frequency spectrum efficiency, 39, 40
  low-mobility, 39t, 41t, 47t, 52f
  miscellaneous, 15, 30, 33, 61, 93, 94, 95, 180
  multi-media capability, 40
  narrow-band, 64–5
  new, 13, 30–1, 243(n44)
  second generation, 39–40, 39t, 41t, 47–48t, 52, 96
  third generation, xiii, 2–3, 6, 14, 18, 28, 31, 39t, 41t, 50t, 52f, 53f, 126, 208–13, 225–34, 234–8
  wide-band, 64–5
Technophone (UK), 63, 154, 155, 168
Tele Danmark, 111t, 113t, 123
Telecel (Portugal), 113t, 142(n42)
Telecom Finland, 111t, 123, 141(n39), 230
(also SIP and SPI) Telecom I (French satellite), 89(n26)
Telecom Italia, 51f, 61, 96, 112t, 113t, 139(n21), 229, 230
Telecommunications (Japanese), 20(n13)
telecommunications, 1, 19(n4), 23, 24, 26, 30, 33
  deregulation, 37
Telecommunications (Japanese), 20(n13)
telecommunications firms, 31
Telefónica, 112t, 113t, 116, 229
Telemig (Brazil), 143(n63)
Telenor, 113t, 123, 141(n39)
Telenor Mobile, 112t
Telepoint, 39t
Telestet (Greece), 113t, 140(n26)
Telettra, 49t, 64, 90(n37), 139(n21)
television, 24, 27t, 35(n3)
  digital, 26, 29, 138
Telezone, 126

Telfort (Netherlands), 141(n35)
Telia (Sweden), 112t, 113t, 123, 229
Texas, 126, 137, 199(n10)
Texas Instruments, 212
Thailand, 43t, 45t, 77, 92(n71–2),
    229
third generation and mobile Internet
    standards and competition in
    third generation infrastructure
    and phones, 206–46
  battle between Qualcomm and
    Ericsson, 208–9
  committee-based competition,
    228–31, 231–4
  competition, 214–18, 225–34,
    234–8
  computing standards, 213–20
  dual-mode phones (market share),
    236–7
  Ericsson-Qualcomm agreement,
    210–11
  global development capability,
    237–8
  handsets, 234–8
  infrastructure, 225–34
  interface competition in
    early 2001, 223–5
  Japanese mobile Internet market,
    220–3
  market-based competition, 226–8,
    231–4
  mobile Internet, 213–20, 220–3
  negotiations over third generation
    standard, 208–13
  service schedules (2001–5), 237f
third generation services, 20(n10)
third generation systems, 78–84, 137
Thomson, 59, 60, 61, 89(n26)
Thomson-CSF, 89(n27)
TMN (Portugal), 112t, 113t, 116,
Tokai, 130t, 132, 184
Tokyo, 69, 130t, 132, 184, 237f
Tops Alliance, 153
Toshiba, xiii, 11t, 91(n61), 92(n71),
    133–4, 149, 150, 184, 187, 187f,
    188f, 194, 197(n3), 199(n10),
    205(n85)
  market share (cellular phones,
    1994–8), 190f

Toshiba-Siemens alliance, 238
Total Quality Management, 30
Toyo Communications, 205(n85)
Toyota, 71, 130t, 131
trade barriers, 240(n12)
trade friction, 31, 131, 132, 156–7
Tsuka Cellular, 130t, 132, 144(n66),
    184
Tunisia, 43t, 45t, 141(n32)
Turkey, 45t, 120t

UAE, 43t, 45t, 120t
UMTS, 209, 212
Uniden, 150, 198(n9)
United Kingdom, 12t, 39, 39t, 41t, 43t,
    45t, 46, 47t, 55, 57, 58, 62–3, 64,
    67–8, 69, 73, 90(n51), 92(n71),
    112t, 114t, 121, 137, 151, 155,
    160, 194, 199(n22), 213, 228, 229
  adopts TACS, 59–60, 88(n20)
project-based companies, 5–6
United States of America, xiii, 3, 6, 7,
    9, 10, 12t, 13–14, 26, 27, 36,
    39–43, 45t, 47t-50t, 52–5, 57–8,
    60, 65, 68, 69, 83–6, 95t, 96–7,
    99–104, 107, 123, 194, 232, 234
  analog market, 16–17, 146, 147f,
    148–57
  DAMPS and GSM markets, 170–2
  digital phone market, 146, 147f,
    169–83
  digital standards, 124–30
  lacks a national digital standard,
    72–6
  third generation technology,
    18–19
United Telespectrum, 97t, 102t, 103,
    138(n7)
Universal Wireless Communications
    Consortium, 240(n8)
Unwired Planet (later Phone.com),
    242(n29)
US Cellular, 102t, 126
US Congress, 210, 241(n14)
US International Trade Commission,
    150
US Justice Department, 57
US Office of Telecommunications,
    20(n12)

US West, 97, 122t, 123, 124, 126, 138(n6), 142(n44), 143(n51)
US West/New Vector, 97t, 101t
US-Japan Telecommunications Agreement (1985), 133
user interface, 162, 163, 164, 165, 166, 170
UTRA, 239(n5)
UWCC (Universal Wireless Communications Consortium), 212, 233
Uzbekistan, 44t
Uzdonrobita (Uzbekistan), 143(n63)

Vanguard, 143(n58)
vendor lock-in, 30
vendor-customer relationships, 93, 95, 95t, 108, 115–16, 124–5, 127–9, 132, 135–6
vendor/service-provider relationships, 233–4
vendors, 100, 138(n10)
video, 19(n1), 24, 26, 27t
VLSI Technologies, 172–3
Vodacom, 141(n38)
Vodafone, 59, 62, 63, 88(n20), 104, 112t, 114t, 121, 122t, 137, 139(n21), 141(n38), 141(n41), 229, 233
VoiceStream, 213
volume discounts, 151–4, 155, 158
volumes, 147f, 157, 175, 186, 191, 195
von Piere, Heinrich, 88(n9)

W-CDMA (Wide-Band Code Division Multiple Access), 9, 12t, 14, 15, 20(n10), 28, 39–42, 50–3, 79, 81–4, 86–7, 92(n71), 94, 131, 133, 206–9, 211–13, 227–32, 235, 236, 237f, 238, 239(n3–4),
    239–40(n5), 240(n7–8,10), 242(n29)
WAP (Wireless Application Protocol), xiii, 216, 217t, 220, 224, 242(n29,35,37), 243(n38)
WAP browser, 236
WAP Forum (1997–), 217t
WAP-NG, 224
Weisshappel, Robert, 174–5
Westel (Hungary), 111t
Western Electric (later Lucent), 97, 138(n4–5)
Western Europe, 48t, 107
Western Wireless, 143(n61)
What Mobile, 20(n13)
WIND (Italy), 141(n35)
Wintel, 24
wireline
    equipment, 31, 117
    industry, 8, 32, 62–3, 107
    Internet, 29
    operators, former, 138(n9)
    service providers, 96–7, 97t, 99
    services, 85, 110
    standards, 46
    switches, 106, 107, 116, 104, 134, 138(n5), 144(n65)
    systems, 26, 38f, 87(n3), 131
wirelines, 37, 78, 88(n9), 92(n69), 95t, 96–7, 115, 117, 126, 160
WML, 224, 236, 242(n37)
World Trade Organization, 210, 241(n14)

X-HTML, 224, 242(n37)
XML, 242(n37)

Yamaguchi (NTT president), 91 (n61)
Yankee Group, 226, 228, 232